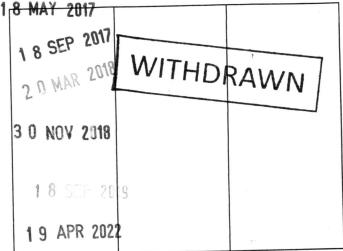

THE RACE FOR
HITLER'S
X-PLANES

THE RACE FOR
HITLER'S
X-PLANES

Britain's 1945 Mission to Capture
Secret Luftwaffe Technology

JOHN CHRISTOPHER

JUNE
1945

First published 2013

The History Press
The Mill, Brimscombe Port
Stroud, Gloucestershire, GL5 2QG
www.thehistorypress.co.uk

British Library Cataloguing in Publication Data.
A catalogue record for this book is available from the British Library.

ISBN 978 0 7524 6457 2

Typesetting and origination by The History Press
Printed in India

CONTENTS

Above: The JB-1 'Bat' manned glider produced by Northrop in 1944 to test the flying qualities of a 'power bomb' inspired by the German V-1 Doodlebugs. At first sight it resembles the Lippisch DM-1 shown on page 170, but the Bat has a conventional tail and swept wings unlike the DM-1's Delta configuration. *Below*: Typical of the scenes encountered by the advancing Allies in 1945, an abandoned airfield littered with a variety of German aircraft including a Messerschmitt Me 262A. (NARA)

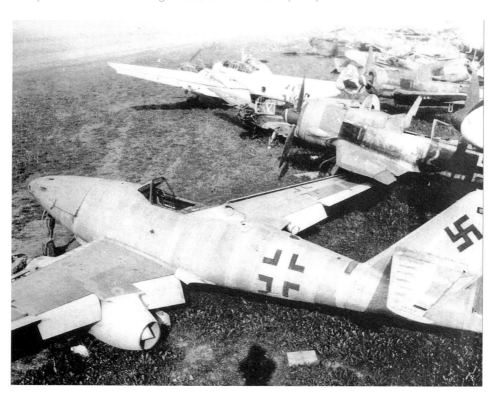

THE SPOILS OF WAR

IN THE LATER STAGES of the Second World War the skies above Europe were filled with death and destruction on an unprecedented scale. Day and night the endless hordes of Allied bombers were pounding Germany's cities and war factories to dust. But as Hitler's thousand-year Reich faced its darkest hour, its *Götterdämerung*, the twilight of the gods, the Führer unleashed an arsenal of deadly *Wunderwaffe*; the wonder-weapons which he believed could turn back the tide in Germany's favour. These included not only the V–1 flying bombs and V–2 rockets, the *Vergeltungwaffen* (meaning 'reprisal' or 'revenge weapons') intended to 'shock and awe' the British into submission, but also a range of highly advanced jet- or even rocket-powered aircraft together with a plethora of guided missiles designed to strike at the enemy's bombers. Such was the extent and sophistication of these weapons that in most cases they were ahead of any technology possessed by the Allies. If the German forces had managed to delay the Allied advance even by just six months or by a year the new weapons might have become available in sufficient numbers to change the outcome of the war.

Fortunately Hitler's war machine came to a grinding halt in the spring of 1945. With overwhelming Soviet forces pushing their way through the streets of Berlin and just a block or two from the Reich Chancellery, Adolf Hitler took his own life on 30 April 1945. General Alfred Jodl, Chief of Staff of German Armed Forces High Command, signed the documents of unconditional surrender on 7 May, signalling the surrender of all German forces to the Allies on the following day.

The conclusion of the war (in the European theatre at least, as the Pacific war still had several more months to run) brought to an end a conflict noted not only for its terrible toll in human suffering, but also for the massive technological strides made in the fields of aviation and armaments. This was particularly so in Hitler's Germany and the legacy of his scientists and engineers was a lexicon of new weaponry including jet-fighters, inter-continental ballistic missiles (ICBMs), guided missiles and smart bombs. Even before the end of hostilities the Allies had recognised that possession of this technology, not to mention the German scientists and engineers, held the key to power in the uneasy post-war peace. Inevitably there were other factors of course. In particular the Americans desperately needed to prepare themselves in case they encountered similar weapons that Germany might have shared with it Axis partners in Japan. Then there were the wider issues of retribution, compensation and commercial gain, not to mention the very

A remarkably intact Messerschmitt Me 262A abandoned in a forest clearing beside the Autobahn. In the final stages of the war some motorways were used as makeshift airfields. *(USAF)*

genuine concern that Germany should not be able to rearm herself as she had done in the decades after the First World War.

It was against this background that the defeat of Germany in May 1945 signalled a frantic technological supermarket sweep undertaken by the Allies and a widespread plunder of the fallen nation's resources. It was as if Germany was a sweet shop and the advanced aircraft and weaponry, the research and production facilities, the papers and documents, even the scientists, engineers and technicians, were the sweets to be stuffed into the victors' pockets. To the Allies these were the rightful spoils of war and in the headlong rush to acquire them the needs of the defeated were cast aside. Time became the enemy. The Allies were in a race not only against looters looking for valuables in the various facilities, but also the wanton vandalism of the slave workers and prisoners who sought revenge against their former oppressors. And, of course, they were in a race against each another. Ostensibly America and Britain collaborated in their efforts, but as for the Russians, that was a different matter altogether. To further complicate the situation, alterations to the Allied Control Zones meant that some areas would change hands within weeks of the war ending.

In recent years much has been published and broadcast on the Americans' efforts to bag the best of the Nazi technology, including Operation Lusty (a somewhat tortuous acronym derived from LUftwaffe Secret TechnologY) and Hal Watson's legendary Whizzers, a team of crack American pilots who scoured the ruined airfields of Germany to secure the latest jet aircraft, such as the Me 262, Arado 234 and the rocket-powered Me 163. The spotlight has also been turned on the German rocketry experts and scientists taken to the USA under Operation Paperclip and their part in launching the space race that put a man on the moon. These have tended to overshadow the less glamorous role played by the British.

During the war the British had been actively engaged in evaluating captured German aircraft, most notably at the Royal Aircraft Establishment at Farnborough, and the round-up of enemy aircraft continued after Germany's capitulation. The British sent technical intelligence teams to work in cooperation with the Americans under the control of the Combined Intelligence Objectives Subcommittee (CIOS). But there was one post-war British mission to Germany that stood apart from the others, and it was the one I stumbled across by chance forty years after the war had ended.

'The Fedden Mission to Germany Final Report' proclaimed the title on the faded tan-coloured cover of the document among a box of papers at a local auction of furniture and general items. Many of the lots in the auction came from house clearances of estates following the death of their owners and the report was with a number of aeronautical reports, papers and photographs relating to the Bristol Aircraft Company. This was located at Filton, just to the north of Bristol and approximately 15 miles from the auctioneers. There was much about this document that attested to its interest and its significance. The word 'Secret' caught my attention initially, and then there was the striking logo adorning its cover. Clearly someone had taken the trouble to design and draft a special logo, an act which seemed whimsical, almost inappropriate, given the official nature and content of the report. (I later discovered that this had been devised by Sir Roy Fedden himself.) This

Messerschmitt Me 163 Komet rocket-powered interceptor. This is V21, the V standing for 'Versuchsmuster' or experimental/test aircraft.

simple graphic device encapsulated the story contained within. Here was the swastika, the instantly recognisable emblem of the hated Nazi regime, with the German eagle pierced through its heart by a spear-like flagstaff bearing a Union Jack, and around the edge were token stars and stripes to represent the USA. Even now the message is blunt, almost shocking. It symbolises the total and absolute defeat of Germany at the hands of the Allies, or, more precisely, the British and Americans, as the hammer and sickle of the Soviet Union are conspicuous by their absence.

Just a few weeks after the end of hostilities Sir Stafford Cripps, Britain's Minister of Aircraft Production, sent a hastily prepared team headed by the renowned engineer Sir Roy Fedden off to Germany to root out whatever they could about the Nazi's secret aeronautical treasures. Among the rubble of the battered cities and airfields, aircraft factories and research centres, they uncovered a wide range of advanced aircraft and power plants. However, this story is about much more than just the aeronautical hardware the Fedden Mission uncovered in Germany. Travelling through this 'conquered and disintegrated country' Fedden's team witnessed the appalling devastation of the war and the impact it had upon the lives of the ordinary people. They also discovered the unremitting horrors of the vast Mittelwerk underground weapons factory tunnelled into the Harz Mountains, where inmates from the Dora concentration camp were worked to death.

It is almost seventy years now since the fall of Nazi Germany and the end of the Second World War. As L.P. Hartley once wrote, 'The past is a foreign country; they do things differently there.' The events of the Second World War seem distant now, but the technological innovations that came out of it, and out of the subsequent peace, have shaped the modern world.

John Christopher, 2013

one

A VERY BRITISH AFFAIR

IN JUNE 1945 London still wore its wartime scars like an old and shabby coat. The rubble-strewn bomb sites, where the walls of ruined buildings looked out like eyeless skulls, had become a familiar part of everyday life for its inhabitants. The euphoria of VE Day, a little over a month earlier on 8 May, had already faded and many just wanted to forget about the war and start rebuilding their lives instead. For most Londoners 12 June 1945 was just another day. They may have read in the newspapers that 'Ike', General Dwight D. Eisenhower, the Supreme Commander of the Allied Forces, was in town to be awarded the Order of Merit by the King and presented with the Freedom of the City at the Guildhall, but nobody cast a second glance at the cars taking Sir Roy Fedden and his newly assembled team of scientists and engineers on the short journey across London from the Ministry of Aircraft Production (MAP) offices at Cooks House in Stratton Street, just off Piccadilly, to RAF Northholt.

Situated on the north-western edge of the city, within the Borough of Hillingdon, Northolt had played an important part in the defence of the capital. Before the war it had been the first RAF station to take delivery of Hawker Hurricanes, with No.111 Squadron receiving four in December 1937. During the Battle of Britain it had been a Sector Airfield of the No.11 Group consisting of several units, including the No.303 Polish Fighter Squadron. From 1944 the reconnaissance squadrons No.16 and No.140 operated both Spitfires and Mosquitoes from Northolt, with No.69 Squadron's Wellingtons joining them later on. It was also home to Winston Churchill's personal aircraft, a modified four-engine Douglas C-54 Skymaster, which was used to fly him to his meetings with the other Allied leaders. But now that the war was over and the fighter aircraft were no longer needed the future of the airfield was uncertain. The camouflage paint that had so effectively protected the various buildings from Luftwaffe attack by making them look like an extension of the houses and gardens that surrounded the airfield on two sides looked faded and was beginning to flake.

The team assembled in the Officers' Mess and Fedden briefed them on the purpose of their mission. Only a few weeks earlier Sir Stafford Cripps, the Minister of Aircraft Production, had called Fedden to his office and instructed him to lead this special mission to Germany. Unlike some of the more thoroughly prepared American teams already sifting their way through Germany, the Fedden Mission was to be a very British affair. Ostensibly its primary purpose was to visit universities, research departments and engineering works in Germany, and to earmark plant, equipment and documents that would be suitable for the new college of aeronautics which was to be established in England. Particular emphasis was to be placed on the developmental work and manufacture of the latest jet engines, as well as the wider subject of fuel injection and ignition for piston engines, and the development and manufacture of variable pitch propellers.

Fedden's team had been hastily but carefully put together from some of the finest experts in their particular fields: Dr W.J. Duncan, Professor of Aeronautics at the University College of Hull and currently seconded to the Royal Aircraft Establishment (RAE); J.C. King of the Structural and Mechanical Engineering Department of the RAE; Flight Lieutenant A.B.P. Beeton of the Engine Department, RAE; and Bert Newport of Rotol Ltd. Organisational backup would be provided by W.J. Stern of the Control Commission for Germany – who would also act as a translator – and Wing Commander V. Cross, Liaison Officer to the Mission, who had been seconded from the Supreme Headquarters Allied Expeditionary Force (SHAEF) in Frankfurt. The pilots flying the two RAF Dakota transport aircraft allocated to the Mission were Flight Lieutenant Reid of the RAF, and Flight Lieutenant Cheaney of the RAF Volunteer Reserve (RAFVR). And then, of course, there was Sir Roy Fedden himself.

1937: Roy Fedden takes centre stage in this group photograph of his Cosmos Engineering team. In 1920 the defunct company had been purchased by the British & Colonial Aeroplane Company. *(RRHT)*

The lightweight and reliable Jupiter nine-cylinder radial air-cooled engine which cemented Fedden's status as Britain's finest engine designer of the inter-war years. This example is displayed at the Imperial War Museum, Duxford.

SIR ROY FEDDEN

Alfred Hubert Roy Fedden was a formidable figure within the world of aeronautical engineering. Born on 6 June 1885, he was the third son of an eminent Bristol family that had done well for itself in the sugar business. He went to school at Clifton College in Bristol, and although he excelled at sporting activities, his academic performance failed to impress his tutors. For a while he contemplated a career in the military, the usual avenue for those labelled as underachievers, but in his heart he yearned for something more practical, something more 'useful'. Then in 1903 his father, Henry Fedden, purchased an 8.5hp two-cylinder Decauville motor car and hired a chauffeur to both drive and maintain it. The car was only the fourth to be registered in Bristol and only the fiftieth registered in the whole of the country. Typical of such early cars, it proved to be thoroughly unreliable and it struggled to cope with Bristol's notoriously steep hills. In fact it broke down so often that Fedden senior soon swapped it for another car obtained from the Bristol Motor Company. Tinkering with these vehicles proved to be the vital spark in young Roy Fedden's choice of career, and much against the expectations of his family he resolved that he would become an engineer. His father was supportive and paid for him to take a three-year apprenticeship with the Bristol Motor Company, and by night he studied automotive engineering at the technical college.

Drawing upon his experiences with the temperamental Decauville, Fedden decided to design a small-engined two-seater that could be driven and even maintained by its owner, and in 1907 he took his drawings for the Shamrock, as it was to be called, to S. Straker at the Brazil Straker car company which was based in Fishponds, Bristol. Liking what he saw, Straker agreed to build the Shamrock and he hired Fedden to head the engineering team. The Shamrock was very well received when unveiled at

On 12 June 1945, the day that the Fedden Mission left for Germany, General Dwight D. Eisenhower was at the Guildhall in London to receive the Freedom of the City.

the London Motor Show later that year. In its production version the little 12 to 14hp four-cylinder car sold for £315, which was considerable less than most cars on offer at the time. It was soon followed by the 15hp Straker Squire with an entirely new 3-litre engine, and this proved to be a hugely successful model with around 1,300 cars sold before the outbreak of the First World War.

In June 1914 Fedden made his first trip over to Germany, primarily to obtain car components from the Bosch engineering company, but it was a chance encounter at Mercedes that was to set his engineering career on a new course. As he later recalled:

> I remember visiting the German Mercedes factory on motor car business, and seeing, what to me at that date, were very large numbers – actually about fifty – of the 75hp six-cylinder in-line liquid cooled aero engines, all lined up in one shop.

So impressed was he by the sight that upon his return he persuaded the directors of Brazil Straker to take on repair work for various aircraft engines. Among them was the American-built OX-5, an early V-8 which powered the Curtiss aircraft being used by the

Royal Naval Air Service (RNAS) to train its new pilots. The OX-5 often proved unreliable and Fedden set about re-designing the engine with the assistance of draughtsman Leonard Butler. The company's role was soon expanded to include building Rolls-Royce aero engines; the water-cooled straight six-cylinder Hawk used to power the SSZ class of coastal patrol non-rigid airships, as well as the bigger V-12 version known as the Falcon for the Bristol Aircraft Company's F2 fighter biplane and the Falcon II and III for the twin-engined Blackburn Kangaroo reconnaissance and torpedo bomber.

Fedden and Butler also set about designing their own aircraft engine, the 300hp Mercury, which was based on an air-cooled radial configuration with the cylinders arranged like the spokes of a wheel in two staggered circles of seven. Air-cooling, it was argued, did away with the weight of the water-cooling systems which were also prone to freezing or overheating in extreme climates. With the radial design all of the connecting rods drove a single crankpin and as a result the crankshaft is shorter and stiffer than with an in-line arrangement. In general a radial air-cooled engine weighs less, has fewer components and so costs less, and performs better. The obvious disadvantage of the radial engine was an increased frontal area resulting in increased drag, but the advantages greatly outweighed this drawback. Following on from the Mercury, Fedden went on to develop the more powerful 450hp Jupiter which featured a single circle of nine cylinders. He also produced a smaller lightweight 100hp engine which was known as the Lucifer and had just three shortened Jupiter cylinders.

Early flight trials with the Mercury, and the Jupiter in particular, were very encouraging but the engines had come on the scene too late to enter wartime production, and the financially struggling Brazil Straker company was purchased by an Anglo-American financial group and re-branded as the Cosmos Engineering Company. With all war work drying up Cosmos went into liquidation and was sold to the Bristol Aeroplane Company (BAC) in July 1920 to form the basis of their new Engine Department at Filton airfield on the northern outskirts of Bristol. At BAC Fedden was given the opportunity and the financial backing to continue with the development of the Bristol Jupiter, as the Jupiter

This Bristol Bulldog Mk.IIA biplane was typical of the RAF's inter-war aircraft fitted with Fedden's Jupiter radial engine.

POPULAR FLYING, *April*, 19

SPEED

PERFORMANCE MANOEUVRABILITY

GREATER STRENGTH

LIGHTNESS OF WEIGHT

SIMPLICITY OF REPAIR

"*Bristol*"

SALIENT FEATURES
OF THE ALL-STEEL

BULLDOG MKIV

SINGLE-SEATER DAY & NIGHT FIGHTER

THE BRISTOL AEROPLANE COMPANY LTD
FILTON HOUSE BRISTOL

The Jupiter-engined Bristol Bulldog was sold to a number of countries and this advertisement published in *Popular Flying* in 1935 featured the 'BU' registration of the Finnish Air Force. Clearly the swastika symbol, shown here in reversed form, was not used exclusively by the Nazis.

was renamed, to its full potential. But BAC had underestimated the engine's phenomenal commercial success when they agreed to pay him a commission on each and every one sold, and as a result Roy Fedden swiftly became the most famous and, in all likelihood, the highest-paid engineer in Britain.

For Fedden the reliability of the Jupiter was paramount. Through extensive testing on rigs as well as on aircraft, any flaws were ironed out. Failed engines would be dismantled and minutely scrutinised to discover the cause, and the failed parts added to Fedden's black museum for future reference. In one exercise six Jupiter engines were disassembled and the parts mixed up and reassembled to confirm the interchangeability of the components. Furthermore, a continuous programme of development and a succession of new models saw improvements both in terms of the Jupiter's reliability and its power output; increasing from 400hp on the early engines up to 500hp on later versions. The Jupiter was widely regarded as the best aero engine in the world for many years from the mid-1920s and well into the early 1930s. Over 7,000 Jupiter engines were built and they were fitted on so many different aircraft, 262 different types in total, that it is hard to single out any particular one. They powered seventeen of BAC's own aircraft, including the famous Bristol Bulldog fighter, plus a host of others produced by manufacturers such as de Havilland, Fairey, Gloster, Handley Page, Short, Supermarine, Vickers and Westland. Then there were the high-profile long-distance airliners, the Handley Page HP.42 and HP.45, eight of which were operated by Imperial Airways on its European services during the 1930s. The HP.42 was fitted with four Bristol Jupiter XIFs of 490hp each while the HP.45, intended for much longer distances, had the more powerful supercharged XFBM 555hp model.

The Fedden and Butler team also produced several successors to the Jupiter. The first of these was the Bristol Mercury, a revival of the old Cosmos Mercury name, followed by the Pegasus. Launched in 1932, both featured the familiar radial configuration, this time with nine cylinders each, and had superchargers to improve performance at altitude. The Bristol Mercury had shorter cylinders to reduce the frontal area and was intended primarily for the RAF's fighter aircraft, whereas the Pegasus was the same size as the Jupiter and was designed for bombers. Later variants of the Pegasus could produce 1,000hp and the long list of famous Pegasus-powered aircraft includes the twin-engined Bristol Blenheim light bomber, the Vickers Wellesley, early versions of the Vickers Wellington, as well as the Short Empire and Sunderland flying boats.

With a general increase in aircraft size and with it an ever-growing demand for more power, Fedden and Butler turned to the sleeve valve for their next engines. This

An Imperial Airways long-range HP.42 biplane fitted with four Bristol Jupiter XIFs. This is G-AAUD Hanno, photographed during refuelling at Samakh, Palestine, in 1931. (LoC)

mechanism consists of a thin tube, or 'sleeve', which sits between the cylinder and the cylinder wall and either rotates or slides so that holes in the sleeve align with the cylinder's inlet and outlet ports. In theory this promised an improvement over the conventional poppet valve system which was considered to have run its course. In practice, however, the sleeves had to be immensely strong and capable of resisting high temperatures, and needed to be made with enormous precision. The direct result of this move to sleeve valves was a whole family of new engines which emerged from Bristol. The Mercury became the Bristol Aquila and the Pegasus was reborn as the Perseus with power outputs in the 500hp to 900hp range. From these grew even more powerful engines with two-row cylinder configurations. The various Taurus models produced 985hp to 1,060hp, the Hercules managed 1,290hp to 1,735hp, while the Centaurus, which was developed from the Hercules, achieved a massive 2,520hp by the latter stages of the Second World War. (It was the Centaurus, or at least eight of them, that would power the huge post-war Bristol Brabazon into the air when it flew for the first time on 4 September 1949.)

The success of the Bristol aero engines, especially the Jupiter, was not confined to the home market. The Jupiter was also licence-built in seventeen other countries including the USA, Japan, the Soviet Union and, significantly, in Germany. In 1924 Ernst Heinkel won the first all-round Germany race, the Rundflug, with a Bristol-engined aircraft. Dornier had produced a number of flying boats powered by Jupiter engines, including the mammoth Do.X which was fitted with twelve Siemens-built Jupiter engines when it first flew in July 1929.

Naturally these overseas business interests enabled Fedden to establish very close working relationships with many of the leading figures within the German aviation community. During the 1920s this had mainly come about through the regular appearance of the German engineers at the Bristol Aircraft Company's Engine Department in Filton, including visitors from the Heinkel, Dornier and Junkers companies. In turn Fedden made several trips to the German companies in the years leading up to the Second World War.

Developed from the Jupiter, later variants of the supercharged Mercury could produce up to 800 hp of power. The nine cylinders are shorter and squatter than on the Jupiter to reduce the frontal area. (Nimbus227)

The introduction of the sleeve valve saw a new family of engines emerge from Bristol including the Perseus which was a reworking of the nine-cylinder Pegasus. *(JC)*

Later, in 1945, he wrote candidly about these pre-war relationships and how he came to be highly respected by his German counterparts, not only for his undoubted engineering prowess, but also because he was a man they had come to trust:

> Herr Koch, chief engineer of the Rohrbach Company, came to Bristol on several occasions and stayed with me. Later he became a prominent Nazi, had a great deal to do with the training of German aircraft engineering personnel, and organised and built the great Heinkel bomber factory at Oranienburg. I believe I was the first Englishman to be taken over to this plant.

On the political front one of his most significant contacts was Erhard Milch. A squadron commander in the First World War, Milch had been a founding director of Deutsche Luft Hansa in 1926 (known as Deutsche Lufthansa from January 1931 onwards). 'He paid several visits to Bristol, stayed with me, and kept up a correspondence on certain of my papers afterwards,' recalled Fedden. In 1933 Milch became Under Secretary of State of the newly formed Reichsluftministerium (RLM), the German Aviation Ministry, answering directly to Reichsmarschall Hermann Göring. In 1939 Milch was also appointed as Inspector General of the new Luftwaffe and in 1942 became Head of Air Armament. Two years later, after failing to oust the increasingly maverick Göring, he re-emerged in a new role as deputy to Albert Speer, Hitler's Minister of Armaments and War Production.

Another distinguished signature in the Bristol visitors' book was Ernst Udet's. Germany's second-highest scoring ace of the First World War, Udet subsequently became the head of aeronautical research and development under the Nazi regime and was once described by Fedden as the mainspring of the Luftwaffe. (Udet committed suicide in November 1941, a fact unknown to Fedden at the time of his German Mission because Udet's sudden death had been explained by the German authorities as the result of an unfortunate accident during the testing of a new aircraft.)

Fedden solved the problem of increasing the number of cylinders on a radial engine by staggering them in two rows. This cutaway of the powerful eighteen-cylinder Centaurus is on display at the Bristol Aero Collection. *(JC)*

The fourteen-cylinder Hercules was the first of the sleeve valve Bristol engines to see widespread use. This example is at the Museum of Flight in East Fortune, Scotland. *(HairyHarry)*

In May 1937 Milch invited Fedden to come over to Germany to see for himself the extent of their new air force. There was to be no concealment, well almost no concealment, as the whole purpose of the trip was to convince the British that they couldn't possibly hope to compete with the Luftwaffe in the event of a war. Milch believed that Fedden, the highly respected engineer, would serve as a willing and credible witness to this fact. Fedden, for his part, seized this opportunity to gather as much useful intelligence as possible on the state of Germany's aviation industry and its rearmament programme. On his arrival, on 17 May 1937, he was met by both Milch and Udet who took him to the German Aero Club where lunch was followed by a lengthy discussion on the state of the German aviation:

Milch knew me, thought my opinion could be trusted technically, and he had sent for me to show me the extent and size of their production. He said that they were so far ahead that they could never be caught up, that they wished to be friends with England if we would fall into line, and he generally endeavoured to impress me with the size of the new air force. About four o'clock he pushed a sheet of paper over to me, and told me to write down where I would like to go. I jotted down seventeen names, covering development, experimental and materials works, never expecting to be allowed to go.

Milch immediately agreed to all of them and over the next twelve days Fedden was taken by Junkers Ju 86 – a twin-engine monoplane originally produced as a fast civil airliner but also capable of operating as a medium bomber – and by official staff car to many of the locations he had listed. In general he was permitted to go where he chose, although this inevitably precluded the more sensitive research and development facilities of which he was not aware and hence did not request to see. As it was, he couldn't get through the whole list during the time available and he went back to Germany in September later that same year to continue his tour.

Fedden returned to Germany once again in October 1938, less than a year before the outbreak of the war, on what was to prove his last pre-war trip. This time the main purpose was to present a paper on sleeve-valve engines at the Lilienthal Gesellschaft conference where, in his role as President of the Royal Aeronautical Society, he was also to present Hugo Eckener of the Zeppelin Company with the Society's Gold Medal. By this stage the once-influential Eckener had been ostracised by the Nazis and the reputation of the giant airships had been tainted forever by the destruction of the *Hindenburg* on 6 May 1937 as it came in to land at Lakehurst, New Jersey. The *Hindenburg's* sister ship, the *LZ-130 Graf Zeppelin II*, had only been launched a month before the 1938 conference, and it would carry out a number of propaganda flights within Germany plus several covert missions to probe Britain's fledgling radar defences. In April 1940 Hermann Göring, who had never bothered to conceal his contempt for the airships, gave the order for both the *LZ-130 Graf Zeppelin II* and its namesake, the old *LZ-127 Graf Zeppelin*, to be scrapped and their hangars at Frankfurt dynamited to make way for his precious aircraft.

Fedden himself was also honoured at a grand ceremonial dinner held during the Lilienthal Gesellschaft conference at the Neues Palais at Potsdam, the former winter palace of the Prussian kings and German emperors. It was here that Adolf Hitler personally presented him with the Lilienthal Ring in recognition of his contribution to aeronautical engineering. Fedden has left us no record of this encounter with the Führer, perhaps because he was more taken aback by a fellow guest at the event, the renowned American aviator Colonel Charles Lindbergh. According to Fedden, Lindbergh was totally mesmerised by the power and output of Germany's aircraft industry and was outspoken on the hopelessness of Britain pitting itself against the mighty Luftwaffe. In his own words, published in his *Autobiography of Values*, Lindbergh later wrote:

> The organised vitality of Germany was what most impressed me. The unceasing activity of the people, and the convinced dictatorial direction to create the new airfields, and research laboratories.

While still in Germany Fedden was offered, and eagerly accepted, the opportunity to inspect several of the aircraft factories he had visited previously in order to ascertain the progress made over the past year, which, as he put it, proved to be 'outstanding'. After each of these trips to Germany Fedden compiled highly detailed reports on his findings, but to his disbelief they were discredited by most of the Air Staff and politicians back in Britain. The official verdict was that Fedden had been duped by the Germans as to the real state of their planning and aircraft manufacturing output. Fedden was branded as a dangerous scaremonger and his valid warnings were never heeded.

Undaunted, Fedden was continuing his work on aero engines at BAC when, on 3 September 1939, Prime Minister Neville Chamberlain announced in a radio broadcast that Britain was at war with Germany. 'We are ready,' the Prime Minister had said, but his words were met with a profound silence at first, followed by a general sense of relief that the period of the so-called phoney war was over. Gas masks had been issued and barrage balloons already flew above London, but in many respects the nation was far from prepared for a war with the mightiest military force ever gathered; a war in which command of the skies would play such a decisive role.

The Bristol Taurus engine was already in production when war was declared. With the Hercules still undergoing testing, work on the big Centaurus engine was put on hold for the time being. In truth the Centaurus was ahead of the game as the newer aircraft types needed to carry this hefty 2,500hp power plant, such as the Hawker Tempest, wouldn't come on stream until later on in the war. By 1941 production of the Hercules was in full swing at Filton, despite the attention and explosives lavished upon the works by the Luftwaffe's Heinkels which caused heavy casualties and, by sheer chance, the destruction of Fedden's house.

The year 1942 proved to be an especially momentous year for Fedden. For a start he was knighted for his services to aeronautics by creating the most successful aero engine of the inter-war years. But satisfying as this recognition must have been, ironically it was Fedden's success that contributed to his undoing at Bristol. The Engine Department was in danger of eclipsing the aeroplane side of the company – a case of the tail wagging the dog perhaps – and he found himself increasingly embroiled in open conflict with the main board. A powerful and charismatic character, Fedden's particular brand of pragmatic single-mindedness and bluntness of speech was often misconstrued and unappreciated by those on the receiving end. There were power struggles, arguments about funding and priorities, and in the end Sir Roy Fedden and BAC parted company. In other words, he was sacked.

At a time of such urgent national need Fedden was not destined to be idle for long and he took up a post as Special Technical Advisor to the Minister (STAM) at MAP. This department had been formed by Churchill in 1940 to preside over an enormous increase in aircraft production, initially to deal with the demand for more aircraft leading up to and during the Battle of Britain in the summer and autumn of 1940. Since 1941 Fedden had already been working closely with MAP in his role as chairman of the Royal Aeronautical Society (RAeS) Committee to the Minister.

At MAP one of the first acts of Colonel John Llewellyn, who succeeded John Moore-Brabazon as the minister in early 1942, was to assign Fedden to head a fact-finding mission to the USA, where he was to learn what he could about the latest American aviation technology and production methods. Between December 1942 and March 1943 Fedden and a small team toured a comprehensive list of research facilities, aircraft and aero-engine plants throughout the USA, including those at Curtiss Wright, Glen Martin, Boeing, Bell, Douglas, Lockheed, Northrop, Fairchild, Grumman and Republic, plus various US Navy and US Air Force establishments. Fedden was immensely impressed by several of the aircraft he saw in production including the P-51 Mustang, the A-26, which later became the B-26 Invader, and the big B-29 Superfortress, but more importantly he felt that the UK aviation industry had much to learn from the size and scope of the Americans' engineering departments – in particular the flexibility of their manufacturing methods and the close liaison between the technical staff and the production departments. He estimated that in general the American companies had between eight and fifteen times as many technical people than was the practice with UK companies. His findings went into a comprehensive report, 'The Fedden Mission to America', but typically of Fedden (who was not known for his brevity) it was a massive tome. Equally predictably, its recommendations were met with resistance by large sectors of the home-grown industry, although some UK companies were keen apply the lessons learnt.

For Fedden his experiences of pre-war Germany and from the wartime mission to the USA reinforced his conviction that Britain had to do much more to bring together the training given by the universities and the practical needs of the aircraft industry. In October 1943 Sir Stafford Cripps, the new minister at MAP, appointed him chairman of an inter-departmental committee tasked with preparing proposals for a school of aeronautical science. Their report, published by MAP in 1944, would lay the foundation for what would later become the Cranfield College of Aeronautics (now known as Cranfield University).

In September 1944 Sir Roy Fedden was sent overseas once again. This time heading a hastily prepared mission to Italy with a view to securing enemy equipment captured in the newly liberated areas. On 29 September he flew to Pomigliano, near Naples, but

The Bristol Beaufighter, derived from the Beaufort torpedo bomber, was a long-range heavy-fighter equipped with twin Hercules engines.

On his mission to America Fedden was impressed by the flexibility of their manufacturing methods and the close liaison between technical staff and production departments. This is Consolidated's Fort Worth assembly plant producing B-24s. *(USAF)*

soon realised that he had been sent on a fruitless task as everything that might possibly have been useful or usable had been systematically destroyed by the retreating German and Italian forces. Following the fall of Nazi Germany in the spring of 1945, Fedden suddenly found himself summoned to the MAP building in Stratton Street once again. This time he was to lead a mission to Germany, and so it was that Fedden and his team found themselves waiting out the weather at RAF Northolt on 12 June.

The Dakota aircraft were finally able to depart from Northolt at 2.15 p.m. Their intended destination was Bückeburg in northern Germany, about 25 miles (40km) to the south-west of Hannover. As most of the conventional airfields were still out of action because of bomb damage inflicted by the Allies, temporary airstrips were built using wire mesh laid out on farmland. The two aircraft landed at 4.30 p.m. in heavy rain, but they were not allowed to stay at Bückeburg and the pilots were instructed to fly on to another airfield. This was just the first of the many difficulties the team would encounter trying to get about in this war-ravaged country. It was 9.30 p.m. by the time they finally arrived at the Tactical Air Force (TAF) Headquarters in Bad Eilsen, weary after their travels but grateful for something to eat and the opportunity to discuss their itinerary with the RAF Liaison officers. Afterwards they were driven to the nearby 2nd Army Group Headquarters at Bad Oyënhausen where they were billeted for the night. The following day was going to be a very important one. Their destination was one of the Nazis' most secret and extensive aeronautical research facilities, the Hermann Göring Institute at Völkenrode. At least, that was the intention.

two

THE REICH IN RUINS

ON WEDNESDAY 13 JUNE 1945 Fedden's team made an early start to get to Army Group Headquarters to obtain travel permits and to make arrangements for the first destination on their itinerary, the secret *Luftfahrtforschungsansalt* (LFA or aeronautical research institute) at Völkenrode. For their first two or three days in Germany they encountered unseasonably cold and wet weather and this may have been why it was decided to travel the 60 or so miles (95km) by road, instead of using the aircraft. Each of the Dakotas carried an American-built Jeep and unloading them was a tricky manoeuvre which entailed making a sharp turn rearwards out of the side of the aircraft's fuselage and then down two narrow and steep wooden ramps. But this operation soon became second nature to the crews, as Fedden noted:

> We were profoundly thankful that we had been given adequate transport, and the method of taking our own Jeeps in the Dakotas was of immense value. At first we had some delays in getting them in and out, but the crews soon became expert, and in a few days it was possible to be on the road in ten minutes or so after touching down.

For this first excursion they also managed to borrow a spare US Army Dodge truck for their 'luggage', which presumably meant the booty they were hoping to bring back with them.

Völkenrode is located to the east of Hannover near the city of Braunschweig, a little north of the Harz Mountains. But getting there was going to introduce the mission to the sort of conditions they would encounter throughout their stay in this battered country. The physical effects of the war were to be seen everywhere, from the countless abandoned vehicles lining the roads to the burnt-out carcasses of the ruined buildings. There were endless delays on the roads, even on the autobahn, caused by bomb damage, obstructions, or where bridges and viaducts had been systematically destroyed by the retreating German army.

'Diversions were usually marked,' wrote Fedden, 'but it was not unknown for the signs to have been demolished by a heavy army vehicle.' Trying to navigate through the towns proved to be even more difficult. In the central area of Braunschweig, for example, 90 per cent of the buildings had been destroyed in the Allied bombing raids of October 1944. By the time of the mission's arrival the mounds of rubble had

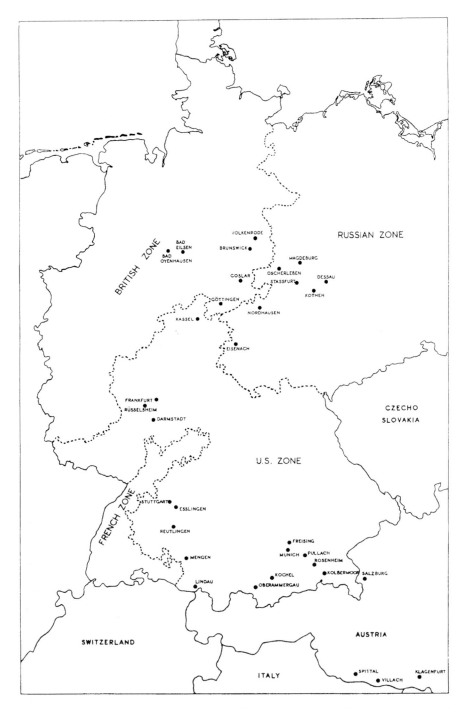

Map from *The Fedden Mission to Germany – Final Report* showing the distribution and clustering of the facilities being targeted by his team as well as the extent of the four Control Zones. Several key sites, such as Dessau and Nordhausen (Mittelwerk), are shown within the Russian Zone, which was extended within days of Fedden's visit.

been cleared from the roads, but without any landmarks to help them it was almost impossible for the drivers to find their way. In the end their journey took almost the entire day and, having averaged less than 10mph (16km/h), they didn't get to RAF Headquarters at LFA Völkenrode until 4.30 in the afternoon. With hindsight they realised that they could actually have flown direct to Braunschweig, the nearest airfield, and then unloaded the Jeeps for the relatively short drive up to Völkenrode. It was a practical lesson in logistics which caused Fedden and his team to reconsider the plans for the remainder of their time in Germany:

> We realised that we had undertaken an ambitious programme, and the map with which we were provided showed no fewer than fifty-two places to visit, but we little knew how great the difficulties would be, and how much scheming we would have to do in order to cover half of what we intended to accomplish … It soon became obvious that the number of visits was too ambitious for the time available and it was therefore found essential to cut down their scope.

The post-mission map, included in the final report, reveals the extent of the itinerary they actually achieved, both in terms of the number of facilities visited but also their geographical distribution across Germany. The 'targets', as they were termed, were divided into three main clusters. To start with they spent six days in the British Zone in central north Germany, with the mission making its headquarters at Braunschweig initially (shown on the map in its Anglicised form as Brunswick) and then at Kassel,

Loading a Jeep through the rear doors of one of the mission's Dakota aircraft. With practice the tricky manoeuvre could be accomplished in around ten minutes.

which is a little further to the south and within the American Zone. From these two locations they also made a number of important excursions north-eastwards, extending up as far as Dessau and into territory which was about to be taken over by the Russians. The second cluster of target sites was also in the American Zone, this time in and around the Munich area of Bavaria in the southernmost part of Germany. Here they were based at the American 3rd Army Intelligence Headquarters at Freising, about 20 miles (32km) outside Munich itself. During this second six-day stint they not only undertook daily excursions within the immediate vicinity, but also went by aircraft to the Stuttgart area further to the west. For the mission's third and final cluster of targets they were based at SHAEF Headquarters in Frankfurt.

Because of the time pressure on their schedule a smaller sub-group returned to Germany later on, from 16 until 25 July, with the primary objective of investigating the 'Hibertus' High Altitude Test Chamber at BMW Munich (see Chapter 12). During this second trip they were based at Freising once again and visited facilities in Munich, Stuttgart, Göttingen, Völkenrode and Kochel. For the sake of clarity, this account of the Fedden Mission to Germany frequently groups the activities and findings of the different trips together, either reporting them within the sections on individual sites or within specific areas of research or development. (The complete Mission itinerary is included as Appendix 1.)

Aside from the obvious practical issues with travelling, the team discovered that they had much to learn when it came to dealing with the inevitable bureaucracy of occupation. Despite receiving the full cooperation of both the American and British officials, plus written authority from SHAEF, obtaining permits for travel invariably took far longer than anticipated. In addition they had to organise appointments and travel permits for the long list of German technicians and engineers they proposed to 'interrogate' and then they had to get these individuals to the various locations when and where they were needed. As virtually all of the aeronautical research centres and industrial plants were at a complete standstill by this time, with the exception of a handful of senior personnel the staff tended to live some distance from where they worked. On several occasions it was found necessary to fetch people from up to 50 or even 100 miles away, again requiring permits as there were even stricter restrictions on travel for German citizens.

There was also the problem of finding accommodation for the mission each night, an especially difficult task in a country bereft of functioning telephones or hotels. They had taken their own tents and rations with them, but for the most part the members of the mission were billeted at American camps where they soon became familiar with the little cardboard boxes containing US Army K-rations and marked 'Supper'. At least they had something to eat and as with so many aspects of life in Germany in the immediate aftermath of war it was a case of adapting to their circumstances as they went along. Accordingly, the biggest change to their method of operating was put forward by Wing Commander Cross, the mission's liaison officer. Instead of moving about as a single unit he proposed sending one aircraft on ahead, a day or two before the main party, in order to organise the permits, accommodation, and so on. It was a strategy that proved to be highly effective and saved them a lot of time throughout the remainder of their stay.

Before and after photographs of Frankfurt illustrating the extent of the damage inflicted on many of Germany's cities. The older timber framed buildings, clustered to the left of the cathedral in the upper image, have been completely destroyed by the bombing. The lower image looks back towards the river with its broken bridges. *(USAF)*

Apart from the engineers and scientists they interviewed, the mission didn't have a great deal of direct contact with German civilians. All contact between the Allied forces of occupation and the local population, even on an official basis, was deliberately limited to what was considered absolutely necessary. Fraternisation was forbidden and Allied soldiers were instructed not to 'shake hands with Germans, visit their homes, play games or walk with them on the streets or elsewhere'. In 1944 the British Political Warfare Executive issued a pocket-sized information booklet, entitled *Instructions for British Servicemen in Germany*, which contained guidelines for the servicemen on what to expect in Germany and how to deal with the situations that they might encounter. It is a slim volume but reveals much about the official attitude of the Allies at the time. From a modern perspective much of its contents read as pure propaganda and racial stereotyping, especially the introduction which was printed in bold type for added emphasis:

For the second time in under thirty years, British troops are entering upon the soil of Germany. The German Army, the most carefully constructed military machine which the world has known, has suffered catastrophic defeats in the field. The civilian population of Germany has seen the war brought to its homes in a terrible form. You will see much suffering in Germany and much to awake your pity. You may also find that many Germans, on the surface at least, seem pleasant enough and that they will even try to welcome you as friends. All this may make you think that they have learned their lesson and need no further teaching. But remember this: for the last hundred years, long before Hitler, German writers of great authority have been steadily teaching the necessity for war and glorifying it for its own sake. The Germans have much to unlearn.

Photographed in July 1945, a tangle of twisted girders at the Fieseler works near Kassel. As well as its producing its own aircraft, the company was targeted because it manufactured parts for the Fw 190. *(NARA)*

Wilhelm Keitel signs the documents of Germany's unconditional surrender at the Soviet headquarters in Karlhorst, Berlin. (NARA)

It goes on to state that, 'there will be no Brutality about a British occupation, but neither will there be softness or sentimentality':

> You may see many pitiful sights. Hard-luck stories may somehow reach you. Some of them may be true, at least in part, but most will be hypocritical attempts to win sympathy. For, taken as a whole, the German is brutal when he is winning, and sorry for himself and whines for sympathy when he is beaten. So be on your guard against propaganda in the form of hard-luck stories. Be fair and just, but don't be soft.

After a brief summary of German history, including the rise of Adolf Hitler and the Nazis, and a description of the conditions in Germany, the booklet returns to its main theme, a warning against the dangers of fraternisation, especially with the women:

> When you meet the Germans you will probably think they are very much like us. They look like us, except that there are fewer of the wiry type and more big, fleshy, fair-haired men and women, especially in the north. But they are not really so much like us as they look … Remember keep Germans at a distance, even those with whom you have official dealings … Numbers of German women will be willing, if they can get the chance, to make themselves cheap for what they can get out of you … Be on your guard. Most of them will be infected. Marriages between members of British forces and Germans are, as you know, forbidden …

That last sentence was also printed in bold type. There would be no sleeping with the enemy. Not for a while at least.

One of the first actions of the Allied authorities in Germany was to implement a programme of denazification. This involved removing former pro-Nazis from positions of authority and eradicating all physical traces or symbols of Nazism. Streets with

Friendly smiles in front of the cameras at least as the 'Big Three', Churchill, Roosevelt and Stalin, meet at the Yalta Conference in February 1945 to discuss Europe's post-war reorganisation. *(US DoD)*

Nazi connections were renamed, all Nazi propaganda was removed from educational establishments, and all Nazi regalia was banned.

For Fedden and his colleagues their first encounter with the German civilians was on the drive to Braunschweig on their first day. They couldn't fail to observe the endless tide of people clogging the roads and filling the towns. These were the DPs, meaning Displaced Persons, a politically innocuous and all embracing term that wrapped up a maelstrom of human stories hidden behind the statistics. The never-ending blur of humanity was too vast to register as individuals, but every now and then a cameo of misery would catch their eye. An old woman pulling a handcart piled high with bundles, a small child asleep in its mother's arms.

The number of DPs was truly incredible. It is thought that approximately 26 million Germans were made homeless as a result of the war, and as many as 12 million had either fled from the advancing tide of the Red Army in the east or were forcibly expelled from Germany's provinces and the former occupied countries such as Poland, Czechoslovakia, Hungary and Romania. This uprooted population didn't just comprise Germans; its number was swollen by hundreds of thousands of former enforced foreign workers, people from France, Holland, Belgium, Russia and Poland, plus concentration camp internees as well as political and other prisoners who had been held by the Nazis. The result was a massive stream of the dispossessed, all striving to make their way home, whatever that had become, as best they could. Put together, this army of lost souls was the greatest movement of people in modern history.

The exodus of civilians from the eastern parts of Germany had begun during the final stages of the war. Under siege, the Nazi regime had paid scant regard to the needs of its civilian population; they were of secondary importance, an unfortunate inconvenience, especially when they hindered the movement of the army. Even in cases where plans had been laid for the evacuation of civilians, discussing such a possibility in the face of

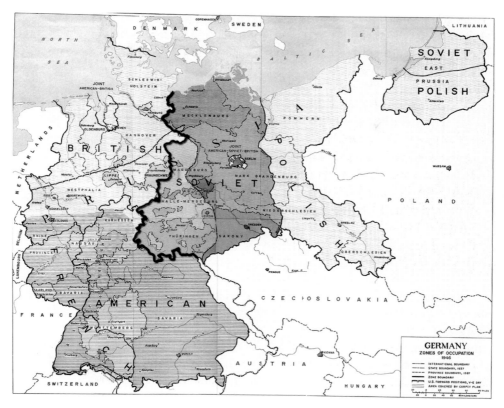

The Allied Zones of Occupation showing the inner German border and the area handed over to the Russians in July 1945. *(LoC)*

imminent invasion would be condemned as 'defeatist talk' and could incur the death penalty. This left the ordinary Germans completely in the dark with nowhere to turn, whilst the Nazi propaganda machine continued to churn out lurid horror stories of what would befall them at the hands of Soviet invaders, in particular with respect to what would happen to the women. Stirring up these deep-seated fears was a deliberate ploy to make the German defenders, both the soldiers and the civilians, hold their ground right to the bitter end. But as it turned out the reality was not that far removed from the propaganda. In an orgy of revenge the advancing Soviet soldiers frequently shot German civilians, looted their homes and burnt whole villages to the ground, while the young girls and women were almost systematically raped, often publicly, and frequently left for dead. Of course it would be unrealistic to suggest that cases of rape didn't occur in the western zones, but it was to a far lesser extent, and under military law an American soldier could face execution if convicted of rape.

Apart from a few older men and young boys, the German DPs consisted almost entirely of women. German men of fighting age – and from October 1944 that included the sixteen to sixty-year-old members of Hitler's *Volkssturm*, a national militia or people's army

– were either dead or they were being held as prisoners of war. Many of the POWs were corralled within large open-air holding camps, which the Allies referred to euphemistically as Prisoner of War Temporary Enclosures. Here they were exposed to the elements and it is thought that thousands of the prisoners succumbed to either malnutrition or disease, especially during the harsh winter of 1945. Many of the POWs were put to work by their captors. At the Yalta Conference the Allied leaders had approved the principle of enforced labour for German POWs, not only in order to repair the damage that the Nazis had inflicted on their victims and fellow Germans but also as a form of war reparation. The three Allied powers handled this in different ways and prisoners held by the Russians, in particular, were very harshly treated with thousands transported to the Soviet Union where they faced years of back-breaking labour in the work camps. Whereas most of those imprisoned by the western Allies were released by the end of 1948, the final repatriation of Russian-held prisoners didn't take place until 1955; ten years after the war had ended.

In addition to the imprisoned soldiers, a further 100,000 German civilians were interned by the Allies in the months after the war because they were either considered to be a threat to security or they were being held for possible trial. The two main architects of the Luftwaffe, Hermann Göring and Erhard Milch, were already in custody. Milch was captured on the Baltic coast on 4 May, while Göring had surrendered to US soldiers in Bavaria on 9 May 1945 (see Chapter 12).

During 1945 the situation with DPs was further exacerbated when Germany was carved up into Allied-controlled zones of occupation. This wholesale rearrangement of Germany's political geography had been agreed some time previously by the 'Big Three' – Franklin D. Roosevelt, Winston Churchill and Joseph Stalin – and it was ratified at the Yalta Conference held in the Crimea in early February 1945. The Allied leaders next met

German officers standing in line waiting for 'C' Rations at a Prisoner of War camp near Hershfeld, April 1945. 'Note their arrogance even after capture', stated the photo caption at the time. *(NARA)*

The programme of denazification saw the removal of all Nazi regalia including named street signs. (NARA)

in July 1945, just weeks after the Fedden Mission's departure, this time at Potsdam, where they continued their discussions on the future of Germany and Eastern Europe. By then there had been some significant changes in their line-up. Following the sudden death of President Roosevelt in April 1945, the USA was represented by his successor, Harry S. Truman, and almost midway through the conference Clement Attlee replaced Winston Churchill after the latter's shock defeat at the hand of the British electorate. That left Joseph Stalin as the only wartime leader still in power. Two of the main policies to come out of Potsdam were the moving of Poland's borders westward, and the approval of a programme of 'ethnic reconfiguration' which would see the forcible deportation of the remaining German nationals and ethnic Germans from the eastern territories. Referred to as 'orderly population transfers' by the Allies, Churchill regarded this process as a vital element in establishing post-war stability, a 'clean sweep' as he put it, to prevent future troubles.

The division of Germany in 1945 saw the British, Americans and Russians each allocated a zone of approximately equal size. The British had the north-west, the Americans the central and southern areas and the Russians took control of the north-eastern zone. Meanwhile the French were allocated a far smaller strip in the south-west of Germany which was created by hiving off territory from the American and British zones. Despite the declared intention of establishing a single unified Allied Control Council across the whole of the country, in practice each of the four powers wielded governmental control within their respective zones. Of particular relevance during the Fedden Mission was an imminent shift of the boundary on the eastern side of the British zone in Russia's favour. This had come about because the invading US forces had over-stepped the mark by pushing up to 200 miles (322km) beyond the boundary previously agreed. Within just a matter of days of Fedden's arrival in Germany the British were due to concede this territory and hand it back to the Russians. This area included the Braunschweig enclaves where the secret LFA research institute at Völkenrode was located, which explains why it was right at the top of Fedden's hit list.

The division of Germany into Allied zones was not a distribution of territories as the spoils of war as such, or at least it was not meant to be, but rather it was intended as a fair distribution of governmental responsibility among the Allies. Having said that, there is no doubt that the prevailing attitude held by the victorious nations was that in defeat the Germans had only got what they deserved, and they would have to pay for what they did, quite literally. With the experience of the war still so raw in the Allies' minds it was never going to be about how to put Germany on its feet again. It was about revenge and recompense. At the Yalta Conference it was agreed in general terms that Germany would 'pay in kind for the war losses caused by her to the Allied nations in the course of war'. This included not only the delivery of goods from production but also, and more significantly in the immediate aftermath, a percentage of usable industrial equipment. The Russians in particular were rigorous in applying this policy and they dismantled and removed complete industrial complexes, right down to the washroom fittings. Similar removals also took place in the American and British zones, albeit on a more limited scale. As for the Nazis' discarded military hardware and expertise, that was regarded as fair game. Such blatant terms as 'war prizes' or the 'spoils of war' might not have been bandied about, but that is exactly what the various Allied technical teams scouring Germany were looking for in the factories, on the airfields and in the aeronautical research centres. (The question of the quantity of hardware and technical knowledge which was removed in this process is examined in Chapter 12.)

It is interesting to note that upon his arrival in Germany in June 1945 Sir Roy Fedden had at first expressed a great sense of satisfaction on seeing the extent of the damage inflicted upon German towns and cities by the Allied bombers. However, this outlook began to wear off after a few days and soon changed. By definition many of the aircraft factories and aeronautical research establishments his team was visiting had been high-priority targets during the Allied bombing campaign and the devastation inflicted was often extensive:

> It is a depressing experience to enter large plants and engineering establishments, even if they belonged to the Germans, and to find them at an absolute standstill. Places with unique equipment and facilities for tackling the most intricate mechanical problems, either on a research or complete production basis, are lying fallow, and in many cases, having been partially destroyed, will soon become derelict wrecks … It is surprising how in a few weeks a production line will deteriorate. Sabotage and looting, which took place by the workers and the troops immediately on the cessation of hostilities, are still evident. And the effect of going into magnificent offices and stores and finding excellent precision equipment, drawings, papers, micrometers, gauges etc, thrown all over the floor in confusion, must actually be seen to be appreciated.

As Fedden mentions, apart from the obvious effects of the bombing, considerable damage and disruption had been caused by a number of groups. To begin with there had been the retreating German forces who deliberately sabotaged aircraft, equipment and plant to make sure they could not be of any use in the hands of the enemy. Then there was the ransacking and sabotage inflicted as revenge and retribution either by those who had been suppressed by the Nazis, in particular by former enforced foreign workers, or by looters looking for valuables to sell. These included the local population, the DPs, and, it has to be admitted, the Allied soldiers themselves who, heady with their victories, were hell-bent on teaching the vanquished a lesson and taking home a few choice trophies. To some extent the revelations of what had been happening in the concentration camps and reports of other atrocities, especially those concerning stories of downed Allied airmen being shot, fuelled a frenzy of anger against the Germans.

In the final stages of the war the British had deployed their Target Force – better known simply as T-Force – to secure important facilities, whether military, scientific or otherwise, and to protect them from looters and saboteurs. There were also fears, unfounded as it turned out, of a campaign of continued covert resistance by Nazi fanatics, a guerrilla war of sabotage and terrorist actions to be conducted by the almost-mythical Werewolf organisation. The lightly armed and highly mobile T-Force operated at the vanguard of the advancing Allied land forces, sometimes ahead of the line and delving deep into enemy territory, to secure and guard targets which had been selected by the experts in the CIOS.

Nuremberg 1945. Some landmarks remain, such as the twin-spired Lorenz Church and the statue of Kaiser William I, but in many cities the streets had been reduced to featureless canyons of rubble. *(US DoD)*

One final element used to justify the Allies' ransacking of Germany's technological jewels was rooted in the widely held view that the German leopard was incapable of changing its spots. At heart the Germans were unrepentant and the ghastly nightmare could start all over again. Fedden expressed himself very clearly in this passage taken from an article written for *Flight* magazine in November 1945:

> Even after a fair interval of time, one's impressions of German aeronautical progress are constantly overshadowed in the mind by the tremendous social, moral and economic problems imposed by the condition of Germany today. I knew several leaders of the aircraft and engine industry for many years before the war, and it was a sombre experience to meet them again after seeing the horrors of Nordhausen, with its incinerators for the corpses and the pitiful shambles of maimed and dying humanity … For the most part these leaders of industry seemed quite unrepentant, and thought it was bad luck they had lost after so nearly winning.

Many argued, Fedden among them, that it was vital that the Allies must get their dealings with a defeated Germany right this time. In particular they must learn from the experience of the First World War and the subsequent Treaty of Versailles, because if they didn't Germany would rise again as a military power. It has been suggested by some historians that it was the terms of the Treaty of Versailles that had actually laid the seeds of German rearmament for the Second World War. In addition to substantial economic reparations the Allied signatories to the treaty had sought to permanently pacify Germany by severely restricting the size of its military forces. The army was limited to 100,000 men and the navy was permitted only six small battleships and thirty other craft, but no submarines. As for the air force, that was to be abolished. It is estimated that between 15,000 and 20,000 German aircraft were scrapped after the First World War. In addition the terms of the Versailles treaty restricted German aeroplane production to civil aircraft only and strict limits were placed on the engine power permitted.

In 1921 the *Reichswehrministerium* (Defence Ministry) had sought to circumvent the restrictions by equipping its security police force with seven air squadrons, but this loophole was soon closed by the Allied Control Commission. Over the ensuing years the aircraft companies, and even the proponents of a new German air force, found ever more devious ways to continue their work either covertly or under the guise of other activities; in particular the training of pilots through the pretext of sport aviation. Within Germany there was an explosion of gliding and private flying clubs which attracted a new generation of young aviators. Further afield, a secret military pilot training base was established in 1924 at Lipetsk, in southern Russia, where the pilots could hone their skills on Dutch-built Fokkers or on a handful of Soviet and German aircraft. Gradually the restrictions were eased. In 1922 the Allies allowed a limited resumption of civil aircraft production and the Paris Aviation Treaty of 1926 actually permitted the manufacture of military aircraft, although for export purposes only. Through these measures the key skills vital for a new German air force were kept alive and when, in January 1933, Adolf Hitler became German Chancellor he immediately instructed Herman Göring to form the RLM. Two years later, in 1935, all pretence was abandoned with the official formation of

After the end of the First World War under the terms of the Treaty Of Versailles the German air force was systematically dismantled and between 15,000 and 20,000 aircraft were scrapped.

the Luftwaffe in a direct breach of the Treaty of Versailles, intended as a show of strength by Hitler.

The rest, as the say, is history. But in 1945 the question facing the Allies was whether German militarism could or would rise from the ashes of war for a second time. Fedden thought so. He expressed his concerns in a secret briefing document prepared in January 1945:

> I have no doubt that Germany is already planning for the next war, and that those who go over there to deal with her, after her defeat this time, will have to be very alive to the fact, and not take an obvious or unintelligent line such as smashing up all her existing types. I do not mean by this that all the heavy industries and aircraft plants must not necessarily be swept away finally; rather I am trying to point out that those responsible for long term policy in Germany are extremely subtle and long-headed people, and, if we are not careful, will manage to work out some quite original plan to counter our stopping the rebuilding of their air force.

What even Fedden failed to grasp at the time is that the Germans had had enough of wars. The greater threat to post-war peace would come from the changing political balance of power and the opposing ideologies of east and west. Even as Fedden's team scooped up the crumbs from the table, the American and Russian technical teams were already scouring fallen Germany to grab the most advanced aircraft, guided missiles, jet engines and rockets that the Nazi scientists and engineers had devised. These machines snatched from the ruins of Hitler's Third Reich would define the weaponry of the Cold War era.

three

WINGS OF CHANGE

ON 13 APRIL 1945, less than a month before the end of the war in Europe, the advancing American forces had stumbled across one of Germany's best-kept aeronautical secrets. On the western outskirts of Braunschweig, near to the village of Völkenrode, they found a collection of buildings, sixty or more, scattered across a wide area of woodland. At first glance many of the buildings appeared to be nothing more than innocuous-looking farmsteads. Only a few rose above the tree canopy, and those that did were hidden beneath concrete platforms covered with several feet of earth and planted with trees to blend in with the forest. This explains how the Germans had managed to hide their most advanced and extensive research establishment: the *Luftfahrtforschungsanstalt* (LFA) Hermann Göring, otherwise known as Völkenrode.

In the aftermath of the First World War German aeronautical research had been left in the doldrums, shackled by the terms of the Treaty of Versailles and lacking either support or funding from the Weimar government. That situation changed abruptly following Hitler's rise to power and his appointment as Chancellor in January 1933, and only months later the RLM had been formed. Suddenly the importance of aeronautical research was being officially recognised by the state and millions of Reichsmarks were poured into expanding the existing educational establishments and research facilities. Huge wind tunnels were constructed at the main centres, the *Deutsche Versuchsansalt für Luftfahrt* (DVL) at Berlin-Adlershof, and the *Aerodynamische Versuchsanstalt* (AVA) at the University of Göttingen. One of the wind tunnels at Göttingen was so big that the Lufthansa pilots were said to use it as a navigational aid because they could easily spot it from the air. However, with the prospect of a war on the horizon, these highly visible city-based institutions might prove vulnerable to aerial reconnaissance and attack by hostile aircraft. What was needed was something altogether more discreet. A little place in the woods, perhaps.

Groundwork on the 1,000-acre site near Völkenrode began in October 1935 and construction of the first wind tunnel commenced in November the following year. A road running between Völkenrode and Bortfeld was diverted to clear the area and the buildings were widely spaced among the trees, grouped into the five main areas of activity that made up the LFA. The Institute of Aerodynamics with five wind tunnels, and the Institute of Gas Dynamics which had a high-speed wind tunnel of its own, were both located at the southern tip of the site. The Institute of Strength Properties, with facilities for static testing, was on the western side, while the Institute of Engine Research was in a detached area on the eastern side. The Institute of Kinematics, which would undertake weapons and ballistic research in its laboratories and using a specially constructed 1,312ft (400m) ballistic tunnel, was in the north-west corner. The buildings were spread out in this way not only to reduce the risk of being observed by enemy reconnaissance aircraft, but also to ensure that the scientists working in any one institute would not be aware of the research going on in another. This was a physical manifestation of the paranoid tendency which permeated the Nazis' weapons programme. An unintended negative result of this policy was that individual teams, be they aircraft or weapons specialists, or even manufacturers for that matter, were unable to benefit from similar work being undertaken by others within the same field.

In addition to these facilities, around 400 houses were constructed at Völkenrode, a little away from the main site, to accommodate a nominal force of 1,500 workers and scientists. There were also various other support buildings such as administration offices, a telephone exchange, electricity generators, canteens, guard houses and so on. To avoid the risk of detection there were no railway lines leading into the site, no overhead power cables and no tell-tale chimneys. All services were brought underground from Braunschweig; even the steam used to heat the buildings. An airstrip was constructed on the outskirts of Braunschweig but was carefully disguised by the planting of patches with several different types of grass seed. So thorough and effective was the subterfuge that

The 'broken back of the Luftwaffe' – British and American personnel examine the remains of a Ju 88 at the Braunschweig, or Brunswick, airfield *(USAF)*

the location of LFA Völkenrode remained secret until the fall of Germany. The Allies did have an idea that such an aeronautical research facility actually existed but had no idea where, as Fedden himself noted:

> British engineers, who had been in the habit of visiting Germany prior to the war, had heard rumours that the RLM was setting up an entirely new research organisation, but nobody knew exactly where it was, or the extent of the equipment and personnel. In fact, rumour had it that it was in East Prussia, whereas other statements were to the effect that such a laboratory had been planned but never started.

Secrecy aside, it was the extent of the site that astounded Fedden and his team when they arrived at Völkenrode on the morning of Thursday 14 June 1945. By then dozens of CIOS technical teams had already pored over the site and the Americans had made themselves at home, even though it was within the British Zone of occupation. As Fedden put it, 'the whole LFA Laboratory seems to have been very finely combed by the American authorities'. The place even had the feel of a US Army base with dozens of white-starred trucks and Jeeps negotiating the maze of wavy tracks that ran through the woods. Some visitors became so lost on the extensive site that signposts were erected in English to help them reach their destinations.

The most obvious jewels at Völkenrode were the wind tunnels, of which there were several, each designated by the Germans and allocated with an 'A' number (as shown on the site map).

A1 was a medium-sized tunnel of the Göttingen type with a circular nozzle 8ft 6in (2.5m) diameter and a maximum air speed of 123mph (55m/sec). It had been in operation since 1937.

A full-size Messerschmitt Bf 109 undergoing testing in the A3 wind tunnel at the secret Völkenrode aeronautical research centre in 1940. *(LoC)*

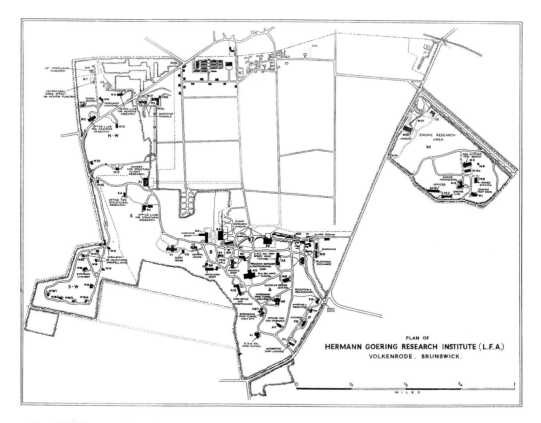

Plan of the Hermann Göring Research Institute (LFA) at Völkenrode. Incredibly this 1,000 acre facility remained secret to the Allies through concealment and the apparent randomness of the layout. On the western side, *left*, starting at the top there is the weapons research area, then structural research with munitions at the bottom. The main aerodynamics area with wind tunnels is central, and engine research is located on the eastern side.

A2 was a high-speed closed-return tunnel with a cylindrical test section of 9ft 2in (2.8m) diameter and 4ft 4in (4m) long. Work on this tunnel had started in 1937 and the first tests were run in 1939. The A2 was especially interesting as it had a maximum airspeed – with test model in place and depending on the dimensions of that model – in the transonic range around Mach 1 to 1.2. (The model was held in place by two carefully profiled struts which were swept back and unshielded.) The return circuit, with provision for cooling air, was located above the working section. The air was supplied by a two-stage compressor driven by a pair of DC motors, each one of 600kw rating. Interferometer and striation apparatus was fitted for visual examination of the airflow characteristics.

The inner surfaces of the A2 tunnel were coated with an application of Keratylene for smoothness and to prevent erosion. However, the tunnel was found to suffer from air vibrations or flutters when operating in the critical range passing from subsonic to supersonic conditions. Because of these problems the scientists at Völkenrode

The mission report states that this is the Rheinmetall-Borsig F25 liquid-fuelled free-flight research model seen at Völkenrode, but in fact Fedden had appropriated a photograph of the test launch of the F55 Feurlilie anti-aircraft missile.

had obtained a free-flight research rocket which was launched almost vertically via a gantry. The model to be studied was attached to the front of the rocket and three cine-theodolites, geared together and fitted with a timer, recorded the flight and provided data to calculate the drag coefficient along the whole trajectory. The rocket Fedden would have seen at Völkenrode was the Rheinmetall-Borsig F25, a single liquid-fuelled engine rocket designed for high-speed research initially, although with the potential for development as a weapon. This had side wings, or fins, and a high-mounted tailplane at the rear. Curiously, the photographs published in the Fedden Mission's final report are labelled as a 'Free flight model for drag investigations at sonic speeds', but actually show the bigger F55. This was a guided anti-aircraft missile known as the *Feurlilie* ('fire lily') which was 15ft 9in (4.8m) long and had a pair of wings at the rear with fins on the tips. Like the F25, the F55 was designed originally to be powered by a single liquid-fuelled rocket engine, but on its first test launch, during which it attained Mach 1.25, it flew with four Rheinmetall-Borsig 109-505 solid fuel rockets instead. So it seems almost certain that for his report Fedden borrowed some photographs of the F55, probably taken as it was being prepared for its first test flight at Pomerania in May 1944, but definitely not showing the smaller F25 research rocket seen at Völkenrode.

The biggest wind tunnel, but by no means the fastest, was the A3; a full-scale Göttingen type with a lateral return, a 26ft 3in (8m) diameter nozzle and a maximum airspeed of 215mph (95m/sec). Importantly, the open working section had a length of 36ft (11m), which was big enough to test a full-size small aircraft. Photographs from around 1940 show a complete Messerschmitt Bf 109 suspended in position in this wind tunnel. The compressor was operated by two 6,000kw DC motors, placed one behind the other and contained in a fairing in the return circuit. This fairing acted as an air intake, continuously removing about 10 per cent of the air in circulation which was then replaced by fresh air for cooling drawn from the measuring chamber.

Fedden was informed that this tunnel had proved very useful in practice, in particular with designing the pressure cowling for the BMW 801 radial piston engine fitted on a number of Junkers aircraft and also on the Messerschmitt Me 264 which had been a potential candidate as an *Amerikabomber*.

THE AMERIKABOMBER PROJECT

The *Amerikabomber* project had called for a long-range aircraft capable of delivering a useful bomb load, say 4.5 tons if we disregard the possibility of an atomic bomb for now, across the 3,600-mile (5,800km) expanse of the Atlantic Ocean. The intention was twofold; to hit back at the Americans and also to tie up their resources in defending the homeland. A number of scenarios were put forward including a return flight, a *Huckepack* or piggy-back configuration in which a larger aircraft would carry a smaller one as far as possible before releasing it, or a one-way trip with the aircraft ditching in the Atlantic afterwards for pick-up by U-boat.

Several aircraft were considered for the *Amerikabomber* project, including the Focke-Wulf Fw 300 which was based on the existing Focke-Wulf Fw 200 Condor long-range

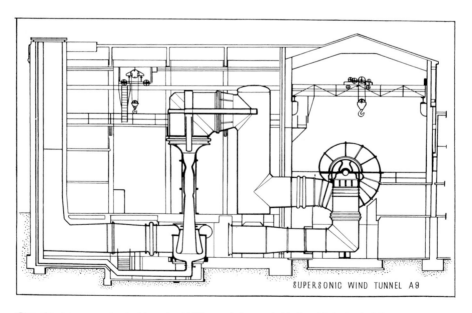

SUPERSONIC WIND TUNNEL A9

One of two supersonic wind tunnels at Völkenrode housed side-by-side in the building shown as A9 on the site map. By coupling the motors from both tunnels Mach numbers of between 1.0 and 1.5 could be maintained.

Photograph from the mission report showing Dr E. Scmidt beside an engine test-bed in the engine laboratory at Völkenrode.

maritime patrol and reconnaissance aircraft, the Focke-Wulf Ta 400, the Junkers Ju 390 which was another heavy transport long-range bomber, the Heinkel He 277 – the nearest the Luftwaffe had to a long-range heavy bomber in production – and the Messerschmitt Me 264. In addition the Horten brothers and the Arado company had put forward proposals for large jet-powered flying wings (see Chapter 10). In the event, a more conventional Ju 390 was selected.

Three prototypes were constructed and some sources have suggested that the second aircraft actually made a transatlantic flight to within 12 miles (20km) of the US coast, although this claim is generally discredited. In the end the *Amerikabomber* raid on the USA was never realised, not through any insurmountable technical barriers but through a lack of will and, by the latter stages of the war, the strain being put on the Nazis' war machine.

Another way of attacking America also under consideration by the Nazis was to deploy rocket-powered aircraft or inter-continental ballistic missiles. Even before the war the scientists Eugen Sanger and Irene Bredt had proposed a winged sub-orbital transatlantic bomber in the form of a lifting body, which they christened *Silbervogel* ('silverbird'). This would have been launched from a 2-mile (3km) track by rocket-powered sled, and once airborne its own rocket engines would have accelerated it to around 13,800mph (22,100km/h) at an altitude of 90 miles (145km). As it gradually descended the *Silbervogel* would have gained lift in the denser air to bounce, like a stone on the surface of the water, in ever decreasing arcs until it had reached it target. The *Silbervogel* never made it off the drawing board.

Plans for a conventional rocket attack were also never put into operation. The A9/A10 *Amerika-Rakete* ('America rocket') was to be developed from the A4 (V2) rocket family as a two-stage missile with inter-continental capability. Another alternative would have entailed launching an A4-type rocket from a U-boat stationed near the American coast, but the problem of fuelling and launching such a complicated weapon from an unstable sea-borne platform were considered too great.

Returning to Völkenrode, the A3 wind tunnel was also used in the development of the Argus pulsejet engine found on the tail of the V-1 flying bomb (see Chapter 7).

Of the other wind tunnels, the A6/7 worked in a different way. An air storage tank with a 35,500ft³ (1,000m³) capacity would be evacuated to about one-fifth atmosphere with the help of a 1,000kw pump. On opening a valve air was sucked through the small working section, less than 16in² (40cm²), for a duration of about 20 seconds. The A9 building housed a pair of supersonic tunnels, side by side. Each one was operated by a 4,000kw motor, and by coupling these motors together either tunnel could be operated with 8,000kw, making it possible to sustain Mach numbers of between 1.0 and 1.5 in continuous operation. However, the working sections were still relatively small at 31.5in² (80cm²) on one, and the open section on the other had a diameter of 35.5in (90cm).

THE SWEPT WING

One of the most important areas of the aerodynamic research conducted in the wind tunnels at the three main research centres, Völkenrode and Göttingen as well at DVL Berlin-Aldershof, was in the development of the swept-wing platform for Germany's new generation of jet-powered aircraft. As the speed of an aircraft increases the effects

Göttingen's big wind tunnel under construction in 1935. It is said that Lufthansa pilots used it as a navigational aid. *(DLR)*

of the compressibility of the air become more pronounced. When the Mach number – defined as the ratio of the flight velocity to the speed of sound – approaches Mach 1 the aerodynamic characteristics of a wing are radically changed. The lift decreases and the drag increases. For conventional straight wings, as featured on just about every propeller-driven aircraft, this radical change in wing efficiency doesn't occur generally until Mach 0.74 and hence it is not an issue. But for faster jets the critical Mach number had to be pushed to higher limits.

The swept-wing, referred to as the *Pfeilflügel* ('arrow wing') by the Germans, was first proposed by Adolf Busemann at an aeronautical conference held in Italy in 1935. Busemann was a professor of aerodynamics at Göttingen University and went on to run the aerodynamics research department at Völkenrode during the war. However, the young engineer's paper was received with only mild interest as it was thought that there was little prospect of any aircraft attaining Mach 1 for some considerable time to come. It was only with the advent of the turbojets that the swept-wing configuration was revisited and wind tunnel testing soon confirmed Busemann's theories.

Of all the Luftwaffe's jets of the Second World War, the Messerschmitt Me 262 is undoubtedly the most famous. But the oft-repeated assertion that this was the first jet to feature swept-wing geometry is incorrect. The truth is that as a result of his wind tunnel research Busemann had suggested that the Messerschmitt designers should use a 35° sweep – the same angle as the later US F-86 Sabre and the Soviet MiG-15 incidentally – but this was not adopted. Instead the production aircraft had a leading edge sweep of only 18.5°, too slight to afford any significant increase in the critical Mach speed. This sweep on the Me 262 was a modification made to counteract the higher than anticipated weight of the jet engines and to realign the centre of lift with the centre of mass of the aircraft. Another claim, that an Me 262 obtained Mach 1 in a steep dive, has never been proved.

Newly completed, Göttingen's massive wind tunnel 6 photographed in 1936. *(DLR)*

Members of the Fedden Mission with Dr Encke, in the white coat, at the AVA Göttingen. Second from the left wearing glasses is Dr W.J. Duncan, next to him is Mr Stern of the Control Commission for Germany.

The maximum level speed of the Me 262 was more in the region of 560mph (900km/h); far short of the nominal speed of sound which is given as 768mph (1,236km/h) in dry air at 20°C. Indeed, tests with series production versions of the Me 262 revealed that a loss of control would occur in a steep dive at Mach 0.84.

The Messerschmitt company did attempt to create special *Hochgeschwindigkeit* (HG) high-speed variants of the aircraft. The Me 262 HG-I V9, fitted with a low-profile *Rennkabine* ('racing cabin'), is reputed to have achieved 606mph (975km/h). The next version, the projected but never built HG-II, was to have had a 35° sweep and a butterfly tail, while the HG-III would have gone even further with a 45° sweep and turbojets jets embedded within the wing roots. The top speed of the HG-III was anticipated as Mach 0.96 at 20,000ft altitude, but this is still below Mach 1. For comparison the rocket-powered Messerschmitt Me 163 B-1 *Komet* exhibited phenomenal rates of climb but even this still had a relatively modest maximum speed of only 596mph (1,060km/h).

Messerschmitt's first true swept-wing jet fighter was to have been the experimental P.1101 which was nearing completion at the Oberammergau works at the time of Germany's surrender (see Chapter 10).

Naturally the Allies showed great interest in the German research into swept wings, and at one point Fedden's team had got one of the wind tunnels working with an airflow model of a swept-back wing aircraft in place when an American delegation arrived on the scene. The Americans frequently included civilian experts from within the aircraft industry in their technical exploitation teams and among this particular delegation was George Schairer. Schairer was involved with Boeing's design work on a new six-engined long-range bomber for the USAF and he showed great interest in the tests. The

Rare air-to-air photograph of a Messerschmitt Me 262A. The shallow sweep of its wings was introduced to realign the centre of gravity and was not sufficient to increase the aircraft's critical Mach speed.

Model of the Junkers Ju 287, with its unusual forward-swept wing geometry, undergoing testing in the Göttingen wind tunnel. (DLR)

next morning the airflow model had gone and Schairer later admitted that he couldn't have left it behind. He sent word back to his design team in the USA to halt all work on a straight-wing design for the bomber and to switch to a swept-back wing instead. Boeing's modified design for the bomber was accepted by the USAF and it became the swept-wing B-47 Stratojet which first flew in December 1947 and went on to become the mainstay of the USAF's Strategic Air Command (SAC) throughout the 1950s and well into the early 1960s.

As this incident with the swept-wing model shows, Britain's closest allies were not against a little 'midnight requisition' of equipment when it suited them. In *American Raiders*, author Wolfgang W.E. Samuel quotes one of the Americans based at Völkenrode at the time: 'The trick was to get whatever test equipment out of the place without the British noticing. As soon as everybody was in bed and the lights were out, we'd

The design of Boeing's post-war B-47 Stratojet bomber was modified to incorporate swept-back wings as a direct result of Germany's wartime research. *(US DoD)*

spring into action.' The 'requisitioned' items would be taken to the airfield where the Americans ran a pair of B-24 and B-17 aircraft like an airline, shuttling back and forth from Völkenrode. At the Potsdam Conference the British complained about these surreptitious appropriations to the USAF's representatives, only to be met by earnest pleads of innocence.

THE FORWARD-SWEPT WING

A radical alternative to the conventional swept-back configuration which was assessed in the wind tunnel at Göttingen was the forward-swept wing. The principle benefits claimed for this were reduced drag, resulting in extra lift at lower speeds during take-off and landing, plus improved manoeuvrability. Unlike with the swept-back wing, the airflow on the forward-swept wing is from the wing tip towards the wing root and fuselage, thus delaying a stall at the wing tips. Shock waves at the wing root do not spread outwards although, conversely, there was a tendency for a stall to occur first at the wing root in a high angle of attack, causing a pitch-up moment further exacerbating the stall. Another advantage of mounting the forward-swept wings further back on the aircraft was that it also freed up space within the fuselage for an unobstructed bomb bay to carry greater loads.

Only one Luftwaffe aircraft featured the forward-swept wing: the Junkers Ju 287, which was developed by Dr Hans Wocke as a testbed for a bomber fast enough to out-run any enemy fighters. The Ju 287 was by no means the Luftwaffe's first jet-powered bomber as the Arado Ar 234 had made its maiden flight more than a year earlier, in June 1943. However, the Ar 234 was too small to be an effective bomber as it was only marginally bigger than the Me 262, and its straight unswept wing limited its speed. The prototype Ju 287 V1 – the V designation on German aircraft standing for *Versuch* ('test aircraft)' – was produced from a mishmash of donor parts. The main fuselage came from a Heinkel He 177 bomber, the tail was from a Junkers Ju 388 and the heavy-duty nose wheels were actually salvaged from crashed American B-24s. The aircraft was powered by four Junkers Jumo 109-004B-1 jet engines, one hung under each wing and the other two in nacelles mounted to either side of the forward fuselage. This unorthodox and unfamiliar configuration looked all wrong, but when flight tests began at Junkers' works at Dessau in August 1944, the aircraft demonstrated good handling characteristics, although further tests suggested that it would benefit from placing more of the engine mass under the wings. Accordingly the second prototype was to have six of the Heinkel HeS 011 turbojets, but because of delays in development the BMW 003 jet engine was selected instead and arranged in groups of three under each wing. It was proposed that a third prototype would have had two engines under each wing plus one on either side of the forward fuselage.

Early in 1945 the advancing Russian forces captured the Ju 287 V1 prototype, which had suffered bomb damage at the Rechlin test centre, as had the unfinished V2 aircraft. Working for the Russians, a large team of Junkers engineers utilised parts from the Ju 287 V2 to create the EF-131 and this was dismantled and taken by railway back to Russia. Test flights with the EF-131 commenced in 1947, but the programme was terminated the following year as the design was already obsolete.

In the decades since the end of the Second World War there have been very few manifestations of the forward-swept configuration. Notable exceptions being Grumman's X-29 research aircraft, of which two were built in the USA in the 1980s, and the Russian-built Sukhoi S-37, later redesignated as the Su-47 Berkut (Golden Eagle), which first flew in 1997. Unlike the Ju 287, both of these designs featured additional canards ahead of the main forward-swept wings.

The Fedden team spent two days at Völkenrode initially, followed up by a second visit to the site by a sub-group ten days later. While their primary interests were focused on the development work carried out in the wind tunnels they also inspected the structures and engine departments. In the Structures Laboratory – shown on the site map as being on the western side – they discovered equipment and samples still in the testing machines, indicating that the research had been directed towards strength of materials and components under alternating stresses, although there appeared to be no strength testing of larger aircraft components. This work was supplemented by photo-elastic research as well as research of stress cracking lacquers, with a view to understanding the phenomenon of stress concentration, which is an important factor where fatigue stress is concerned. Unfortunately, Fedden was unable to interrogate any of the laboratory staff on this matter. Included on his inventory of equipment in the lab were 60 ton and 20 ton Schenck-Erlinger horizontal push-pull pulsators, plus other vertical pulsators and

The Messerschmitt Me 264 four-engined long-range maritime reconnaissance aircraft was a candidate for the proposed Amerikabomber project capable of attacking New York.

impact and fatigue testing equipment. In the main this equipment was in good condition, although Fedden did observe that most of the recording instruments had been damaged prior to their visit.

The team members were then guided around the Motor Laboratory by Dr E. Schmidt, who seemed to be in frail health. In the photograph of Dr Schmidt standing beside an engine test-bed he looks drawn and he is shown resting on a stick. In contrast with the other laboratories Fedden thought the engine department was generally lacking in modern equipment. It did contain an altitude test bed, however, which he suggests was 'better than anything we have in this country' but not as advanced as the equipment they would later see at BMW in Munich. Like the remainder of the Völkenrode departments, the Motor Laboratory gave every appearance of being under-staffed in Fedden's opinion: 'On the other hand a considerable volume of work had been in progress on basic research of a more ambitious nature than has been attempted in this country during the war.'

The extent of this work covered turbine and stator blade forms, including research using optical interferometers to make airflow around wings or turbine blades visible, temperature measurements at high altitude at Mach 2, the conductivity of liquids at varying temperatures, heat exchangers, ceramic turbine blades, hollow liquid-cooled turbine blades, plus the study of plain bearings for rotor mountings, piston cooling, air-cooled finning on cylinders, liquid cooling, turbulence and detonation. The tests on various materials and methods of cooling turbine blades were of special interest given the shortage of certain strategic materials towards the latter stage of the war (see Chapter 4).

Dr Schmidt was pleased to show them the equipment used in developing water cooling for his turbines. Fedden considered Dr Schmidt to be one of the leading authorities on heat exchangers for different types; air-to-air, gas-to-air, oil-to-air, and air-to-liquid. This work was very important as the heat exchanger's effectiveness would be a critical factor in future high-performance turbine power plants. In terms of specific equipment in the Motor Laboratory, Fedden was particularly impressed by an interferometer used in the optical investigation of high-speed flow phenomena in connection with turbine blades. However, as he curtly commented in his report, 'It is understood that the instrument has since been removed by the Americans.'

On the Friday evening, 15 June, the team departed from the Braunschweig airfield at 7.15 p.m. for the 80-mile flight to Kassel, south-west of Göttingen, and overnight they billeted at the American Intelligence Centre, Camp Dantine. The next morning the party split into two; one group going to the Junkers jet engine factory in Magdeburg, while the remainder returned to Göttingen where they made arrangements for Professor A. Prandtl and his colleagues to be available for interrogation the following day. At Göttingen Fedden's team inspected another impressive collection of wind tunnels; the mission report lists more than ten, plus several water tunnels which were used in fluid motion research. The largest of the wind tunnels had a large working section, which could be used either open or closed, 15ft 5in (4.7m) high by 23ft (7m) wide. One of the smaller tunnels working on the vacuum storage tank principle was capable of supersonic speeds up to Mach 3.2.

Weapons testing inside the Institute of Kinematics K1 1,312ft (440m) ballistics research tunnel at Völkenrode, 1940. *(DLR)*

The line-up of scientists they met at the AVA included Prandtl who was in charge of the laboratories, A. Betz who worked with the wind tunnel equipment, J. Stüper who was an expert pilot as well as a scientist, L. Ritz who was working with heat exchangers and low temperature research, specialising on jet-engine projects, W. Encke a leading authority on compressor and turbine design, and H.G. Kussner who was an expert in flutter. It is interesting to note that Fedden always uses the term 'interrogate' in regard to the German scientists and engineers, even though he had known many of them personally from before the war. The term is an extension of the language of the soldier, the language of a victor talking about the defeated. Of the Göttingen people he readily admits that they were, 'a first class team of experimental aerodynamic research workers'. And in general the mission concluded that it was preferable to interview the Germans at their laboratories or works rather than take them to London for questioning:

> … it is better that engineers and scientists should be interrogated on their own ground, where they can refer immediately to drawings, samples and to the workshops, and where information given by one man can be checked up with that given by another on the same job. The mission has interrogated many technicians in Germany and in particular cases, it is believed, have got different stories from those which have been given by senior executives sent over to London. It was found possible to check up by referring the problems to the factory, and by interrogating two or three people on the same job. The information that it was able to glean directly in Germany may be nearest to the truth.

Despite this note of suspicion, the mission found that most of the German engineers were more than willing to cooperate with the Allies:

> Generally speaking, and with a few exceptions, the mission believes that the engineers, technicians and executives who were interrogated, and who showed them around the laboratories and plants, wished to be helpful, and to give constructive answers to the points raised … It was sensed that there was considerable apprehension on the part of the German scientists and engineers as to their future. Several spoke of their desire to move their staffs and equipment to America, or particularly to Canada.

Their concern was understandable as the Russians, for their part, had no qualms about taking any scientist or engineer they thought might be useful back with them to the Soviet Union. In contrast the other Allies, especially the Americans, had to find ways to legitimatise any transatlantic brain drain, lest they should be accused of bringing former Nazis into the country. And while it was simple enough to load the captured equipment and documents straight on to a truck or aeroplane and take it out of Germany, moving people would take a little more time to organise.

four

ENTERING THE JET AGE

THE STORY OF Germany's jet engines is inseparable from that of the aircraft they were intended for. Those which actually flew operationally under jet power were the experimental Heinkel He 178 and He 280, the Messerschmitt Me 262, the Arado Ar 234 and the diminutive Heinkel He 162 *Volksjäger*. Experimental aircraft to fly were the Horten tail-less Ho 229 and the forward-swept Junkers Ju 287 testbed. In addition to these there was a diverse range of proposals for future jet aircraft and some were actively under development by the end of the war, most notably the Messerschmitt P.1101.

German interest in turbojets can be traced back to the early 1930s, when Hans von Ohain began his research at the University of Göttingen. While von Ohain was aware of the work of the British jet pioneer, Frank Whittle, he did not appear to have had any comprehensive information on Whittle's designs and the two engineers are generally credited with producing their engines concurrently. By 1935 von Ohain had been able to demonstrate the principle of his turbojet and the following year he attracted the interest of the Heinkel company for whom he produced the Heinkel-Hirth HeS 1 engine. (The Hirth company had been founded by Hellmuth Hirth in 1920 as a manufacturer of engine components. Following his death as the result of an aircraft accident in 1938 the RLM nationalised the company, and in 1941 it was merged with Heinkel who used the Hirth facilities for von Ohain's work on jet engines.)

The HeS 1 featured a centrifugal compressor, annular combustion chamber and radial inflow turbine, and it was fuelled by hydrogen. Producing a static thrust of around 551lb (250kg) the HeS 1 was successfully bench-tested in 1937 and it led directly to the development of the first turbojet flight engine, the HeS 3. This was basically a tidied up and more compact version of the HeS 1, which had also been converted to burn liquid fuel instead of hydrogen.

The Heinkel company carried out this work on jet engines of its own volition, but in 1938 officials at the RLM instigated two lines of development that would ultimately come together in the world's first operational combat turbojet, the Messerschmitt Me 262. Hans Mauch and Helmut Schlep of the RLM power-plant development division had initiated an official jet engine programme, while Hans Antz of the

Kassel's Koenigstrasse rendered almost unrecognisable by the Allied bombing raids. *(NARA)*

airframe development department started a complementary programme for jet and rocket-powered airframes. Both of these were visionary steps taken at a time when the Luftwaffe was demonstrating its aerial supremacy through conventional piston-power, and in official circles the jet initiatives were greeted with very little enthusiasm. With the beginning of the Blitzkrieg matters were so clearly going Germany's way that few in authority could envisage a time when the Fatherland would need such aircraft to defend itself. Indeed, apart from Heinkel the other aircraft companies were not that interested either. With development of a jet engine already well in hand, Heinkel was ahead of its competitors, Junkers and BMW, and in the summer of 1939 an HeS 3B was mounted within the prototype Heinkel He 178. Apart from the motive power this was a fairly conventional-looking aircraft, quite small with a metal fuselage, high-mounted straight wings and a retractable undercarriage including rear drag wheel (although in the trials the front wheels remained fixed in the down position). At the nose there was a gaping hole, the intake for the single HeS 3B engine which was contained within the fuselage. On 27 August 1939 the He 178 took to the air with Heinkel's test pilot Erich Warsitz at the controls of world's first turbojet flight. In general the He 178 performed well, attaining speeds of up to 375mph (598km/h), but it was let down by its short combat endurance of only about ten minutes or so. This may explain why a demonstration of the new aircraft in front of RLM officials in November 1939 failed to impress.

Above: The Heinkel He 178 made the world's first jet-powered flight in August 1939 but failed to impress officials from the RLM.

Right: Its successor, the twin-engined He 280, was airborne two years later but its introduction was hampered by delays with the HeS 8 turbojet. *(USAF)*

Undaunted, Heinkel pushed on with its successor; a twin-engined jet fighter this time, at first designated as the He 180, although this was later changed to the He 280. This design had a more slender fuselage, the engines were mounted on the low wings, and at the back of the fuselage was a dihedral or twin tail. To provide clearance for backwash from the engines the He 280 had a retractable tricycle undercarriage. It was also the first aircraft to be equipped with an innovative compressed-air powered ejector seat. Although the He 280 prototype airframe was ready by the summer of 1941, aside from some gliding tests the first jet-powered flight was held up by delays in the completion of the more powerful HeS 8 turbojet, and it wasn't until 3 April 1941 that test-pilot Fritz Schäfer finally flew it under jet power. Unfortunately for Ernst Heinkel the hold-ups with the engines would prove costly as he was now in direct competition with his old rival Willy Messerschmitt.

THE ME 262

Unlike Heinkel, Messerschmitt's involvement had come about in direct response to the RLM's airframe development programme which called for a jet aircraft capable of flying for at least one hour and at a speed of 528mph (850km/h). Chief of development at Messerschmitt was Robert Lusser, and heading up the design team on the jet aircraft was Dr Woldemar Voigt. Under the project designation P.1065 – later to become the Me 262 – they had submitted their design proposal to the RLM in June 1939. This was for a twin-engined aircraft with engines mounted within the wings, and with the ministry's approval a wooden mock-up had been completed by March 1940.

Messerschmitt had no direct involvement in the design of the jet engines and the RLM awarded contracts to both Junkers Motoren (otherwise known as Jumo) and

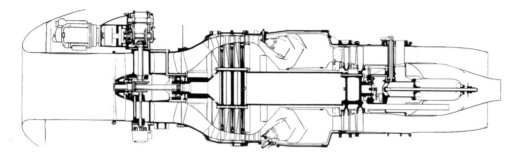

Diagram of the Heinkel-Hirth HeS-011 advanced turbojet with a three-stage axial compressor and, <u>below</u>, a cutaway of the real thing. The HeS-011 was not ready to enter production before the war ended. *(USAF)*

At its Stassfurt facility the Fedden Mission came across a quantity of smashed BMW turbojet engines and components.

BMW to develop a suitable turbojet capable of producing a static thrust of 1,496lb (680kg). This was despite the fact that the Heinkel company was already making progress with its von Ohain designs. Because Messerschmitt's airframe programme was ahead of engine development the engineers revised the positioning of the engine pods, no longer embedding them within the wings but slinging them underneath to allow for repositioning if required. This would also make it far easier to replace them; an important factor given the relatively short time period between major services. As it turned out the BMW 109-003s did prove to be heavier than anticipated and accordingly the wings of the Me 262 were swept back by an angle of 18.5° to properly position the aircraft's centre of gravity. This did not mean that the Me 262 had a true swept-back wing as explained in the previous chapter. (The RLM used the same '109' prefix for the turbojets as already allocated to rocket engines, but for the sake of clarity this prefix is generally not used when referring to the turbojets.)

For its turbojet BMW concentrated on a counter-rotating compressor design at first with the intention of eliminating torque, but this was later abandoned in favour of the simpler axial-flow engine which became the BMW 003. Running for the first time in August 1940, its output was a meagre 331lb (150kg) – disappointingly only half the level that had been expected. The 003 was first tested in flight mounted beneath a Messerschmitt Bf 110, although this aircraft flew using its piston engines and the jet was only fired up for a limited duration. Further technical delays on the 003 meant that the

BMW 003 axial-flow turbojet on display in the Luftwaffenmuseum, Germany. *(MisterBee1966)*

prototype Me 262, the V1, had to begin its testing programme fitted with a Jumo 210 piston engine in the nose. Once the BMW 003 engines were ready the Me 262 V1 first flew under jet-thrust in November 1941, but turbine failures occurred on both engines shortly after take-off. It was a major setback for BMW and it took them a further two years to raise the output of their engines to 1,760lb (800kg). Consequently, by the time the 003 entered any sort of production run in 1944 the Jumo 004 engines were already powering the Me 262s.

Under the guidance of Dr Anselm Franz the Jumo 004 utilised an axial compressor design which allowed a continuous straight flow through the engine. The 004 ran on three types of fuel: J-2, a synthetic fuel produced from coal; diesel oil; or aviation gasoline, although the latter was not ideal because of its extremely high rate of consumption. The first of the Jumo turbojets, the 004A, had begun bench-runs in November 1940 although it was not until 15 March 1942 that it was ready to be test flown beneath the Messerschmitt Bf 110. The Jumo engines were subsequently fitted to the Me 262 V3 prototype for that aircraft's first true jet flight, which took place on 18 July 1942. The RLM immediately placed an order for eighty of the engines and by October that same year the designs for the production version, the 109-004B, were completed. The first of the production engines were delivered early the following year and successfully test flown on Me 262 V1 on 2 March 1943. Unfortunately a series of engine vibration problems held up full production until early 1944 and this had a knock-on effect delaying the introduction of the Me 262 into service.

The world's first operational jet squadron, *Erprobungskommando* 262, or Ekdo 262, was formed in December 1944. Based at Lager-Lechfeld in Bavaria, the squadron was an

A member of Fedden's team examines a damaged compressor ring from a BMW 018 turbojet at Eisenach.

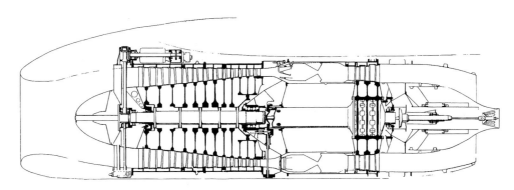

Drawing of BMW's experimental 018 turbojet.

experimental proving detachment for the Me 262 and would also be used to train a core of jet pilots. Ekdo 262 was equipped with the Me 262A-1a, commonly known as the *Schwalbe* ('swallow'), which was built in both fighter and fighter/bomber versions. It was the most common type produced and was equipped with four short-barrelled MK108 30mm cannon embedded within the nose. The Me 262 soon proved to be an incredible aircraft. Legendary German fighter ace Adolf Galland described the experience of his first taste of jet flight as if being 'pushed by angels'. The Allied bomber crews quickly came

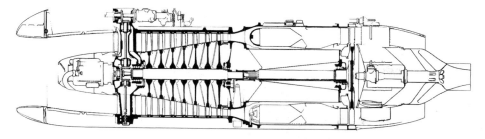

Full production of BMW's 3306 turbojet was said to be still a year away by the war's conclusion.

to recognise its distinctive shark-like snout and slightly swept wings and they marvelled at its incredible speed; up to 560mph (900km/h) in level flight. By the end of the war around 1,430 of the Me 262s had been built, but despite its undoubted superiority it was a case of too little too late to turn the fortunes of war in Germany's favour.

THE ARADO Ar 234

The second jet to enter service with the Luftwaffe was the Arado Ar 234, otherwise known as the *Blitz* (derived from Blitz-Bomber meaning 'lightning bomber', although strictly speaking this means that the Blitz name should only be applied to the '*Schnellbomber*' Ar 234B variant). This twin-engined jet had begun life in 1940 in answer to an RLM specification for a high-speed reconnaissance aircraft with a range of 1,340 miles (2,156km). At that point it was unclear which of the two main jet engines, the Jumo 004 or BMW 003, would become available in time, but in the event it was to be the 004 once again. In appearance the Ar 234 was a high-wing design with an engine pod slung under each wing and it had a long slender fuselage with a rounded front canopy. To keep the aircraft below the RLM's target weight of 17,600lb (8,000kg) the engineers at Arado had fitted early examples with a jettisonable three-wheeled landing trolley and triple landing skids, one skid under the fuselage and another under each engine pod.

Delays with the development of reliable turbojet engines held up the first flight and it wasn't until 15 June 1943 that AR 234 V1 took off from the Rheine airfield equipped with a pair of Jumo 004B-0 engines.

The sixth prototype, V6, was powered by four BMW 003A-1s instead of the two Jumos and these were mounted in individual nacelles, whereas the V8 prototype had two pairs of 003A-1s installed within twinned nacelles. These two prototypes were the world's first four-engined jets and the V8 became the first to fly, on 1 February 1944, followed by the V6 just a couple of months later on 8 April. However, it wasn't all plain sailing for the Ar 234. The last of the A-series prototypes fitted with two 004B-1 turbojets, the V7, suffered a port engine fire during flight testing and Arado's chief test pilot, Flugkapitän Selle, was killed as he attempted to land the aircraft. After this incident the AR 234 was fitted with a conventional retractable undercarriage. By then

As photographed by the Fedden Mission, bomb damaged Jumo 004 engines scattered around the factory yard at Magdeburg.

the RLM had come to recognise the aircraft's potential as a fast bomber and the V9, the prototype Ar 234B, first took to the air on 10 March 1944.

The V9 was equipped with cabin pressurisation and an ejector seat. On the V10 prototype bomb racks were installed beneath the engine nacelles as the restricted space within the aircraft's slender fuselage was mostly occupied by fuel tanks.

In subsequent flight trials V15 and V17 were fitted with just two BMW 003A-1 turbojets to investigate problems with the engine's thrust control, but these engines proved to be difficult to restart in flight after a flame-out, and the first pre-production versions of the Ar 234B-0 left the production lines at Alt-Lonnewitz with the Jumo 004 engines installed.

In the meantime, several of the prototype aircraft had entered active service in a reconnaissance role. Flying at a height of around 29,000ft (9,100m), the V7 became the first German jet to fly over the UK. Apart from engine flame-outs and the requirement for frequent engine overhauls, operationally the Ar 234s performed well and were generally much liked by their crews. There was an issue with excessively long take-off runs but this was addressed by fitting rocket-assisted take-off (RATO) units (see Chapter 9).

THE HEINKEL He 162

The last of the German jet aircraft to enter service was the diminutive Heinkel He 162 which carried a single BMW 003 engine mounted on its back. It was designed in response to a competition launched by the RLM in August 1944 to create a *Volksjäger*, a people's fighter, which could tackle the Allied bomber formations. (The He 162 is also covered in greater detail in Chapter 9.)

From Fedden's perspective the advent of the jet age threatened to undermine the dominance of the piston-driven aero engines, especially his beloved air-cooled radials which had been the cornerstone of his own career. But technological evolution could not be ignored and, as he observed in his pre-mission briefings, jet propulsion was obviously going to be the subject for 'the most intensive study':

> We know of two gas turbine units being made in Germany, Jumo 004, used in the Me 262, which is in service in fairly large numbers, and the BMW 003, which is just coming into service in the Arado 234. The Daimler-Benz and Heinkel-Hirth companies are also believed to be producing the BMW unit. Heinkel-Hirth built their own design of unit two or three years ago, but this has presumably proved unsuccessful so far. Brown-Boveri are also making some form of gas turbine. [A German subsidiary of the Swiss company which made electric motors for locomotives and developed steam and gas turbines to power ships and, during the war, some U-boats.] It is anticipated that present German policy is to make jet propelled fighters the sole instrument of their first line fighter strength, and recent experiences by our bomber crews tend to confirm this.

This extract reveals that his pre-mission information on specific jet projects was still very sketchy at the time, which was only to be expected as examples of the aircraft had yet

Me 262 V3 photographed at Leipheim prior to the first flight on 18 July 1942. Note the tail-dragger wheel arrangement raising the nose up into the air.

The 10hp Riedel two-stroke starter motor concealed within the intake cone of the Jumo 004. The ring of the starter handle protrudes on the right. *(JC)*

to fall into Allied hands for closer examination. An insight into the level of Allied data on the jets can be gauged from a confidential report on Jet Propelled Aircraft which was issued by the US Army Headquarters 115th Anti-Aircraft Artillery Group, in March 1945. Clearly it was essential that the anti-aircraft units were able to correctly identify the various new aircraft in order to deal with them and safely distinguish friend from foe. In the introduction to the report Colonel Peter S. Peca emphasised the significance of the German jets:

> A steady rise in operational flights of German jet propelled aircraft over the western front has been noted since the first of this year. It is possible that as the war continues, the German jet propelled aircraft will become a serious menace to both air and ground operations. Due to the high speed and reduced noise level of jet aircraft, you will find them more difficult to detect, engage and destroy than the conventional type aircraft. You must be continually alert; learn to recognise these plane's in a split second; utilise completely your AAAIS and other warning; and use your fire control equipment properly.

The last sentence was underlined for emphasis. Presumably the reference to the 'reduced noise level' really meant the reduced time in which to identify the fast-moving jets.

The report went on to provide information and, in most cases, reasonably detailed drawings, plan views and silhouettes of the key aircraft; the Messerschmitt 262, Arado 234, Messerschmitt 163A (it does point out that this was a short-duration rocket-powered aircraft for the 'home-defence' of specific sites) which were all listed as being both 'fighter and fighter-bomber aircraft', and the Heinkel 280 'fighter'. According to the document a P-47 Group had reported an encounter with an He 280 over the Rhine. However, this would have been impossible as only nine prototypes had been built and after the project was cancelled by Milch in March 1943 these were used only for experimental purposes. In all probability, the sighting over the Rhine was a misidentification of an Me 262.

THE HEINKEL He 343

Under the heading 'Experimental' several aircraft were listed, the He 343, Horten 3 and Dornier 325, but here the report strayed into the realms of speculation. The Heinkel 343 was described as a multi-seat fighter with a mid wing, the leading edge swept back and the trailing edge tapered. It was of all-metal construction, with the exception of the control surfaces, and it had a conventional tailplane mounted fairly high. 'Thought to be a four-jet aircraft, but twin-jet units may be prototypes. Prisoner of war interrogations have definitely confirmed the existence of this aircraft.' In truth the German POWs had been leading their interrogators astray and there was zero chance that the anti-aircraft gunners would see one of these. The He 343 had begun development in early 1944 as a type of enlarged Ar 234, and at least parts for the prototype, if not the whole aircraft, were in production when the project was cancelled at the end of 1944 due to the Emergency Fighter Programme. Post-war, the He 343 was the basis for the Illyushin IL-22, the first of the Soviet jet bombers when it flew in July 1947. The Il-22 is said to have led on to the twin-engined Il-28 of 1948.

THE HORTEN Ho 3

The Horten 3 was described by Fedden as 'reportedly a rocket-propelled version of the unmanned aircraft also assumed to be in existence as a jet-propelled type'. Again a mishmash of half-facts. The Horten III was an unmanned glider built in 1938, while it was the Ho 229 (or Go 229) prototype H.IX V2 which had first flown with two Jumo 004s in February 1945. This flying wing was not combat-ready by the time the war ended.

THE DORNIER Do 325

Last on the list was the Dornier 325, described as 'a suspected jet-propelled aircraft in experimental stage'. Clearly a reference to the double piston-engined Do 335 which was very fast but not a jet.

And what of the Allies own jets? Several were under development and even in production before the cessation of hostilities, but none saw active service over in the European theatre. Three Allied jets were included in the report to avoid possible misidentification as hostile aircraft. These were the Bell P-59A, the Curtiss P-60A Shooting Star and the British Gloster Meteor.

With events moving so rapidly in the latter stages of the war it was a race for the Allies to bring their data on the German jets up to date. Fedden was well aware that there was much to learn when his mission team reached Germany, as he revealed in the following handwritten caveat in the margins of his personal copy of the pre-mission briefing notes:

I would recommend that we do not accept too readily the idea that Germany is basically behind on this vital subject, because knowing something about the technicians who have been working on this development, and the length of time they have been on the job, I would be inclined to weigh this up very carefully and consider whether we have fully appreciated all of the contributing factors.

Although the Fedden team would examine various aspects of piston engine development in Germany (see Chapter 5), the terms of reference outlined in the introduction to the Final Mission Report also gave prominence to the investigation of gas turbines and jet engines under the following terms:

To endeavour to make a broad review of their relative development in Germany in comparison with this country, and to ascertain the cost of manufacture and general technique of jet engines, as compared with piston engines in Germany.

Clearly, even as the world stood at the threshold of the jet age it would take time for the more entrenched aeronautical community to come to terms with the impending paradigm shift from piston to jet.

Once in Germany Fedden's team of experts targeted the three principle players in jet development and production: Junkers, BMW and Heinkel-Hirth. The first on the Mission's itinerary was the Junkers works at Magdeburg.

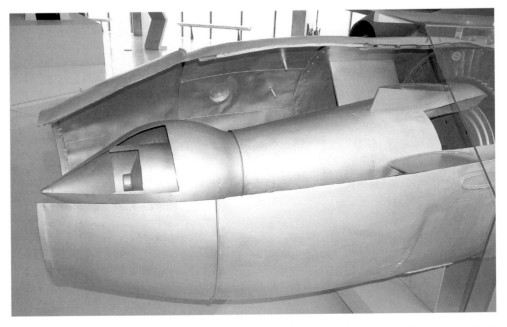

The Zwiebel, or 'onion', located at the rear of the Jumo 004 could be moved forward or aft to alter the exhaust area and hence the thrust. *(JC)*

An abandoned Me 262A found intact in April 1945 by advancing US 9th Army troops at an airfield near Stendal. *(NARA)*

THE JUNKERS WORKS, MAGDEBURG

On Saturday 16 June they had divided into two groups after having been billeted overnight at the American Intelligence Centre, Camp Dentine, 15 miles from Kassel. One aeroplane flew north-east to Oschersleben and that group then went by Jeep on to Magdeburg, while the others were flown to Göttingen to continue investigations there.

Located on the River Elbe, Magdeburg is now the largest city in the Saxony-Anhalt region within unified Germany, but in the summer of 1945 it was inside the territory already allocated to the Russians, along with the Junkers main plant at Dessau. Consequently there was precious little time left to the Americans and British before it was handed over. The Junkers works at Magdeburg had been used for the manufacture and overhaul of the Jumo 004 jet engines. Fedden found that although the works did contain several piston engine test-beds there was no evidence of any experimental or development work having been undertaken on the jets. In general the works had been extensively damaged in the Allied bombing raids and the mission photographs show a number of bomb-damaged Jumo 004 engines strewn about in the outside areas.

Dr Franz, Junkers' chief technician at Magdeburg, was not available to meet the British delegation and instead the former production director, Otto Hartkopf, dealt with them in his capacity as acting works manager. Hartkopf began by explaining that all of the drawings relating to the jets had already been removed by the Allies. Hartkopf said that over 5,000 of the engines had been produced overall (although the actual figure is now thought to be nearer the 8,000 mark). As well as the Magdeburg site a series of additional factories had been planned in order to raise manufacturing output up to an ambitious figure of 5,000 engines per month. This programme was well in hand by the time the war ended and more than 1,500 Jumo 004s were being delivered each month.

The production series Jumo 004 turbojet weighed 1,543lb (700kg) and produced 1,984lb (900kg) of thrust at 8,700rpm. It consisted of an eight-stage axial flow compressor, multiple combustion chambers built up from sheet steel and axially positioned around the body of the engine, and a single-stage turbine incorporating hollow blades. The engine had two interesting features. The exhaust had a variable geometry nozzle which could be adjusted by the movement of a restrictive body nicknamed the *Zwiebel* ('onion'). This varied the jet exhaust cross-sectional area for thrust control. And concealed within the intake cone there was a 10hp Reidel two-stroke engine which was used as a starter engine, the ring of its starter handle protruding at the front. The compressor casing, of cast magnesium, was split axially into two halves, each one having bolted to it the half sections of the stator assemblies. (Fedden comments that this is one aspect of the design that did not appear to have been executed very satisfactorily.) The first four stators consisted of profiled alloy blades located in their mounting rims by welds, while the last five stators were pressed sheet blades which were located on the rims by bending over and welding. The compressor blades were also of alloy and dovetailed into slots on the compressor discs and locked into position by small axial screws, half in the blade root and half in the disc. The compressor discs were, in turn, assembled onto a steel shaft and fastened by twelve radial set screws.

Jumo had been experimenting with various construction methods for its compressor blades, although it is not clear whether this was an attempt to solve particular problems or simply to improve the production process. In early models the turbine blades had been of solid steel, but on later versions the blades were hollow, formed from sheet metal and welded along the join line on the tapering edge. Their roots were formed to fit over rhomboid-shaped studs on the turbine wheel to which they were pinned and brazed.

BMW'S WORKS AT EISENACH AND STASSFURT

To investigate production of BMW's 003 jet engines the Fedden Mission travelled to two separate locations, Eisenach in the foothills of the Thuringia Forest, and Stassfurt, which is between Nordhausen and Dessau. Both of these establishments were within the soon-to-be Russian zone. On Monday 18 June, the mission had split into two once again, with one party travelling southwards by road to the BMW jet engine works at Eisenach. BMW's jet engine research had originally been undertaken in Berlin, under the control of Mr Bruckmann and his assistant Dr H. Oestrich. Since 1942 Bruckmann had taken charge of the company's piston engines, and it was in that capacity that the Fedden Mission met with him in Munich (see Chapter 5) but he was also an enthusiastic advocate of the jet engine for high-speed aircraft. In particular he foresaw a potential application for turbine engines to drive propellers, in other words turbo prop engines.

Fedden reports that Bruckmann was of the opinion that they would eventually come into widespread use for long-range aircraft once the development of suitable heat exchangers had been brought to fruition:

> He stated that it would be a relatively simple matter to design a 5,000hp piston engine now, but that a propeller turbine engine would probably take five years' development to arrive at an equivalent fuel consumption.

Oestrich, who had taken over responsibility from Bruckmann for the BMW jet division, had previously been a 'piston man' at Spandau in Berlin, the former Siemens works which were absorbed by BMW in 1938. He had started working on jets in 1939 and as with the other German engineers he had chosen the axial flow compressor design because of its smaller diameter.

At Eisenach the mission also interrogated Dr Schaaf, the managing director, as well as two directors listed as Dr Fattler and Dr Stoffregen. They said that around 11,000 men had been employed at Eisenach, with 4,500 of them working in a camouflaged factory located within the side of the hill, producing the Type 132 nine-cylinder piston engines and parts for the 801 fourteen-cylinder engine. The remainder worked in the town itself at the factory that had produced motorcycles and aero engine components up until 1944. It was then that BMW had been instructed to concentrate on the jet engines with 003 production planned at Eisenach, Spandau, Nordhausen and later Prague, to meet the overly ambitious target output of about 5,000 to 6,000 engines per month. In the event, because the BMW 003 lagged behind the Jumo 004, many more Junkers engines were completed by the end of the war than the BMW 003s.

The Lockheed P-80A Shooting Star first flew in 1944, but the Americans had no jets in service by the end of the war. This example was photographed at the Ames Aeronautical Laboratory, Moffett Field, in 1946. *(Nasa)*

Several models of the BMW 003 were produced although they were basically variants of the 003/A1. The main difference between it and the Jumo 004 is that the BMW engine used an annular combustion chamber containing sixteen individual burners instead of separate chambers. The BMW 003 was approximately 4in (10cm) smaller in diameter – an important factor for a high-speed aircraft – and despite its lower thrust the engine's reduced weight and diameter resulted in similar aircraft speeds.

The BMW 003's compressor casing was not split and there were other details on the compressor parts that differed from the Jumo 004. According to Fedden the 003s were generally better executed in detail. The stator blades – stationary fans between each pair of rotors which realigned the gas flow to more effectively direct it towards the blades of the next rotor – were all dural alloy pressings inserted into magnesium rings with provision for expansion, the blades being bent over and spot-welded to the inner ring but still free to expand in the outer ring. The compressor rotors were also alloy, mounted in annular grooves in magnesium rotor wheels and pinned in position. The rotor wheels were assembled on the shaft with the stator rings loosely in position before the whole assembly was inserted into the cast magnesium compressor casing. In the initial versions the rotor blades had a tendency to fracture after only a few hours of running; most probably the result of bending fatigue caused by a resonance effect in the wake of the three bearing supports. Despite efforts to cure this by increasing the number of supports to four, the only reliable solution was to considerably stiffen the blades of the first stage.

Originally the compressor had six stages but this was subsequently increased to seven, with the intention of taking it to eight in later models. The BMW 003 used hollow turbine stator blades with air-cooling for the blades bled from the fourth stage of the compressor, apparently consuming about 5 per cent of its capacity in the process. The turbine blades were dovetailed into shaped groves within the turbine wheel and secured by end plates. In the 003/A2 series the number of blades was reduced to enable further strengthening of the root fixings.

Arado Ar 234 jettisoning the launch trolley, with landing skids extended beneath the fuselage and engine pods. Despite the weight penalty this system was replaced by a retractable undercarriage.

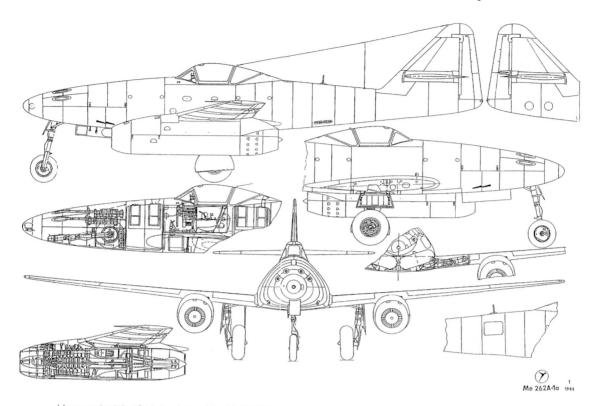

Messerschmitt's 1944 drawings of the Me 262A-1a.

The BMW 003 turbojets underwent several improvements during development. The models AO, A, A2, E and E2 were the production types and featured only minor changes, while the 003/C and D versions incorporated major modifications to increase thrust from 1,768lb (800kg) to 1,990lb (900kg) and finally to 2,762lb (1,250kg), the latter incorporating eight compressor stages and a two-stage turbine.

The Fedden Mission learnt that an experimental version of the 003/A had been produced incorporating a special non-expendable rocket motor fitted in the rear end to provide an additional 2,762lb (1,250kg) of thrust for take-off or rapid climb as well as dash on-demand at critical moments in combat. This was not a separate or jettisonable unit like the RATO assistors, but was a permanent fixture fed by fuel pumps. The duration of these rockets was determined by the capacity of the tanks carrying the special fuels (see Chapter 9). One Me 262 fitted with this unit is claimed to have climbed to a height of 40,000ft (12,000m) in just three minutes.

Fedden states that the mission found the quality of the work at Eisenach to be excellent. But the long delays in development meant that the 003 lost out to the simpler Jumo 004 on the main jet types, the Me 262 and the Ar 234. Apart from a handful of tests on various Me 262 prototypes and experimental aircraft such as the Horten Ho 229, the only production aircraft to fly with the BMW 003 were the He 162 and some four-engined versions of the Ar 234. It is estimated that around 500 of the engines were built, mostly 003-A1s and a few of the A2s. However, production at the Eisenach factory had been severely disrupted by the Allied bombing raids.

The day after the Eisenach trip the mission inspected an underground BMW jet engine plant at Stassfurt. This had been set up in 1944 within a salt mine 0.75 miles (400m) underground and was to have been used for the machining operations on the BMW 003 and, possibly, final engine assembly as well. Mr Stoffergen explained that 1,700 machine tools had been installed on the site and around 2,000 people were employed there, but by the time of Fedden's visit widespread looting had left the underground factory in a state of utter chaos. He did manage to obtain some information on BMW's experimental 018 engine which was generally along the lines of the 003 but with a twelve-stage axial flow compressor and a three-stage turbine giving around 7,770lb (3,500kg) of thrust. Development of the 018 had commenced in 1940, although a complete engine had not been produced and the workers had destroyed the remains of an 018 compressor and a number of jet engines before the place was overrun by the Allies. Fedden did examine some examples of the compressor blade forgings and also a blade from the third stage of the turbine.

THE HEINKEL-HIRTH WORKS, KOLBERMOOR

On the afternoon of Thursday 21 June members of the Fedden mission visited the third of the main jet companies. They travelled on from the BMW rocket development department in Munich south-eastwards to Kolbermoor, near the Austrian border, to the Heinkel-Hirth works.

The HeS 011 is generally considered to be one of the most advanced of the German turbojets produced during the Second World War, but, although it was intended for a number of proposed aircraft, it was not ready for mass production and only nineteen examples were finished by the fall of Germany.

During their investigations the Fedden team paid particular attention to the production of the turbojets and the comparative costs of piston versus jet engine. Lengthy interrogations were conducted with key personnel: Mr Schaaf, managing director of BMW, Mr Dorls, the planning engineer who had been with the company for over ten years and was closely involved in piston engine production, and also Mr Hartkopf, the works manager at the Junkers works who had extensive experience with both piston and jet engine production. From information supplied by Dorls they compiled a table which clearly demonstrates the difference in material costs between the types of engines:

Junkers	type 213 piston engine	35,000 Reichsmarks
BMW	type 801 piston engine	40,000 Reichsmarks
Junkers	109-004 jet	10,000 Reichsmarks
BMW	109-003 jet	12,000 Reichsmarks

These figures for raw materials showed that the jets could be manufactured for approximately half, if not a third, of the cost of a piston engine. The process of constructing the jet engines was also much more straightforward, as Fedden stated:

> The mission was impressed with the simplicity and straightforward methods of production, especially of the BMW jet engines. Relatively speaking, there are no very special machining operations or expensive tooling required. The Mission saw few special machines for turbine manufacture except for the seven spindle indexing machines for cutting the slots in the compressor hubs, made by the Magdeburg Junkers production plant which was previously a large machine tool manufacturing concern.

Other specialist tools included a Deckel copying machine for the forming of blades which was seen at Stassfurt, and a treble balancing machine. Otherwise all turning work was very simple and the hollow blade and other sheet metal work on the engines was tooled on plant previously used in the production of motor car body panels. Despite earlier comments, in general Fedden considered the standard of workmanship at both BMW and Junkers to be of a reasonable standard 'but quite ordinary and commercial, and definitely of a lower order than that of current British piston engines'. Once again Fedden harks back to the piston engine as the only point of reference with which he was familiar. But as the German production engineers explained, one of the big advantages is that they had been able to employ a 'lower grade' of labour in manufacturing the jets. In many cases this can usually be taken as a euphemism for enforced or slave labour. The mission was also able to make a comparison of labour times, including manufacture of individual components, assembly and shipping, plus testing. For the BMW 801 fourteen-cylinder radial engine this came to 1,400 hours per unit, while for the jet it was only 375 hours; a considerable saving.

One of the biggest engineering issues in producing the jets had been the acute shortage of important strategic materials. The early pre-production engines, in particular the Jumo 004s, had been built without restrictions on the use of materials such as nickel and cobalt. For large-scale production the hot metal parts were changed to mild steel protected by a coating of aluminium, or hollow turbine blades produced from folded and welded Cromadur alloy which had been developed by Krupp. As a consequence the engines had become cheaper to manufacture but their operational lifespan was shortened:

> It appeared from the comparative performance of German and British engines, that the performance of the German types had suffered from the necessity of conserving alloys, which led to the development of cooled blades. Apart from the loss of performance due to bleeding air from the compressor, the use of the variable exit nozzle may well lead to turbulence losses in the jet. In an attempt to restore the situation the German designers appear to have sacrificed efficiency so as to achieve a low pressure drop across the chamber and this may have aggravated their troubles in connection with unstable combustion under altitude conditions.

One big disadvantage with the jet engines had proven to be the short periods between overhauls. At Junkers the Mission was informed that about 300 engines had been back for repairs, some of them being overhauled more than once. The engineers admitted that the engines were lasting for between thirty and fifty hours between overhauls – some sources suggest even less at only ten to twenty hours for the Jumo 004 – and that thrust would start to fall off after this period. It was a similar situation with the BMW 003 which, the engineers claimed, required attention every fifty hours. Set against this they were very satisfied with the short turnaround times. The usual practice was to replace any damaged blades and rebalance the rotors, although the combustion chamber, tail cone, automatic governor and starter also required attention. In general the combustion chambers needed servicing every twenty to fifty hours and had a life of around 200 hours. But it was the turbine blades that bore the brunt of the damage, mostly caused by foreign matter entering the engine or by abuse on the part of the pilots resulting in the overheating of the turbine blades. Replacing the blades was a straightforward task which, Fedden was informed, could be handled by women and slave labour. In terms of costs, Fedden was surprised by the low wages for even the skilled workers: 'These wages appear to be in the order of a half of those in the Coventry area.'

It is interesting to note that the engine life and time between services could be significantly affected by the way they were handled. It was suggested that a skilled pilot could coax up to twice the endurance time out of them. This was because the early jets had a sluggish throttle response and in the hands of an impatient or inexperienced pilot it was a common mistake to open up the throttle too quickly, thereby injecting too much fuel into the engine before it had been able to speed up. The result was a build up of heat before the cooling fans could remove it, leading to a softening of the turbine blades and possibly damaging the combustion chambers. To counter this, the engineers had been working on a delayed-action control to limit the time of acceleration from idling speed to maximum rpm.

The final and sobering comment on the German jets comes from the pages of the Mission Report:

Series production of jet engines in large quantities was undoubtedly in a more advanced state in Germany than in Britain and the USA, and had the war continued and had their factories not been overrun, they would have been producing several thousand jet engines per month by this autumn [1945]. By the middle of 1946, the output would have been at a rate of 100,000 jet engines per annum, at least.

five

PISTONS AND PROPS

GERMANY'S ROLE in conventional piston engine development during the Second World War is often overshadowed by that more showy upstart, the turbojet. But given Sir Roy Fedden's considerable contribution to aero engines during the inter-war years, you can be sure that he was not going to give the German piston engine builders a miss. Of the main engine companies in Germany, Junkers, BMW and Daimler-Benz were considered to be the most important, certainly in Fedden's opinion, as they had continued with piston engine development throughout the war and had supplied engines for all of the first line fighter and bomber aircraft of the Luftwaffe. At the height of wartime production, these three companies had employed between 150,000 and 170,000 people and, with the help of the shadow firms, they were delivering in the order of 6,000 to 7,000 engines every month. The Allied bombing campaign, however, dented these prodigious output figures, reducing them to about one third, as Fedden confirmed in conversation with a number of the German engineers encountered during the 1945 mission:

> Most people commented on the efficiency of our 'communications' bombing, which they said was far more disastrous from an engine output point of view than actual bombing of works. Few works could not be repaired or dispersed in a comparatively short time, but the bombing of rail heads, trains, lorries, roads, etc, absolutely paralysed production and efficiency.

JUNKERS FLUGZEUGWERKE, DESSAU

On Monday 18 June members of the Fedden Mission travelled by road from Kothen to Dessau to interview technicians at the Junkers Flugzeugwerke in Dessau. All new Junkers aircraft, right back to the Ju 60 single-engined airliner of 1932, had first flown from here and by the outbreak of war the works had expanded to cover a massive area. Even so, actual aeroplane production was increasingly transferred to other sites in order to meet the high demand for Junkers' flagship aircraft such as the Ju 87 *Stuka* – short for *Sturzkampfflugzeug*, meaning 'dive bomber' – and the twin-engined Ju 88 light bomber. Inevitably the conspicuous complex of buildings at Dessau attracted the attention of the Allied bombers and in one particular attack, on 30 May 1944, the works were virtually wiped out. Fedden reports: 'Damage was so extensive that little of value could be seen in a quick look round, which was all that was possible with the imminent approach of the Russians.'

The engine company, Junkers Motoren, otherwise known as Jumo, had separated from the aircraft part of the company in 1923. Their primary piston engine of the Second World War was the Jumo 211, widely considered as a rival to Daimler-Benz's DB 601. German aero engines were designated by a three-digit number with the first digit identifying the manufacturer: 1 or 8 for BMW, 2 for Junkers, 3 for Bramo, 4 for Argus, 5 for Hirth, 6 for Daimler-Benz, and 7 for Bückner or Klöckner-Humbolt-Deutz. The following two numbers denote the individual engine series.

The Jumo 211 was an inverted V-12 in-line liquid-cooled engine giving between 986hp on the earlier A model and up to 1,479hp on the final P version. Total production of the 211 series was over 6,000 engines and in addition to the Junkers Ju 87 and Ju 88 it powered, among others, the Heinkel He 111E, H and Z, the Ju 90 and the Ju 52.

The Jumo 213 grew directly out of the 211 design, with the open cycle water cooling replaced by a pressurised cooling system that emulated the DB 601. This reduced the amount of water coolant required, making the engine both smaller and lighter. Other improvements boosted the power by 500hp, resulting in the Jumo 213 in its various derivatives becoming one of the most sought-after piston engines towards the end of the war. Over 9,000 Jumo 213 engines were built. They were fitted to a long list of Luftwaffe aircraft including the redoubtable Heinkel He 111 bomber, the Junkers Ju 88, Ju 188 and Ju 388 twin-engine multi-role/bombers, the single-engined Focke-Wulf Fw 190D and Ta 152 fighters, the Ta 154 night-fighter, and also the Messerschmitt Me 209(II) which was a proposed beefed-up version of the highly successful Bf 109. Messerschmitt had wanted the DB 603 engine for the Me 209(II), but as this was in short supply the Jumo

Early Luft Hansa Ju 52/3mho featuring Jumo 205 air-cooled six-cylinder inline diesels. Later versions were fitted with BMW 132 radials based on the Pratt & Whitney Hornet.

213 was substituted instead. The prototype made its maiden flight in November 1943, but in the event only four Me 219(II)s were completed before the project was cancelled in 1944. After the war the Jumo 213 also appeared on some versions of the Nord Noroit, a French-built flying boat.

In their discussions with Dr A. Scheibe, the technical director in charge of Jumo piston engine development, Fedden's team learnt that out of a large number of Jumo 213 projects, three definitive series models could be singled out for attention: the 213A, the major production version with one-stage two-speed supercharger; the 213E with intercooled supercharger, basically a high-altitude version of the 213A; and the projected 213J, two-stage three-speed, but with a different ratio and four valves instead of three per cylinder. Its weight with intercooler was 2,325lb (1,055kg) and the power output was 2,350hp for take-off at 3,700rpm. The 213J had not entered production by the time the war ended. The mission team later came across several brand new Jumo 213-Bs, still crated up, in the Junkers factory at Magdeburg. Other Jumo piston engine projects, such as the ill-fated Jumo 222 with twenty-four cylinders, and the diesel developments, had stagnated in the latter stages of the war with all effort being concentrated on the 213 series.

On 1 July 1945, Dessau was officially handed over to the Soviet Military administration and in 1946 Dr Scheibe and his team went to the USSR where they continued with the development of the Ju 287 (see Chapter 3).

BMW WORKS, MUNICH

In contrast to Junkers' bomb-damaged plant at Dessau, the British team managed several trips to inspect the BMW works in Munich, mostly between Wednesday 20 June and Sunday 24 June 1945, and again during a supplementary visit to Germany in July. This gave them the opportunity to speak to a number of the BMW engineers. In charge of piston engine development at BMW Munich was Dr Amman, aided by his chief assistant Mr Willich, and Mr Sachse who had been the senior engineer up to 1942 before he started his own works at Kempten, Bavaria, for the manufacture of automatic controls. The chief engineer and technical director in overall charge of BMW's jet, piston and rocket development was Buno Bruckmann, an old friend of Fedden's and a man very familiar with the Bristol Jupiter engines which were being built under licence in Germany before the war. (Along with the former managing director Dr Popp, Bruckmann was imprisoned by the American authorities shortly after the mission's first visit to Munich. Fedden noted, 'We gather the grounds are subversive activities, but as far as we know no charges have been preferred.')

Piston engine development at Munich was focussed on three main objectives: Developing the 801 up to the limit, getting the eighteen-cylinder 802 engine into production, and continuing development of the big twenty-eight-cylinder 803 engine.

The BMW 801 was an air-cooled radial engine with the cylinders arranged in two rows of seven. A staggering 61,000 BMW 801 engines were built, the largest number

Cover of <u>Der Adler</u> for November 1941 shows Ju 88 fuselages nearing completion. Around 16,000 of the multi-role twin-engine aircraft were built.

of any German wartime radial engines. It was provided with a single-stage centrifugal supercharger with two automatically changing speeds, and a direct fuel injection system. The 801A, for example, weighed 2,669lb (1,213kg). Best known as the power-plant for the Focke-Wulf Fw 190, the BMW 801 was also fitted to the Blohm und Voss lop-sided BV 141 reconnaissance aircraft, the prototype BV 144 which was intended as an advanced post-war airliner, the Dornier Do 217 twin-engine bomber, a whole family of Junkers including the Ju 88, Ju 188, Ju 288 and Ju 388, as well as several candidates for the *Amerikabomber* project. These included the Heinkel He 277, which was a four-engine heavy-bomber derived from the fire-prone He 177 but never completed, the Ju 290 four-engined heavy-bomber and its offshoot, the six-engined Ju 390, plus the Messerschmitt Me 264 previously mentioned.

The 801 had not been in production when the war started, but with pressure coming from the RLM development was accelerated under the direction of Sachse. This included testing the complete power plant at LFA Völkenrode. Through extensive wind tunnel exploration it was thought possible to make considerable improvements regarding the drag of the piston engines, and a reduction in drag to the extent of 150 to 200hp was considered a definite possibility on the 801 engine installation for the

The Junkers engine plant at Dessau was conspicuous from the air and is shown during an attack by Allied bombers on 16 August 1944. *(NARA)*

Focke-Wulf Fw 190. The wind tunnel testing also enabled the engineers to maximise the use of positive air pressure built up in the cowling in front of the engine to cool the cylinders, cylinder-heads, crankcase and so on.

The 801–1 was the turbo-blower version. The blower was mounted high up behind the engine, with its axis sloping forward at about 30° from the vertical. The turbine wheel had hollow steel blades, similar to those in the jet engines. Fedden saw a number of these engines abandoned and left in the open on Kassel airfield. The final production version of the 801 series was the 801-E which had a pressure die-cast hydronalium cylinder head, chromium-plated cylinder barrels and exhaust valves, and stronger pistons. The 801-E, which had not entered production, incorporated a strengthened crankshaft necessary for power in excess of 2,000bhp. It was anticipated that this engine would be rated at 2,600bhp with methanol-water injection.

The BMW 802 was an eighteen-cylinder engine of 'interesting and unorthodox design', as Fedden put it, attributed to Dr Sachse. A two-stage three-speed blower gave a rated altitude of 32,000ft (10,000m) and the maximum speed was 2,700rpm. The engine weight was 3,380lb (1,530kg). Emphasis had been placed on the manufacture of the complete power plant with clean air flow throughout. The unusual front and rear valve

Post-war scrapyard heaped with unwanted German aero engines. *(NARA)*

position was extended to give the shortest and straightest possible air and exhaust passage, and the positioning of the blower on the front was adopted for the same reason. Air entering the power plant was compressed by a fan and stator ring, then taken off by the blower and dealt with separately. The remaining air divided into three parts passing through the intercooler boxes, the front row cylinder baffles and the rear cylinder baffles. These three streams of air then joined up behind the rear cylinders and were ejected by the exhaust gasses. With this design the ejector thrust and mechanical work to the fan just balances the total internal drag. Several of these engines were made in 1942, but development over the remaining few years of the war was dropped in favour of the 801. Fedden observed:

> Dr Amman himself thought the 802 was a good engine, and that if more power was to be the goal, then they would have done better to have gone to the 802, rather than flog the 801, which was now pushed to the limit. He thought that 3,000bhp would have been obtained fairly easily.

Fedden personally considered the 802 to be one of the most interesting piston engines seen in Germany and well worth following up.

The BMW 803 was a project put forward by the Siemens part of the BMW organisation in Berlin, but it was not well received by the Munich team and was still languishing in the very early stages of development by the war's end. The 803 was described by Jane's *All the World's Aircraft 1945/6* as having 'the appearance of two fourteen-cylinder engines joined together', which is pretty much what it was. Designed by Dr Spiegel, it consisted of two fourteen-cylinder units which ran independently but coaxially, the idea being that one unit could be cut out if required. (In tests it was subsequently found that the bearings of the idling engine tended to break up under these conditions.) The two coupled units drove twin coaxial propellers on the front end and a pair of blowers side by side at the back. Each fourteen-cylinder unit consisted of seven radially disposed twin in-line liquid-cooled units, which were detachable with the barrels and valve gear. There were two valves per cylinder, operated by an overhead camshaft, each driven by a bevel-geared radial shaft. The capacity of the whole twenty-eight cylinders was 83.6 litres and 3,700bhp was anticipated for take-off at 2,700rpm. The prototype weighed 7,714lb (3,500kg) complete with propellers, but this was more heavily built than the production versions would have been. Fedden understood that only about twelve 803s had been built and the team saw examples in pieces at the Munich works, but they remained unimpressed by the engine and described it as a 'pedantic compromise'. The Mission Report stated:

> Its layout and design appeared clumsy and rather indifferent, and gave the impression of having been designed by one with an air-cooled radial mentality, yet without the courage of his convictions.

DAIMLER-BENZ HEADQUARTERS, UNTERTÜRKHEIM

There hadn't been enough time for the Fedden Mission to visit the Daimler-Benz works during their first visit to Germany, but a group was despatched to the Untertürkheim on the second, supplementary trip in July. Located on the edge of Stuttgart and right beside the main railway line, Untertürkheim remains the headquarters of Daimler AG to this day, but back in the spring of 1945 the works presented a scene of utter devastation. Due to the level of bombing the production had been almost entirely stopped between 1943

Heinkel He 111 being stripped by American personnel. (NARA)

and 1944, although the aero-engine factory had continued to function as Daimler-Benz's engine development centre.

Prior to leaving for Germany Fedden had been briefed on various Daimler-Benz developments with information mostly obtained from the interrogation of German personnel held in London. However, he was left with the impression that some of this information did not fall in line with what they were being told by the general manager, W. Haspel, or the chief designer, Dr E. Schmidt, over in Untertürkheim.

The Daimler-Benz DB 603, a liquid-cooled in-line twelve-cylinder inverted V-12, was a successor to the earlier DB 600 and DB 601 engines. The latter was basically a redesign of the DB 600 incorporating direct fuel injection and improved supercharging capacity. The racing version of the DB 601, which set a World Speed Record of 469.2mph (750.7km) in a Messerschmitt Bf 109R in 1939, was specially boosted to develop a maximum of 1,800hp at 3,500rpm as opposed to the 1,050hp at 2,400rpm for the then standard engine. The DB 603 had commenced production in May 1942. It powered a number of aircraft including the twin-engined Dornier Do 217 fighter/bomber N and M versions, the Heinkel He 219 Uhu night-fighter, Messerschmitt Me 410 heavy-fighter, the Do 335 tandem-engined heavy-fighter, and the single-engined Focke-Wulf Ta 152C high-

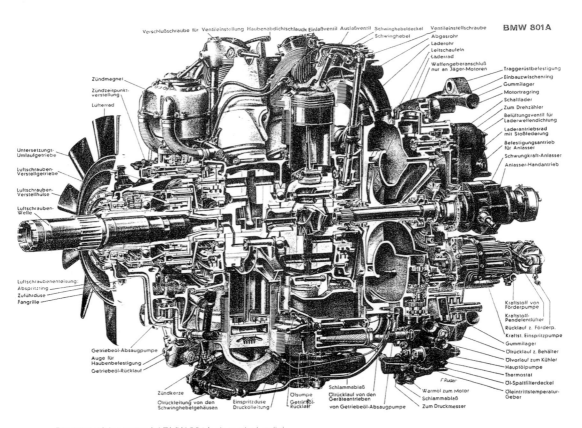

Diagram of the powerful BMW 801A air-cooled radial.

altitude fighter interceptor. (The Ta 152C only entered service in January 1945.) By the latter stages of the war the development of the DB 603 had, pretty much, been pressed to the limit, resulting in a take-off rating of 2,400bhp. A later version, designated as the DB 603N, was upgraded with a new cylinder head and a two-stage two-speed blower, although without intercooler, giving 2,800 to 2,900hp. But it never entered production.

It is interesting to note that the quest to reduce drag, resulting in the cramping of the engine, had caused considerable headaches for the engineers at Daimler-Benz, in particular when it came to its maintenance or installation. Unlike BMW they had never been given the opportunity to conduct full-scale testing in the LFA Völkenrode wind tunnels. Despite this, an experimental installation of the DB 603E in a Focke-Wulf Fw 190 had, it was claimed, resulted in a speed of 420mph (676km/h) at 18,000ft (5,500m). Although this was not that much faster than the standard Fw 190 A–8 fitted with the BMW 801 D–1 at 408mph (656km/h), it was only a whisker slower than the 426mph (685km/h) claimed for the Jumo 213 A–1 engined Fw 190 D–9.

Fedden was informed that all work on the DB 604, a twenty-four-cylinder 43l X-configured engine, had been stopped in 1940 by the Air Ministry which did not consider the design to be sufficiently promising to merit further resources. He also learned that some studies were undertaken on an even bigger thirty-six-cylinder engine as well.

During the war years the production of Daimler-Benz engines had peaked in the summer of 1944 when around 3,000 were produced by 50,000 people working at the parent and subsidiary firms.

THE SWING-PISTON ENGINE

An alternative approach to the piston engine was the Lutz toroidal or swing-piston engine which the mission had come across in the engine department at Völkenrode, albeit in pieces. The concept of the toroidal is not dissimilar to Felix Wankel's rotary engine which it pre-dates. Wankel's design featured a three-sided rotor which moved about an eccentric shaft within an oval-shaped chamber to create a cycle of three combustion chambers, directing the force of the gas pressure to drive the shaft directly. In the swing-piston engine the pistons move in a circular motion inside a ring-shaped cylinder, moving towards or away from each other to provide compression and expansion. During the war Otto Lutz had developed an experimental six-cylinder toroidal in association with the Bussing Company of Braunschweig. The aim was to create an operational system consisting of compact multi-sectioned units, but Fedden was characteristically scathing regarding its potential as an aero engine:

> It is understood that experimental work was being done by Junkers and also by Bosch and Mahle. Opinions varied considerably as to the promise this work held out, but the general feeling was that it introduced rather more new problems than it solved old ones, and that its chances of success in the aircraft field were not particularly rosy.

The concept has recently enjoyed something of a revival and Raphial Morgado's Massive Yet Tiny (MYT) Toroidal engine won first prize in the 2005 Emhart-Nasa Tech Briefs Design Contest.

Fedden felt that at the time of Germany's collapse the best that the aero engine industry could offer were the twelve-cylinder liquid-cooled and the fourteen-cylinder air-cooled series in the power range of 2,000 to 2,4000hp:

> They had a number of other developments, but, as happened in other countries, they had found high power piston engine development very slow and extremely difficult. They were also hampered by a number of bad technical decisions from the RLM, and a policy of stopping and starting certain production types. Furthermore, their development was being harassed all the time in continually increasing measure by our bombing. Under wartime conditions they could not see that a 5,000hp engine could be got into series production in less than four years, and this would probably have been the Jumo 222 or the BMW 803 in their opinion, although the latter appeared to the Mission to be a poor effort which was unlikely ever to become a classic type.

In 1944 the RLM ordered that all development work on piston engines should be halted in order to concentrate efforts and resources on the turbojets. Spurred on by an increasing atmosphere of panic, limited piston engine development recommenced in January 1945, but the drive seems to have been spasmodic.

Summing up his impression of German piston engine development Fedden concluded by saying:

> It is not felt that there is much to learn from Germany about piston engine development, of a general policy nature, except the emphasis placed on the results of full scale wind tunnel tests, for both air-cooled and liquid-cooled types, the necessity for foolproof single-lever

Preserved
BMW 801 D2.
(Rottweiler)

control, and the feeling that fuel injection had not only been worth while, but becomes progressively more important as the number of cylinders increases. All this lines up well with our own reactions to the problem of the higher power piston engine.

ENGINE IGNITION, FUEL INJECTION AND VARIABLE PITCH PROPELLERS

In addition to the engines themselves, the Fedden Mission also examined German development work on engine ignition, fuel injection and variable pitch propellers. When it came to fuel injection the mission had little to report as they had been unable to get hold of the right people at Junkers, or at Deckel in Munich, although in Stuttgart they had more luck and were able to talk to Dr Heinrich, a designer from the Bosch injection development department at Reutlingen. In general Heinrich said that, apart from producing larger capacity units, their efforts to make improvements to the fuel injection pumps had not borne fruit. The closed Bosch nozzle, as used on the BMW 801, had performed well enough, he admitted, although it was complicated to manufacture. At Dessau, Junkers had tried various types of nozzles but stuck to the open type fitted on the Jumo 213.

On the subject of sparking plugs Fedden's experts fared better, with information obtained from BMW, Daimler-Benz and Bosch, although not from the other two major plug manufacturers, Beru and Siemens. Apart from special projects the main development work had been on improved operation at higher altitudes or under hotter engine conditions, either through better electrical insulation or more efficient cooling.

All work on propellers was halted once the turbojets had been allocated the highest priority, but it was picked up later on when the development of piston engines resumed. The only propeller activity investigated by Fedden's team was that of the Vereinigte Deutsche Metallwerke (VDM) company. At Göttingen they had been able to talk to Dr J. Stüper who had done a considerable amount of test flying as part of the development of VDM's braking propeller. This consisted of three blades connected by links through the hub to the inner member of a large bearing, which slid on an extension at the rear of the hub. An outer bearing member is fitted in a hinged yoke which is tilted by threaded rods controlled by two electric motors to alter the pitch of the propellers. The rate of pitch change was 2° per second for constant speeding and 60° to 100° per second for reversing. Its main purpose was as a brake in the windmill brake position. According to Stüper the system had been very satisfactory and production was due to start in early 1945 for the Dornier Do 335, Do 317 and the Fw 190.

The mission also spoke to Dr Eckert, technical director of Continental Metall Gesellschaft (CMG), an off-shoot of VDM which had taken over the propeller work, although forgings were still being supplied by VDM. He confirmed Stüper's observations on reversing propellers and added that they were considering replacing the electric motors with hydraulic cylinders to enable counterweights to be dispensed with.

CMG had another type of reversing propeller under construction with the gearing rearranged in such a way that, with a four-bladed prop, it would be possible to put the propeller into braking pitch by decreasing pitch on two blades while simultaneously increasing it on the other two blades. The main advantage of this would be the elimination of the over-speeding of engines during braking.

CMG had also commenced research into hollow steel blades. On the first trials the welding on the leading and trailing edges failed. They then tried a blade made up of a hollow rectangular tube with the edges welded on. Like many other firms CMG had suffered badly as a result of the Allied bombing campaign and had been forced to move its machine shops several times. Fedden inspected one which had been relocated to a railway tunnel at Kasselborn, about 22 miles (35km) from Frankfurt, but found little of interest.

The forging of the metal propeller blades was done by VDM at their works in Heddernheim on the north-west edge of Frankfurt. The process of making a propeller began with a 31in (80cm) cylinder of metal alloy, about 13in (33cm) thick, which was heated to 750°F (400°C) and extruded into oval sections 5.9in (15cm) on its widest axis and 19ft 8in (6m) long. These lengths were cut into six, heated again to 750°F (400°C) and passed through rollers to produce tapered forging blanks. These were heated, to 840°F (450°C) this time, and formed into shape by a massive 15,000-ton press. The largest propeller made by VDM was a four-blader of 14ft 9in (4.5m) diameter for the DB 613 engine. Towards the end of the war a shortage of aluminium necessitated the increased use of wooden blades.

As previously mentioned, BMW's Bruckmann had also advocated the development of turbine engines to drive propellers, which he thought would eventually come into common use for long-range aircraft.

Focke-Wulf Fw 190A. The A series was fitted with variants of the BMW 801 radial. *(USAF)*

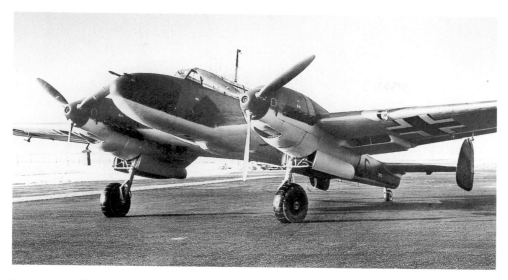

Messerschmitt Bf 110 with a pair of DB 601 liquid-cooled inverted V12s.

THE DORNIER Do 335 *PFEIL*

Of all of the Luftwaffe's piston-engined propeller-driven aircraft the most unusual, but also the fastest – and potentially the fastest piston-engined fighter ever – was undoubtedly the Dornier Do 335. Known as the *Pfeil* ('arrow'), this featured a distinctive tandem push-pull configuration with engines and propellers at both the front and back. Its origins can be traced back to Claude Dornier's earlier experiments with tandem engines on most of his multi-engined flying boats, including the mighty Do.X which had been fitted with Fedden's Jupiters at one stage.

On the Do 335 one DB 603 engine was mounted in the nose in the conventional manner, with a second one within the fuselage behind the cockpit driving a propeller in the tail via an extension shaft. Dornier had patented this configuration in 1937 and a concept demonstrator was built by Schemp-Hirth, the *Göppingen Gö 9*, which flew successfully in 1940. The RLM, however, showed little enthusiasm for a tandem fighter and required Dornier to concentrate its efforts on its range of bombers. Then in May 1942 Dornier's updated version of the push-pull configuration, the P.231, beat off the competition in meeting the ministry's requirement for a single-seat high-speed bomber/intruder. The P.231 became the Do 335 but by the autumn of 1942 the RLM had decided that the bomber/intruder was no longer required and instead a multi-role fighter based on the same general layout should go ahead. For a fast fighter aircraft there were distinct advantages in the tandem design, in particular the power of a twin-engined aircraft without the greater frontal area and associated drag of mounting an engine on each wing. It also placed the weight of the engines on or near the aircraft's centreline, increasing the roll rate and eliminating the asymmetrical thrust normally caused by a single-engine failure.

The push-pull configuration of the Dornier Do 335 looked all wrong, but the reduced drag resulted in an extremely fast fighter aircraft. Only a handful were built. *(NARA)*

In terms of appearance the Do 335 looked like no other aircraft. For a start it was very big for a fighter; 45ft 5in (13.85m) long and, riding on a tall tricycle undercarriage, it was high at 16ft 4in (5m) to the top of the cruciform tail fin. This tail extended below the fuselage to protect the rear propeller from possible ground strikes. In the event of a pilot bail-out, explosive bolts would jettison the upper tail and rear propeller, although at least one aircraft was fitted with an ejector seat.

Flight testing commenced on 26 October 1943 when the Do 335 V1 prototype took off from Dornier's Oberpfaffenhofen airfield. Despite the loss of the second prototype due to a fire in the rear engine, the aircraft demonstrated good handling qualities with an exceptional rate of climb, reaching 26,250ft (8,000m) in under fifteen minutes, and a blistering maximum speed of 474mph (763km/h) at 21,300ft (6,500m). Production of the Do 335 A-1 began in late 1944, and several variants were planned including two-seater night-fighter and trainer versions. The Do 335 B-1 saw an upgrade in weaponry from the 15mm MG 151/15 cannon to the 20mm cannon, and the Do 335 B-2 was to have an additional pair of 30mm MK 103s installed in the wings. The Do 335 B-3 was basically a Do 335 B-1 fitted with the more powerful 2,100hp DB 603LA engine.

By the time the US Army overran the Oberpfaffenhofen factory in April 1945 just a handful of the Do 335 fighter-bombers and two A-12 conversion trainers had been completed. Including the various prototype aircraft a total of only thirty-seven Do 335s were ever built and the sole surviving example, a Do 335 A-0 pre-production model, is displayed at the Smithsonian National Air and Space Museum in Washington D.C.

six

DISPERSAL OF PRODUCTION

STRATEGIC BOMBING aims to systematically destroy those resources which will most weaken an enemy by denying them the materials or weapons they need to continue a war. One of the main objectives of the Allies' Combined Bomber Offensive, launched in the summer of 1943 and carried out during the last two years of the war, was to shut down Germany's aircraft industry and to cut off the flow of usable aircraft to Hitler's fighter squadrons. Preventing or disrupting the development of new aircraft or aero engines was never a specific item on the agenda, but it was an inevitable by-product of the intensive onslaught unleashed upon the aircraft and engine plants.

During their time in Germany the Fedden Mission came face to face with several examples of the destructive power of the Allied bombing raids and also the measures taken by the Germans to circumvent their effectiveness. Of the various plants they visited, without exception those which had been known to the Allies had been severely damaged. As Fedden commented in the final report, 'Several of the places it was hoped to examine were found to be so badly bombed that there was nothing to be seen'. The Junkers works at Dessau, for example, were so extensively damaged that little of value could be found, and it was a similar story at the Jumo engine plant at Magdeburg, used to manufacture and overhaul the Jumo 109-004 jet engines. 'A number of wrecked jet engines, destroyed in the air raids, were seen lying about,' observed Fedden. Of the Daimler-Benz Untertürkheim plant in Stuttgart he wrote, 'These works had been very badly damaged and production had been almost entirely dispersed during 1943-44.' It was the same at the Bosch works at Stuttgart and with BMW at Stassfurt. Only the most secret sites, such as the LFA research institute at Völkenrode or Messerschmitt's experimental and design department which transferred to Oberammergau in October 1943, and the carefully concealed or dispersed facilities, such as the Mittelwerk at Nordhausen, that had escaped unscathed. Everywhere else the devastation to industry and the transportation infrastructure was absolute and, as this excerpt from an official US government report on the effects of the strategic bombing campaign testifies, no country could carry on functioning for long under these circumstances:

Wrecked Me 262s amid the rubble of the bombed Messerschmitt factory at Obertraubling in Bavaria. *(LoC)*

Even a first class military power – rugged and resilient as Germany was – cannot live long under full-scale and free exploitation of air weapons over the heart of its territory. By the beginning of 1945, before the invasion of the homeland itself, Germany was reaching a state of helplessness. Her armament production was falling irretrievably, orderliness in effort was disappearing, and total disruption and disintegration were well along. Her armies were still in the field. But with the impending collapse of the supporting economy, the indications are convincing they would have had to cease fighting – any effective fighting – within a few months. Germany was mortally wounded.

So why was it that the Luftwaffe, equipped with the world's first operational jet fighter in the Me 262, not to mention rocket-powered interceptors and all manner of guided weaponry, had been unable to hold back the enemy bombers? For the answer to this question we need go back to the beginning of the war when the role of Germany's newly formed air force had been defined as supportive to the army within Hitler's doctrine of lightning-fast Blitzkrieg offensives. It was all about quick-fire attack. All evidence suggests that Hitler regarded the war in the west as being over by October 1940. Yes the British were a nuisance, but what harm were they likely to cause? Reichsmarschall Hermann Göring once famously boasted that no enemy bomber would ever reach Germany's industrial heartland. 'If one reaches the Ruhr,' he joked, 'my name is not Göring. You may call me Meyer' (a highly derogatory term). And when Hitler's forces were poised to seize Leningrad and Moscow it must have seemed that the war in the east was about to be successfully concluded too. At that point Germany was not under any direct threat, neither was there any expectation of conducting a prolonged bombing campaign on an enemy's industrial base and, accordingly, there was no great impetus to step up aircraft production. In this situation the German aircraft industry was meeting the Luftwaffe's existing production requirements with comparative ease. In fact it was operating with 100 per cent excess capacity as it was customary for aircraft plants to work on only a single daytime shift basis. Neither were women brought in to boost the workforce, as was the case in both Britain and, later, the USA.

But the cracks in this strategy of complacency through strength had already begun to appear by the autumn of 1940. Only a matter of months after Hitler had abandoned Operation Sealion – the intended invasion of Great Britain – the RAF hit back, commencing with a number of daylight raids against Germany's industrial centres in an effort to weaken the economy and undermine the morale of the German population. Unfortunately for the British airmen their own losses on these missions were extremely high while the tonnage of bombs dropped was quite small, especially when compared with the combined bomber offensive of the final year of the war; only 16,000 tons dropped in 1940 and 46,000 tons in 1941, as opposed to a staggering 676,000 tons in 1944. While the physical damage inflicted in those early raids was not particularly significant perhaps, the appearance of the British aircraft above the Fatherland undermined public confidence and was a source of huge embarrassment for Göring. It wouldn't be long until the Germans began deriding the regular wailing of the air-raid sirens as the 'horns of Meyer'.

Me 262 aircraft found by the advancing Allies at a 'Waldwerk' or forest factory near Obertraubling. *(NARA)*

Me 262s under cover: The entrance to the low buildings of the forest factory has been carefully concealed under camouflage netting. *(NARA)*

The biggest shake-up of the German armaments industry came unexpectedly in February 1942. Following the sudden death of Fritz Todt in an aircraft accident Hitler immediately promoted Albert Speer, the Reich's chief architect at the time, to take charge of the *Reichsministerium für Rüstung und Kriegsproduktion* (RfRuK or Reich Ministry for Armament and War Production). This may have been a deliberate pre-emptive ploy to prevent the power-hungry Göring from claiming Todt's ministerial powers for himself, but Speer was both loyal to the Führer and a very capable organiser. He immediately set about rationalising the nation's war production, centralising control and achieving a threefold increase in output through the elimination of inefficiencies and improving the utilisation of existing industrial plant and facilities. Then, on 30 May 1942, the RAF made the first of its controversial 'thousand plane' raids on German industrial and urban centres, starting with Cologne and followed two nights later by an attack on Essen. This was followed up in the summer of 1943 when the port of Hamburg was singled out for one of the most devastating attacks of the entire war, carried out over three successive days and resulting in the destruction of around one-third of all the houses in the city and the deaths of 60,000 to 100,000 people. The Nazi leaders were shaken to the core, as Speer later confided: 'I reported for the first time orally to the Führer that if these aerial attacks continue, a rapid end to the war might be the consequence.'

And the odds were already stacking up against the Nazis. Back in 1941, on 7 December, aircraft of the Imperial Japanese Navy had launched their notorious surprise attack on the US naval base at Pearl Harbor, Hawaii. The following day President Roosevelt signed his country's declaration of war against Japan. In loyalty to their Japanese ally, both Germany and Italy reciprocated by declaring war on the USA on 11 December 1941. It is said that

Hitler was furious with the Japanese for dragging the US into the war when he had yet to gain full control of continental Europe, but he still believed that American bombers would never dare to attack Germany. He was wrong.

Under the Combined Bomber Offensive (CBO) the might of the RAF and the USAAF, backed up by the USA's formidable industrial base, were brought together to strike at the heart of Germany. At its peak this entailed a round-the-clock offensive with the RAF attacking at night and the USAAF by day. As far as targeting the German aircraft industry was concerned, the bombing offensive can be divided into two distinct periods. The first half, starting in April 1943 and through to May 1944, is referred to as the High Priority Campaign and focussed on the aircraft industry and the U-boat bases as the main strategic targets. The second half of the Combined Bomber Offensive, described as the Low Priority Campaign, took place from June 1944 right through to the end of the war in April 1945, and although the aircraft industry was still targeted it was no longer a main priority as a strategic target.

The first phase of the High Priority Campaign, beginning in April 1943 and continuing up to the autumn, saw bombing raids on those plants manufacturing the Messerschmitt Bf 109 and the Focke-Wulf Fw 190 fighter aircraft, plus one attack on an engine plant and several on the ball bearing plants at Schweinfurt. At this stage in the war these locations were at the extreme range that the Allied bombers could reach when still flying with protection from fighter escorts. Official records state that the first phase ended with 'no discernible results' in terms of disruption caused, but it did incur heavy losses for the Allies. Accordingly, over the winter of 1943 and into 1944, there was a brief hiatus in the proceedings to allow time for a build-up of heavy bomber strength and to await delivery of America's new P-51 Mustang long-range fighter which would be able to escort the bomber formations right into the heart of Germany. The P-51D was a formidable aircraft with a maximum range of 1,650 miles (2,755km) when equipped with external fuel

A pair of Jumo 004 engines discovered in one of the forest factories. *(USAF)*

tanks, and an impressive maximum speed of 437mph (703km/h) at 25,000ft (7,620m). Performance-wise, they were more than a match for the Messerschmitt Bf 109s and they just had the edge on the Focke-Wulf Fw 190s.

The CBO resumed in the new year, with deep penetration raids carried out under fighter escort, and from 20 to 25 February 1944 the bombs rained down upon twenty-three of Germany's airframe plants plus three of the aero-engine works. March to May 1944 saw the heaviest bombing of aircraft targets of the whole campaign. Every single aircraft plant was hit and by late April Germany's synthetic oil plants were beginning to replace the aircraft factories as strategic targets.

While these heavy attacks left the airframe plants at Marienburg, Augsburg, Wiener Neustadt and Dessau as smoking ruins, the raids were still regarded as failures in strategic terms as they caused only minor disruption to the fighter aircraft output. The Allies had failed to appreciate the tremendous recuperative powers of Germany's aircraft industry, which was partly due to its inherent spare capacity and the fact that the machine tools were remarkably durable even though the buildings might be in ruins. More often than not it was a case of just clearing the rubble and starting up again.

In response to the onslaught Germany's *Jägerstab* ('fighter staff') was formed in February 1944 and the responsibility for aircraft production was wrested from the Luftwaffe and placed in the hands of Albert Speer's Ministry of Armaments and War Production. Speer faced two very different problems: how to increase aircraft production – in particular for the fighter aircraft – while also protecting the plants from further bombing damage. The solution was to be implemented in three stages: firstly, decentralising aircraft production through dispersal; secondly establishing safe facilities underground either in mines or tunnels; and finally instigating an ambitious plan to construct six large and impregnable weapons plants. Dividing the manufacturing process into smaller and less vulnerable units also established multiple supply sources not only for components and parts, but for the sub-assembly and final assembly of aircraft. If one site was hit then another could take on the work.

An American serviceman examines an unfinished Me 262 at an underground assembly plant near Kahla. *(NARA)*

DISPERSAL

Dispersing production was the quickest policy to implement. Over the next twelve months twenty-seven of the main airframe plants were split and relocated to around 300 smaller facilities, and the fifty or so engine plants were scattered to more than 200 different locations. The process of dispersal was aided by the ministry but the actual expense remained the responsibility of the individual companies, although they had little choice in the matter. Likewise, the workforce had to do what it was told and had to put up with moving to the new locations. A limited amount of dispersal had already taken place before 1944. The first important aircraft factory to be dispersed had been the Focke-Wulf plant in Bremen. Located in the north-west part of the country this was considered to be especially vulnerable to attack and following RAF raids in 1940 and 1941 its production facilities were divided between several sites at Marienberg, Posen, Cottbus and Sorau, all of which were deeper within Germany to the east and south-east of Berlin.

Messerschmitt's plants had been heavily hit in the latest round of Allied raids, and the large areas of forest in the Augsburg area offered the obvious means of concealment via dispersal to a number of Waldwerke, or forest factories. In no time there were more than a dozen such factories hidden in the woods and the plant at Horgau, about 7 miles (11km) west of Augsburg, was typical of one of these set ups. Located beside the autobahn, it consisted of twenty-one timber buildings, including barracks for 845 workers, which were painted green and hidden from view beneath a combination of camouflage netting and overhanging foliage. Production work was carried out on a two-shift basis, assembling wing panels, nose and tail sections for the Me 262 which were then transferred to a nearby final assembly plant. The concealment of the forest factories was so successful that none was detected by aerial reconnaissance during the war, although Allied fighters did attack a number of Me 262s half hidden along the motorway. The autobahn served as a makeshift runway to send the aircraft on their way to the operational bases and the Fedden team reported seeing several Me 262s still on the stretch between Stuttgart and Munich, although it should be remembered that the Luftwaffe also made operational use of autobahn runways towards the end.

During the summer of 1944 the Germans had a brief respite from the incessant raids as virtually all Allied air power was concentrated on establishing air superiority in preparation for the D-Day landings at Normandy and the subsequent breakout. Then in September the CBO resumed with jet aircraft production given a priority second only to the oil plants. The list of specific targets included jet airframe and engine factories, conventional aircraft engine factories, fighter airframe factories, any airfields particularly associated with jets, and all airfields with concentrations of fighter aircraft. In most cases each target was attacked on a handful of occasions, although some were subjected to multiple attacks – possibly up to eleven times. This onslaught resulted in considerable damage to the buildings and facilities, but once again the effect on production was minimal as most plants had been dispersed by this time and several of the underground sites were starting to become operational.

GOING UNDERGROUND

The initial movement below ground had commenced as early as 1943 when orders had been given to identify suitable underground locations following the RAF's Operation Hydra raids on the V-weapon research station at Peenemünde. The damage caused had been immense and for the Germans it demonstrated the vulnerability of such large above-ground facilities. Accordingly production of the V-weapons – both the V-1 flying bombs and the V-2 (A4) rockets – was transferred to an extensive network of tunnels burrowed into the Harz mountains near the village of Nordhausen. (These works were visited by the Fedden Mission to Germany and its findings are described in Chapter 7.) Once the German High Command had given priority to the production of jet fighter aircraft a number of airframe and engine plants were also moved underground. The scale of the underground sites varied enormously depending on whether they were natural caves and quarries or more extensive mine workings which, in certain cases, were massively extended or adapted for their new roles. Usually these sites are referred to by the nearest village (the choice of village appears to vary with different sources of information) and they were also allocated misleading codenames to throw Allied intelligence off the scent. Old mines and tunnels were usually named after various animals or fish, for example, while new tunnel systems were given geological designations.

Production of Junkers aircraft was relocated to a deep salt mine at Tarthun, about 12 miles (19km) to the south-west of Magdeburg. Work began on preparing the site in March 1944 and production had commenced by December that year. In a series of tunnels and galleries occupying an area of about 200,000ft² (18,580m²), the 2,400 workers worked in shifts on the Heinkel He 162 *Volksjäger*. One photograph, taken after the site was discovered by the 1st US Army in April 1945, shows a gallery with over thirty He 162 fuselages all neatly lined up in a row. Apparently the moisture-absorbing qualities of the salt resulted in very satisfactory working conditions, although the capacity of the lone elevator cage made access awkward. Junkers occupied further underground facilities near Halberstadt in the Champignon Caves, a system of old quarry workings, codenamed *Makrele* ('mackerel') I and II, for the manufacture of aircraft parts and fuselages for both the He 162 and Ju 88.

The aero engine companies also sought safety underground. Production of the Jumo 109-004 turbojet was moved into the north end of the Nordhausen complex, and to the Malachit (malachite) tunnels under the Takenberg hills, also near Halberstadt and slightly further to the west of the Tarthun mines. This extensive grid of interlocking caves was created by excavating new workings, started in June 1944, connected to an entrance from an existing sandstone quarry. The aim had been to manufacture turbine components for 1,000 engines every month but production only commenced in April 1945. Daimler-Benz moved part of its plant into a 500,000ft² (45,000m²) gypsum mine near Heidelberg, codename Goldfish, and BMW occupied railway tunnels at Markirch, near Strasbourg.

With hindsight, it would have been far more effective if the Allies had gone for the aero-engine manufacturing plants or the foundries that produced specialist castings for the jet engines from the outset and before they went underground. Albert Speer himself commented on this point after the war:

We were surprised for a long time that you attacked the airframe production and not the motor production. There were only a few big factories ... If you had attacked the motor factories at first and not the airframe, we would have been finished.

Dispersing and hiding the production facilities obviously provided protection from the bombs, but it also concealed them from prying eyes, as this official US government report later confirmed:

After the industry dispersed, however, the quality of our intelligence deteriorated. We not only did not know the locations of many important units in the dispersal pattern, but we seriously underestimated the production capabilities and recuperability of the German industry.

Dispersal did cause its own problems, however, as Fedden noted:

We were told of organisations which had been dispersed to four different sites in fourteen months. It would be common for a firm to have hardly been settled down in a new place, before they had to be moved to another.

The dispersal had other effects including a dilution of technical talent, an increase in the need for indirect workers engaged in transportation and handling, and it placed a far greater reliance on the transportation system, in particular the railways. Furthermore, as the bombing offensive continued and the disruption increased the aircraft companies faced delays in the supply and delivery of essential materials, in particular aluminium, magnesium and high-strength steel alloys. For airframe construction this was mitigated to

He 162 Volkjäger fuselages being assembled at Junkers' underground facility at Tarthun. (NARA)

some extent by the simplification of designs and the greater use of more readily available materials such as steel or wood. As for the turbojets, the requirement for nickel and cobalt was minimised as much as possible and new methods of heat-proofing were developed including aluminium coatings to protect steel fan blades against oxidisation.

Inevitably the headlong rush to meet production targets and the problems caused by the new working situations resulted in issues concerning the quality of workmanship. The cracks were starting to show, literally. On an aircraft such as the Me 262 a smooth finish is important to minimise drag, but increasingly the gaps between badly fitting panels were being smoothed over with a filler paste. Fedden reported:

> A shortage of raw materials and difficulties from our bombing attacks made many changes necessary. The chief engineer of BMW said that during the war he had had to change the steel of his poppet valves ten times, and his crankshafts three times, necessitating check tests in every case.

But time and time again the clear message was that it was the destruction and disruption of the transport infrastructure that had the greatest effect on productivity and effectiveness:

> Several of the firms said that the bombing of their communications was more serious than the bombing of the factories as, with few exceptions, the factories could be got going again comparatively quickly. The bombing of communications however was fatal, and cut down, for instance, piston engine production, from the spring of 1943 to the spring of 1945, to one third of what it had been previously.

When the Allies shifted their focus to attack the transport infrastructure, in particular the railways, bridges and marshalling yards, and also the oil and synthetic fuel plants, the problems of moving components, materials or completed aircraft were further compounded. Monthly production figures for synthetic fuels fell from 316,000 tons to 17,000 tons by September 1944, and output of aviation fuel fell from 17,500 tons to a meagre 5,000 tons. In the spring of 1944 Germany's consumption of oil was already exceeding production and by the end of the year virtually all of the reserves had been used up. For the beleaguered Luftwaffe the run-in time for new aircraft engines was cut from two hours to ninety minutes, and all pilot training was drastically reduced to save precious fuel. Synthetic rubber production also suffered from the attacks on the oil industry.

IMPREGNABLE WEAPONS PLANTS

In the end the dispersal measures proved self-defeating. The ultimate way to circumvent some of the production and infrastructure difficulties was to centralise production centres, either in huge bunkers or underground, where every aspect of an aircraft's production could be carried out at a single well-protected site. In 1944 work began on a series of semi-subterranean bomb-proof bunkers in the Landsberg area, near Kaufering in Bavaria, specifically for the large-scale manufacture of the Me 262. These new facilities were part of a project named *Ringeltaube* ('wood pigeon'), instigated by Albert Speer's ministry. Three cavernous arched bunkers, each 1,300ft (400m) long and 278ft (85m) wide, were to be constructed starting with the first, codenamed '*Weingut II*' ('vineyard II').

It was built by heaping up tons of excavated gravel to create a former or mould for the vast semi-cylindrical concrete roof which consisted of 8in (20cm) of light cement interlaced with iron rods, capped with a further covering of heavy concrete. This was considered adequate to resist even the RAF's 6-ton bombs. Once the concrete had set the gravel was then removed and used in the construction of the other parts of the structure. *Weingut II* was so vast that the plans included an underground runway for the departure of the finished Me 262s, although assistance from liquid-fuelled rocket-assisted take off (RATO) units would probably have been essential.

Responsibility for construction lay with the Organisation Todt, while the SS managed an army of 10,000 slave workers made up of Russian prisoners plus thousands of Jewish inmates brought from concentration camps such as Dachau. Working fourteen-hour shifts, seven days a week, conditions for the workers were appalling; their average life expectancy was measured in weeks. It is estimated that 30,000 people were employed in the construction of *Weingut II* and that between 10,000 and 20,000 perished in the process. (The involvement of slave labour in the armaments industry is discussed further in Chapter 7.) *Weingut II* had not been completed by the time it was occupied by American troops in April 1945.

When reviewing the effects of the CBO and the German's dispersal programme as a whole, it is worth noting that official Allied sources estimate that 18,000 aircraft of all types were denied to the Luftwaffe in the period of intensive attacks between July 1943 and December 1944, of which 78 per cent, or 14,000, would have been fighters. Ironically, however, German aircraft production actually increased dramatically after the CBO had commenced. For example, figures for fighter aircraft production show a total of just over 2,700 in 1940, but an almost tenfold increase to approximately 25,000 in 1944, and even 5,700 for the first few months of 1945 alone. Of course there are no figures for jet aircraft production prior to 1944, but in total by the end of hostilities almost 1,300 Messerschmitt Me 262s had been produced, 364 Me 163Bs and around 116 Heinkel He 162s. The Arado Ar 234 is classified as a bomber, and of these 214 were built. This gives an estimated total figure for German jet or rocket-powered aircraft of around 2,100. And that was despite the problems of maintaining production through the bomber offensive and the disruption and disadvantages of the dispersal programme. The potential for further increases was summed up by Fedden:

> The German jet engines, Junkers and BMW, were primarily designed for very large production. From an examination of their designs as well as the tooling equipment and factory layout, it appears quite possible that their estimated production of about 100,000 jet engines a year by the middle of 1946 would have been realised if they had been allowed to continue.

Hidden in the woods beside the Autobahn, this abandoned Me 262 has been stripped of its Jumo 004 engines. (NARA)

Seen from the purely engineering point of view the German aeronautical designers had produced a dazzling array of advanced and exotic flying machines in the most difficult of conditions. Fedden again:

> The Mission did feel that the German aircraft industry was in the midst of some extremely interesting new developments, and that, had they been able to proceed with their new prototypes undisturbed, they would have had, within a short time, a family of very high performance interceptor fighters, as well as a family of very high speed bombers in series production.

Primarily it was through the wrecking of Germany's manufacturing base and transportation infrastructure that the Allies ensured this didn't happen. The official view is that the Combined Bomber Offensive had probably shortened the war by 'some months'. It doesn't sound that much perhaps, but as Fedden concluded: 'The members of the Mission have come back thankful that the war ended when it did.'

seven

A VISION OF HELL

ON TUESDAY 19 JUNE the whole of Fedden's team, including the pilots and crew, travelled to Nordhausen in the mountainous Harz region. Some of them went with the two Dakotas direct to the landing strip outside Nordhausen, while the others travelled the 50 or so miles (80km) by road from Stassfurt where they had inspected the BMW jet engine plant the previous day. It must have been a very pleasant journey as the Harz is an exceptionally scenic area, where the thickly wooded slopes are dissected by rocky gorges and valleys of rich farming land. The regional capital, Halberstadt, had been severely damaged by air raids but for the most part there was little of the widespread devastation they had experienced in the industrial areas to the north. Fedden noted that it was 'a very hot and brilliantly fine summer's day'. However, the British team had little time to enjoy the mountain scenery for they were about to descend into what can only be described as a man-made vision of hell:

> The Mission had been told that at Nordhausen there was a large underground factory, and that they would see extraordinary production methods, but they had no idea that they would be brought face to face with such an undertaking. Although members of the Mission had read a good deal about the concentration camps of Germany, Nordhausen was not officially regarded as such, but as one of the most modern production factories. The reaction of the Mission to this visit to Nordhausen was one of the utmost revulsion and disgust. Such a place must be visited to be believed, and it is hoped that nothing can compare with it elsewhere in the world.

Although Fedden refers to it as Nordhausen, taking the name from the nearest town, the subterranean factory tunnelled under the Kohnstein mountain was officially known as the Mittelwerk, meaning middle or central works. The site, including the nearby concentration camps which housed the workforce, was uncovered by the advancing American troops of the 3rd Armored Division on 11 April 1945. US Army Intelligence knew that there was something unusual in the area. It was only with the discovery of the thousands of dead and sick prisoners in the outlying camps and barracks that they began to grasp the true scale of what they had stumbled upon.

The Mittelwerk was the largest and most notorious of the German subterranean arms factories. Its chief function was the assembly of the main elements of Hitler's much

American personnel in front of the camouflaged south entrance to the Mittelwerk weapons factory concealed beneath the Kohnstein mountain near Nordhausen. *(NARA)*

vaunted *Vergeltungwaffen*, the vengeance or retaliation weapons, principally the V-1 flying bomb and the V-2 (A4) rocket. There was also a third and lesser-known V weapon, the V-3 super-gun, although this had no connection with the Mittelwerk as it was of necessity constructed at a fixed site near the Channel. The V-3 was a long-range cannon with a series of propellent charges spaced along the barrel's length which were fired in sequence to maximise the finned projectile's velocity. Under the German codename *Tausendfussler* ('millipede') – because of the gun's appearance with the charge chambers sticking out like legs on the long barrel – work had commenced in the autumn of 1943 to construct up to five V-3 guns in quarries located near Mimoyecques in the Pas de Calais. The 490ft (150m) barrels were placed within sloping tunnels aimed directly at London. Some test firings had been conducted at the Hillerben artillery proving ground near Magdeburg, but the Mimoyecques guns had yet to fire in anger when they were put out of commission on 6 July 1944 by Tallboy deep-penetration bombs delivered by the RAF's 617 Dambuster Squadron.

In contrast to the V-3, the other two V weapons, the V-1 and V-2 (A4), were more flexible in their deployment and consequently they proved to be far more deadly and difficult to defend against.

THE V-1

The first to be deployed, but by only a matter of months, was the V-1 flying bomb. Developed by the Luftwaffe, as opposed to the V-2 (A4) rocket which was regarded as a long-range artillery weapon and hence the province of the army, this was the precursor to the modern cruise missile. Back in November 1939 the RLM had issued a requirement for a remote-controlled aircraft capable of carrying a payload of 2,200lb (1,000kg) over a distance of 310 miles (500km). In other words far enough if launched from occupied Europe to reach Britain, in particular London. Fritz Gosslau of the Argus Motoren company had already conducted some work on a remote-controlled surveillance aircraft, the AS 292, and Argus combined with Lorentz AG and Arado to produce a joint design for such a flying bomb. In April 1940 Gosslau presented the plans to the RLM as Project P35 'Erfurt' (the name of the capital city of Thuringia). The Air Ministry decided not to go with this design because of concerns about the viability of the remote-control aspects as they feared it might prove vulnerable to electronic jamming.

Nonetheless, Gosslau pressed ahead with his developmental work, abandoning the remote-control system in favour of an autonomous pilot-less aircraft. For expertise in designing a fuselage Heinrich Koppenburg, the head of Argus, recruited the assistance of Robert Lusser, who was a chief designer with Heinkel and had taken up a position with the Fieseler aircraft company. Lusser simplified and improved Gosslau's design, principally making it into a single instead of twin-engined craft, and the revised project was re-submitted to the technical department of the RLM in June 1942. It was approved

Around 25,000 inmates died at the notorious Mittelbau Dora camp built to house slave workers for the Mittelwerk. Many were killed by the fleeing SS guards and as the result of an Allied air raid. *(NARA)*

by Ernst Udet and the Fieseler company was appointed as the main contractor to build the Fieseler Fi 103, as the project was now designated.

The Fi 103 was a pilot-less aircraft with a wingspan of 17.6ft (5.37m) and measuring just over 27ft (8.3m) from nose to tail. The fuselage was of welded sheet steel while the wings were constructed from plywood and slotted on to a main metal spar extending from the fuselage. The payload, a not inconsiderable 1,900lb (850kg) of Amatol-39 explosive, was contained within the warhead, and propulsion was via a single pipe or tube-like engine supported at the rear of the fuselage by a small tail. This was the Argus pulsejet, a type of engine sometimes referred to as a resonant jet. In flight, fuel was drawn past hinged flaps at the front of the pipe by the aircraft's forward motion. Initial ignition was by an automotive spark-plug, but otherwise it required no source of ignition once it got going as each pulse of fuel, coming at a rate of fifty per minute, was ignited by the heat of the previous one. Each combustion shut the flaps at the front, forcing the exhaust to be expelled out of the back of the tube to create thrust, and the cycle recommenced. This meant that the pulsejet engines were extremely simple devices with very few moving parts. They were also light in weight and could run on a low-grade petroleum fuel. Furthermore, in comparison with the later V-2 rockets, they were relatively cheap to produce.

V-1 assembly line at Nordhausen. The flying bombs lack their wings and nose cones at this stage. The wings would be slotted on to the circular spars. *(NARA)*

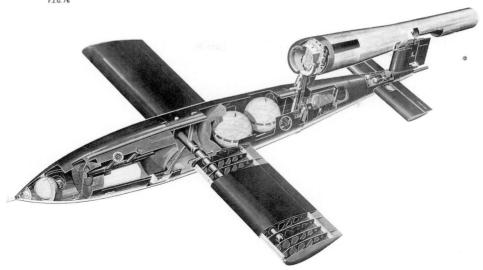

FLYING BOMB
F.Z.G. 76

Cutaway diagram of the Fieseler Fi-103 V-1 with Argus As 014 pulsejet. *(USAF)*

Because of the apparent advantages of the pulsejet concept, tests were also conducted to investigate their potential as propulsion units for conventional aircraft, as well as for road vehicles and even on an experimental high-speed attack boat, but the excessive vibration and high noise levels made them unsuitable for more sustained use. Even for the unmanned V-1 the Argus As 014 engine suffered a drawback in that it did not generate sufficient thrust for the missile's stubby wings to attain take-off speed. The V-1 had a stall speed of around 130mph (200km/h), and accordingly they were launched on an inclined 'ski ramp'. The missile was mounted on a trolley launched by a piston-driven steam catapult, although this is something of a misnomer as they actually used T-Stoff and Z-Stoff fuels consisting of hydrogen peroxide and potassium permanganate.

In flight the V-1s attained an airspeed of around 400mph (640km/h), cruised at between 2,000 and 3,000ft (600-900m), and had an operational range of about 160 miles (250km). Their altitude was regulated by a weighted pendulum and gyroscopic system to control pitch, while a gyrocompass controlled the yaw and roll via a linkage to the small rudder in the tail. An odometer activated by an anemometer – a wind gauge driven by a tiny pair of propeller blades located on the tip of the nose – determined when the missile had travelled the predetermined distance to its intended target. The odometer could be adjusted to take account of the wind speeds on a particular day, and some V-1s were also fitted with radio transmitters for position verification.

By the end of 1943 around 100 V-1 ski ramp launch sites were under construction along the northern coast of France. It was the presence of these conspicuous ramps, pointing straight at London, that alerted the Allies to the threat of the V-1s and RAF Bomber Command initiated a series of intensive bombing raids to knock them out.

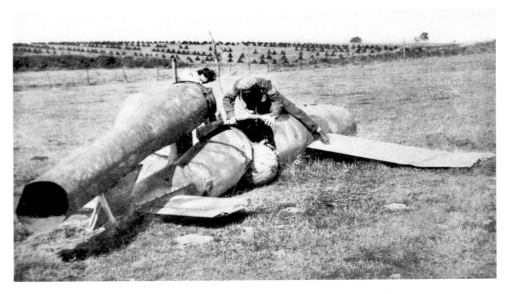

The Allies obtained detailed information on the V-1 flying bombs from examples which fell to earth intact near the launching sites. *(CMcC)*

In response the Germans abandoned the sites – an action unknown to the Allies who kept pounding away – and opted instead for less permanent and better concealed launch facilities.

The first V-1 attack on London took place on 12 June 1944, just a few days after the D-Day landings at Normandy. The notion of vengeance weapons suddenly became far more than a matter of propaganda or rhetoric and Hitler saw them as an effective act of retaliation against the Allies. The attacks soon intensified and at the height of their deployment more than a hundred V-1s were hurtling across the Channel every day. At the receiving end people living in London and the south-east of England quickly came to recognise and dread the distinctive sound generated by the pulsejets. Described as being like the throb of a noisy motorbike it inspired the British nicknames of Buzz-bombs or Doodlebugs, the latter being a general term for a buzzing insect. (The Germans had their own names including *Kirschkern*, 'cherrystone', and the *Maikäfer*, 'maybug'.) But the worst sound of all was the terrifying silence that followed the moment when a V-1's engine cut-out, signalling its imminent descent. The cut-out was not intentional as the missile was designed to strike the ground in a powered dive, but the sudden tilt caused by the automatic release of two spoilers on the elevator resulted in a momentary starvation of fuel in the pipelines. This fault was rectified on later models.

To deal with this new form of aerial bombardment the British developed a number of countermeasures. These began with detachments of the Royal Observer Corps stationed along the Channel coast to provide the earliest possible identification of the incoming missiles. Next in line came the anti-aircraft batteries, although in practice the gunners found the small, fast-moving targets extremely difficult to hit at first. The introduction of proximity fuses raised their success rate enormously and by the end of August 1944 around 80 per cent of the V-1s were being destroyed. To back up the AA guns, an inner barrage of 2,000 balloons was deployed to the south-east of London to entangle the intruders in a curtain of wires, and around 300 V-1s were accounted for in this fashion. For the balloon crews Doodlebug catching was a hazardous activity as a snagged V-1 was liable to fall to the ground close to the balloon winch.

The other defence was to scramble fighter aircraft to intercept the missiles. Only thirty Hawker Tempests – one of the few aircraft capable of sufficient low-altitude speeds fast enough to catch them – were assigned to the task initially, but they were later joined by P-51 Mustangs, Supermarine Spitfire Mk XIVs and, during the night in particular, by de Havilland Mosquitoes. In addition the new British jet, the twin-engined Gloster Meteor, was rushed into service, but although it had the speed to catch the V-1s its cannon were prone to jamming and only thirteen kills were attributed to the world's first jet-on-pulsejet encounters. Shooting a V-1 out of the sky was always potentially dangerous for the pilots, and often failed anyway, so an alternative tactic was to chase a missile and manoeuvre into a position with one of the aircraft's wing tips just inches above the V-1's wing, using the airflow to tip it upwards to override the gyros and send it off into a dive. (Not, as sometimes suggested, by physically flipping its wings.) More than 1,000 V-1s were brought down by the aircraft interceptors.

V-1 being wheeled tail first out from a concrete storage bunker. The wings were fitted on site prior to launching. (CMcC)

The British had one final card up their sleeve. If they couldn't destroy all of the flying bombs then they would lead them astray through deception. By misleading the Germans regarding the locations of V-1 impacts they caused them to adjust the settings, which had the effect of making the missiles come down in less densely populated areas. This was achieved in part by a news black-out on the identification of specific impact sites and, more significantly, by feeding false intelligence back to Berlin via a number of turned German agents. To add a degree of authenticity information on some of the location of undeniable and well-known V-1 impact sites was included in these reports. By this late stage in the war it had become virtually impossible for the Luftwaffe to carry out reconnaissance flights over England to verify the information, so these reports were largely taken at face value.

Approximately 9,500 of the V-1 missiles were launched against London and south-east England before the various launch sites in France had been overrun by Allied ground forces in October 1944. Further attacks continued on a reduced scale with the missiles either air-launched from beneath bomber aircraft flying over the North Sea or, during February and March 1945, several hundred longer-range F-1 variants were launched from sites in Holland. The final V-1 to fall on English soil came down at Datchworth, Hertfordshire, on 29 March 1945. By then almost 23,000 people had lost their lives in the V-1 attacks, and over a million homes had been destroyed. It is estimated that without the policy of deliberately diverting the missiles away from central London the casualty figures might have been much higher, possibly by as much as another 50 per cent.

THE V-2

The V-2 was not a successor to the V-1; it was developed entirely separately and its origins go back to the 1920s when the imagination of a young man named Wernher von Braun was captivated by Hermann Oberth's book *Die Rakete zu den Planetenräumen* – The Rocket into Interplanetary Space. From 1930 von Braun attended the Technical University of Berlin where he assisted Oberth in the development of liquid-fuelled rocket motors. Walter Dörnberger, an artillery captain in the German Army, recognised the potential of the rocket as a weapon of war and arranged an Ordnance Department grant for von Braun to work within the army's fledgling rocket programme at the Kummersdorf testing site. By late 1934 von Braun and Dörnberger's group had successfully launched two liquid-fuelled rockets, the A1 and A2, which attained heights of 7,200 and 11,500ft (2,195 and 3,500m) respectively. These were the first in the series of the 'A' or Aggregat rockets, the German term referring to a mechanism or mechanical system. The next step on the evolutionary ladder was the A3, a much bigger rocket with an engine that burned oxygen and alcohol to generate 3,300lb (1,500kg) of thrust for a duration of forty-five seconds. A triple-gyroscope was devised to control its trajectory by deflecting the jet vanes. By late 1937 test firings were being undertaken at the army's new rocket development and test centre at Peenemünde, a remote site on the island of Usedom, off Germany's Baltic coast. (The Luftwaffe shared part of the test site.) The first

A V-1 launch ramp at Belloy-sur-Somme. *(CMcC)*

launches suffered from a variety of teething problems, including premature parachute deployment and engine failures, and the rockets crashed soon after launching. The most likely cause was identified as being the guidance system and work on the A3 rocket was abandoned in favour of the full-scale A4 and also the A5 which was a smaller test version of the A4.

The A4 had been developed specifically as a ballistic weapon with a range of about 109 miles (175km) and a payload of 2,200lb (1,000kg) of Amatol explosives. In order to achieve this goal the A3's troublesome motor was redesigned by Walter Thiel, and following an extensive series of test firings of the A5 version the first successful launch of the A4 took place on 3 October 1942. The rocket performed flawlessly this time and came down 120 miles (193km) away after attaining a height of 260,000ft (80,000m); it was the first man-made artefact to penetrate the edge of space. After watching the pencil-thin plume of flame disappear into the heavens, Walter Dornberger proclaimed the day as 'the first of a new era in space transportation, that of space travel'. With stars in their eyes the missile's proponents were more than happy to ignore its destructive nature and the dreadful cost in human misery to achieve it.

Having previously experienced indifference from Adolf Hitler, who believed that such a weapon was not needed as the war would be concluded very swiftly, the A4 programme was suddenly accorded the highest priority. The V-2 — as it was christened by Joseph Goebbels' *Reichsministerium für Volksaufklärung und Propaganda* (the Reich Ministry for Public Enlightenment and Propaganda) — stood almost 46ft (14m) high. At the tip was the warhead, next came the automatic gyroscopic control systems, then the fuel tanks

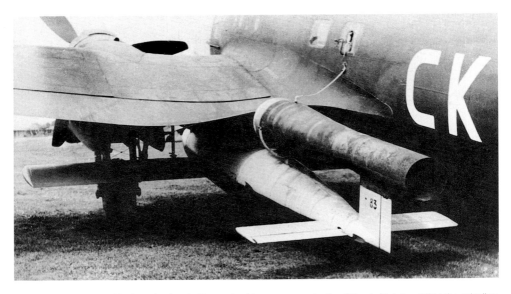

Once the land-based V-1 launch sites in France had been overrun by the Allies in October 1944 the missiles were air-launched from modified Heinkel He 111 bombers over the North Sea.

– which accounted for the bulk of the missile's volume and weight with an upper tank holding a 75 per cent ethanol/water mixture and in the lower tank liquid oxygen – and at the base there was the rocket motor, exhausts and the four control fins. Despite its deadly intent the V-2 had an undeniably pleasing aerodynamic profile. It was, in essence, the shape of the future.

From the moment of launch the rocket was propelled for up to sixty-five seconds under its own power before continuing on a free-fall trajectory to its target. It was guided automatically by rudders located on the trailing edge of the tail fins, and by four internal vanes directing the exhaust gasses. Its LEV-3 guidance system consisted of two free gyroscopes – one for vertical and one for horizontal guidance – and an accelerometer to control the engine cut-off at a pre-determined velocity.

An assembly line had been set up at Peenemünde by mid-July 1943 but barely a month later, on the night of 17/18 August 1943, the RAF unleashed Operation Hydra as the first strike in the Allies' Operation Crossbow strategic bombing campaign, aimed specifically at destroying the V-weapon programme. An armada of 596 heavy bombers pounded the research centre at Peenemünde. Although the deputy director Walter Thiel (the engineer who had also designed the motor for the Wasserfall anti-aircraft missile) was killed in the attack, along with hundreds of civilian workers, Hydra failed in its objective as the V-2 programme was set back by about only six to eight weeks. Ironically its main outcome was to accelerate the drive to disperse and protect V-2 production underground.

The initial intention was to launch the V-2 rockets from a number of fixed bases in northern France, and processing and launch facilities were constructed in the Pas de Calais for this purpose. At Watten a massive *blockhaus* ('bunker') was constructed in the form of a concrete box 302ft (92m) long and 92ft (28m) high. The facility included a liquid oxygen plant and the rockets would be delivered by train for final assembly, fuelling and arming, with an anticipated launch rate from the site of up to thirty-six per day. Constructed by the Organisation Todt with walls of reinforced concrete up to 23ft (7m) thick the *blockhaus* was considered impregnable, but the Allies struck with Barnes Wallis's Tallboy earthquake bombs before the construction work was completed and the concrete had had a chance to fully harden. The *blockhaus* was put out of action, and obviously it had become too conspicuous to fulfil its intended role. But just as the pyramids outlived the Pharaohs this massive structure will remain as a relic of the Third Reich for hundreds if not for thousands of years to come. Likewise the nearby 'Coupole' V-2 facility at Wizernes, constructed within a disused chalk quarry and capped by a shallow concrete dome 276ft (84m) across, also fell victim to the Crossbow raids before becoming operational.

With the large static sites attracting too much attention the Germans changed to individual mobile launch batteries which were known as *Meillerwagens* after the trailer vehicles used to transport the missiles. The V-2 had been designed with transportation on the existing railway system in mind, which meant that they could be sent to any number of locations very easily and then transferred to the *Meillerwagens* to be launched from the cover of wooded areas. Painted in camouflage colours, or dark olive green, and given the transient nature of the mobile launch pads, the V-2s were virtually immune from observation and attack by Allied aircraft.

On the receiving end the V-2s were both undetectable and unstoppable. They fell to earth at 2,200mph (3,550km/h) – approximately four times the speed of sound. There were no warnings, no air-raid sirens, and for the victims on the ground it was as if the explosion was instantaneous. The only defence was to repeat the policy of falsifying information on the impact locations and to conduct an all-out bombing campaign against the V-2 installations, although the Mittelwerk remained unknown to Allied intelligence and as it was located deep beneath the Kohnstein mountain it was virtually impregnable anyway.

Apart from the issue of its impunity from defensive measures, the value of the V-2 as a strategic weapon is highly questionable. Starting in September 1944 more than 3,000 V-2s were launched, with about half that number targeting London while the bulk of the remainder fell on Allied-occupied Antwerp, with a further seventy-six in France and eleven launched against the advancing Allied forces at Remagen within Germany itself in the final stages of the war. It is estimated that around 2,750 civilians lost their lives in the attacks on London and another 6,500 were injured. Set against this the weapon was extremely expensive to construct and consumed significant quantities of increasingly scarce materials and resources. The V-2 programme is said to have cost Germany more than the Americans invested in the Manhattan Project to develop the atomic bomb. Individually each V-2 missile cost around twenty-five times more than a V-1 but only delivered a comparable payload. Furthermore the V-2's warhead did not have a proximity fuse and the missile's incredibly high rate of descent meant that it exploded when already embedded into the ground with much of its destructive energy being dissipated. As a

General Dornberger shakes the hand of Gerneral Hjanssen on the occasion of General Fellgiebel's visit to Peenemunde in October 1944. Fellgiebel is between the two officers and beside Wernher von Braun who is wearing a dark suit. *(NARA)*

vengeance weapon it clearly had a devastating effect on its victims. However, it wasn't until 10 November 1944 that Winston Churchill announced in Parliament that England had been under attack from the rockets 'for the last few weeks' as he put it. By that time the war was clearly moving in the Allies favour and its end was in sight. There was absolutely no possibility that the V-2 campaign could have changed the outcome.

V-WEAPON PRODUCTION AT THE MITTELWERK

In September 1943, only a couple of months after the RAF's Operation Hydra raids on Peenemünde, the Mittelwerk had been incorporated as a private company and a contract for the construction of 12,000 V-2 (A4) missiles was awarded on 19 October 1943. The immediate task was to significantly extend the existing tunnel network, making it suitable as a full-scale arms factory.

Some tunnelling had commenced back in August 1936, before the outbreak of war, working from an Anhydrite mine on the north side of the mountain. Ostensibly this was to create a bomb-proof store for chemicals, oil and gasoline, although some sources also suggest that the intention was to store chemical weapons or poisonous gases here. The firm responsible for that construction work had been a government company called *Wissenschattliche Forschungsgesellschaft*, also known as WIFO. For its new role as a weapons factory a second phase of extensive excavation was started in 1943 to create an overall floor area almost 6,500,000ft² (600,000m²) once completed. According to post-war Allied intelligence reports only 1,780,000ft² (165,000m²) was actually in use by the time the Mittelwerk was overrun in April 1945. The layout consisted of two main parallel tunnels, known as 'A' and 'B', each large enough to accommodate double railway tracks running their length. These main tunnels were connected at regular intervals by a series of parallel transverse tunnels to form what looked in plan form like a shallow S-shaped ladder. A 1945 CIOS report on underground factories in Germany provides further details:

> The general layout and production arrangements were based on two main tunnels, each about a mile long and 30ft [9m] wide, extending from one side of the hill to the other, thus giving double entry on both sides. These two main tunnels were connected via forty-six cross-galleries, known as Halls or Kammer, each one about 520ft [160m] long and 30ft [9m] wide. The two primary tunnels were used for main and inter-bay transport. Prepared roads giving access to the four main entrances permitted the use of road transport both to and throughout the main tunnels.

Constructing the tunnels was reasonably straightforward from an engineering point of view as the anhydrite had a particularly fine-grain crystalline structure well suited

Photograph of the V-2 rocket engine assembly line at the Mittelwerk, taken from the mission report.

to tunnelling and it could stand unsupported over widths of 30 or 40ft (9 or 12m). In spite of occasional rock falls the galleries were unlined, although steel supports and cross beams were placed to strengthen particular areas where the roof was weaker. To provide ventilation eight vertical shafts led upwards to the surface. Once the tunnels were operational a system of air heater batteries positioned within the ventilation system provided heating, the warmth being circulated by the movement of the air. To prevent the air from becoming stale a system of extractors ensured that fresh air was supplied at a rate of about 33,550,000ft³ (950,000m³), which roughly equates to one complete change of air every hour.

Transverse tunnels numbered 1 to 17, starting at the northern end of the complex, had been completed in 1937. A second phase of excavations saw the remaining ones constructed in two stages, with numbers 18 to 36, and later 37 to 46, finished by March 1944. All of this work took a vast labour force consisting of concentration camp inmates who were overseen by the SS under the command of General Hans Kammler. According to the Nazis' war productions minister, Albert Speer, the use of prisoners for the work was considered to be a reliable means of ensuring that the Mittelwerk remained secret from the rest of the world. Initially the workforce came from the Buchenwald concentration camp and it was made up of a variety of nationalities, including large contingents from Russia and Poland. Many were Jewish, but not all. There were also a number of political prisoners, including members of the French Resistance for example. At first these *Häftlinge*, meaning 'detainees' or 'inmates', worked, ate and slept in the freezing unheated tunnels for weeks on end without respite, digging and clearing the works. Throughout this process the atmosphere was thick with gypsum dust and blast fumes, and many hundreds, possibly thousands, of the workers never saw daylight again.

Once the excavation work had been completed the prisoners were rehoused in a new camp built close to the mouth of the tunnels and known as Dora. Its name was

Another Mittelwerk image from the mission report, this time of an unfinished V-2 rocket.

The rear section of a V-2 stranded on a train near Bronkirchen, 5 April 1945. *(NARA)*

later changed to Mittelbau-Dora. Until the new camp opened in November 1944 with its own incinerators, the bodies of those who perished were transported back to Buchenwald for disposal. At Mittelbau-Dora there were around fifty-eight barracks on the main site, and in addition there were up to forty or more sub-camps scattered in the area around the mountains. Once the tunnelling work had been completed the inmates were reassigned to build the V weapons. In July 1944 the Nordwerk, or 'north works', occupying transverse tunnels 1 to 20 were allocated to Junkers for jet and piston engine production and this appears to have been run independently, without SS involvement. Meanwhile, the V-1 flying bomb assembly commenced in October 1944 in the tunnels vacated by the excavation teams at the southern end of tunnel A. At the end of January 1945, fifty-one V-1s were shipped from one of the Fieseler factories to Nordhausen for completion and by February the Mittelwerk had become the sole factory producing the flying bombs. In the final months of the war Taifun anti-aircraft missiles were also being produced at the site. But the main product to emerge from the Mittelwerk remained the V-2 rocket and it is estimated that around 4,575 were completed in the six months between August 1944 and March 1945.

The tunnels were organised as a vast production line with Tunnel A used to bring in and transport the components and materials to where they were needed, while the main assembly took place in Tunnel B, running from north to south. The transverse tunnels

The massive 'blockhaus' at Watten in the Pas de Calais was intended as an impregnable launch facility for the V-2 rockets. *(JC)*

were used for the more detailed work, checking and installing components, as well as for storage. Each missile was mounted on a railway bogey for its journey on the production line principle. At the south end of the tunnel system Hall 41 had been excavated up to 50ft (15.2m) in height to allow for each missile to be raised into the vertical position for final testing of the gyroscopes and guidance systems.

It was a colossal undertaking and according to the CIOS data the labour force at any one time was in the region of 12,000 people, of whom three-quarters were foreign or slave workers, and an estimated 2,000 were free workers. Working in two shifts of twelve hours straight, they were supervised by German engineers under the ever-present scrutiny of SS guards. The type of task each man was assigned depended very much on his skills. Those with any sort of engineering or technical background were selected to inspect parts, sub-assemblies or conduct tests, and in many cases these workers were from among the better educated French prisoners. The less skilled, notably the Russians and Poles, were assigned to the more physical duties such as transporting and moving the components and materials. This was particularly back-breaking work and it is said that these prisoners were treated far more harshly by the guards and consequently they were 'used up' very rapidly.

Aware that the rockets were intended to kill Allied personnel or civilians, some prisoners attempted to sabotage them. This might involve accepting sub-standard parts for example, or perhaps making inadequate welds that would result in the missile failing. But it was a desperately dangerous game to play. Prisoners involved in electrical assembly were required to identify their work by inserting slips of paper and if a component failed it could be traced back to them. The penalty for sabotage was death, not just for the perpetrator but often for the rest of their immediate group of co-workers. Group hangings were common and usually conducted in full view of the others. Sometimes they were carried out using the rocket hoists in Hall 41 with the condemned men slowly raised into the air to suffer a lingering and painful death. Their bodies would be then left dangling from the hoist for several days as a deterrent to the others.

It is estimated that as many as 60,000 people passed through Mittelbau–Dora and the associated sub-camps. Of these around 25,000 inmates died, either from malnutrition, disease, exhaustion or from the vicious beatings inflicted by the guards and the executions. As the Allies advanced towards the area, in early April 1945, many prisoners were also killed by the SS in their panic to evacuate the camps, and others died as the result of RAF

Cutaway revealing the V-2's complex rocket engine. This preserved example is displayed at the Imperial War Museum, London. *(JC)*

bombing raids between 1–4 April after the rows of huts were mistaken for factory or military facilities. Some of the most enduring and pitiful images of concentration camp inmates and the rows of emaciated corpses come from Mittelbau–Dora.

When the Fedden Mission arrived at the Mittelwerk it was only a couple of days before the area was scheduled to be handed over to the Russians. The site was occupied by a handful of US army personnel, but otherwise it was unguarded. The area surrounding the main entrance into the tunnel complex was littered with V-2 components, fuselage rear sections, complete with their fins, lying sideways on wooden frames ready to be transported, plus rows of combustion chambers and nozzles standing upright, slightly taller than a man. The entrance itself was disguised by crude wooden scaffolding covered by camouflage netting. On entering the tunnel it took several minutes for the visitors' eyes to adjust from the harsh sunlight outside to the deep gloom within, but once inside they found that the production areas were surprisingly well lit by overhead electric lights. When the American troops first discovered the tunnels they had found them abandoned, but left as if ready for the next shift with the lights and ventilation systems still running.

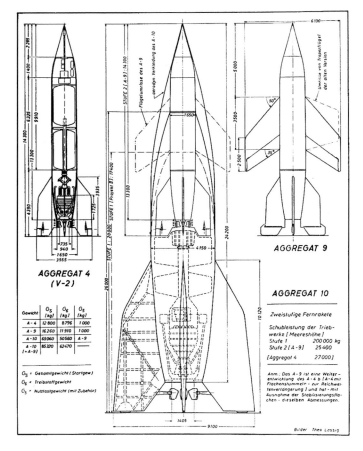

Drawing of three members of the Aggregat rocket family. The Aggregat 4, the V-2, is shown alongside the proposed Aggregat 9, or A4B, which was to be a longer-range version of the A4. In the centre is the A10 intercontinental missile intended to attack the USA.

The Mittelwerk tunnel system is so vast that Fedden's team could only explore a part of it:

> Its extent and area were such that it was impossible to gain anything but a very rough idea of its size and capacity, and there was nobody to explain the details, except one of the directors of the BMW factory, who had only been there on one or two occasions before.

In the southernmost tunnels there were hundreds of wingless V-1 missiles. The wings would only have been attached once they had been transported to the launch sites. A little further into the tunnels they came across the stores of unused V-2 components, including the liquid oxygen tanks, and in Tunnel B they found examples of the completed rockets. On one the Americans had scrawled 'Hands off don't move', although who the message was intended for is hard to say. In the ten weeks or so since its discovery the Allies, particularly the Americans, had been busy stripping this technological Aladdin's cave of its contents before the area came under Russian control. It is estimated that they transported around 300 rail-car loads of V-2 hardware and components back to the USA, not all of it from the Mittelwerk as many V-2s were also captured intact, having been stranded in transit by the devastating disruption caused by the intensive bombing of the German railway system. Moving through the interconnecting tunnels Fedden also saw some of the production lines where the more intricate components had been assembled by the enforced workers. Some of the halls housed huge machine tools which had been brought from Peenemünde and these included Weingarten hydraulic presses more than 20ft (6.1m) tall. At first Fedden was true to the remit of his mission and wrote of his experience in the Mittelwerk purely as an engineer:

> It is difficult to explain in writing the impressions the Mission received, coming in from brilliant sunshine and beautiful country, having been through this enormous labyrinth, containing the most expensive equipment and tooling for making these various aircraft munitions on an unparalleled production basis, as regards fool-proof slave labour production. To go from store to store, which had been looted by the slave workers and the soldiers, and to find the most up-to-date and brand new equipment lying strewn about the floor in hundreds, such things as micrometers, gauges, very expensive precision equipment, Bosch fuel pumps, electric starters, etc. in the utmost confusion – must be seen to be appreciated.

Nonetheless he and his team were not immune to the human tragedy they were witnessing: 'This factory is the epitome of megalomaniac production and robot efficiency and layout. Everything was ruthlessly executed with utter disregard for humanitarian conditions.' They also saw for themselves something of the conditions in the Mittelbau-Dora concentration camp:

> The record of Nordhausen is a most unenviable one, and we were told that 250 of the slave workers perished every day, due to overwork and malnutrition. Some of the Mission visited a slave workers' encampment, talked to a Dutch doctor who had been there throughout

the war, and saw many of the wretched inmates who were in an appalling state, although receiving every medical attention now. They also saw stretchers heavily saturated in blood, a room in which there was a slab on which the bodies were drained of blood, and the incinerators in which they were burnt. These are all facts which require to be seen to be fully appreciated.

Undeniably the V-2 had set in motion a leap in technological development that has gone on to shape post-war history and our modern world. Yet the German rocket programme came at an inconceivably high price in terms of the loss of life. The story of the Mittelwerk is one written in human suffering and misery and the mathematics reveal a chilling statistic. Each V-2 missile came at the price of six human lives. In fact more people died in building the V-2 weapons than were killed by their deployment and it has been suggested that the main product to come from tunnels of Mittelwerk was not the V weapons, it was death itself. Naturally the Fedden team was in sombre mood after its descent into the darker regions of human depravity. In the Final Report Fedden wrote: 'This terrible and devilish place has now passed into Russian hands and it is sincerely hoped that our Allies will deal with it in a proper and adequate manner.'

They did just that. As with the other Allies before them the Russians took whatever technology was of value. Then in 1948 the south portal to Tunnel A was blown up and the Mittelwerk and its dark history lay largely forgotten for several decades. In 1991 the tunnel complex was designated by the Germans as an historic site to protect it from further damage by surface mining in the area. There is now a small museum area in the southern part of tunnel A, with access via a transverse tunnel. Many parts of the underground site remain inaccessible and some chambers, including Hall 41, are partially or completely submerged under water. A memorial to the thousands who died has been created at the site of the Mittelbau-Dora camp, but the legacy of the Mittelwerk does not rest there. The on-going story of the post-war exploitation of the secret Nazi rocket technology and the competition between the former Allies to grab the best of the German scientists, and their involvement in the use and treatment of a slave workforce, is continued in Chapter 12.

eight

HITLER'S SMART BOMBS

THE FEDDEN MISSION came away from Nordhausen having seen for themselves the starkest extremes of the Nazis' secret weapon programme. On the one hand they had witnessed the abject horror and depravity of the slave labour system, while, on the other, they could not fail to marvel at the most technologically advanced weapons programme the world had ever seen.

The following day they flew south to Munich, where they inspected the BMW engine works and billeted overnight at the American 3rd Army Intelligence Centre at Freising. On Thursday 21 June the mission divided into two groups, with four members of the team departing by road to Rosenheim and the BMW rocket development department at Bruckmühl. As chief engineer and technical director in charge of BMW's jet, piston and rocket development, Bruno Bruckmann accompanied them, explaining that BMW's intensive development of rockets had started in early 1944 on RLM orders. It was conducted under the control of an engineer named Szibroski, an SS man who had disappeared before the American Army arrived in April 1945.

Many of the German rocket projects had their origins in the early stages of the war, or even before it in some cases, but the impetus to wheel them out had come with the intensification of the Allied strategic bombing campaign. As we have seen, the V-1 cruise missile and the V-2 ballistic missile were dedicated offensive weapons and had no defensive role to play, but rocket-power could be used very effectively to augment the existing ground-based anti-aircraft defences of the Luftwaffe's flak regiments, or to fill the gaps left by the increasingly overstretched fighter aircraft. In addition to their use as surface-to-air anti-aircraft missiles, the range of other applications included aircraft-launched weapons – either air-to-air against other aircraft, or air-to-surface against ground targets or shipping – and even surface-to-surface as a form of artillery. When combined with a variety of guidance systems this array of missiles became the first generation of smart bombs, although, lacking the technology to home in on a target autonomously without human guidance, it might be more accurate to describe them as semi-smart bombs.

Press photograph released in November 1944 of an HS 293 anti-shipping missile with Walter 109-507 B liquid-fuelled rocket motor.

THE BMW TYPE 109-718

As it turned out the first rocket motor the Fedden Mission was shown by Bruckmann wasn't a weapon at all. The BMW Type 109-718 liquid-fuelled rocket – 109 was also the RLM prefix for rockets – was a small non-expendable assistor unit designed to be used in conjunction with the BMW 003 jet engine to which it was fitted at the rear end; a configuration known as the BMW 003R. The internal and external main chambers were liquid-cooled by one of the fuels, nitric acid, passing round a spiral tube inside the outer member. The whole engine unit weighed 176lb (80kg) and gave a thrust of 2,755lb (1,250kg) for three to five minutes. The fuels used were nitric acid and a mixture of hydrocarbons. Fuel consumption was 5.5kg per 1,000kg of thrust per second, and it was estimated that with two of these assistors a Messerschmitt Me 262 could climb to 30,000ft (9,150m) in three minutes.

Unlike the expendable RATO units, this was specifically intended for rapid climb or bursts of speed in an emergency. The 109-718 had the potential to turn a jet fighter into an ultra-high-speed interceptor while at the same time conserving the rocket fuel through intermittent operation, unlike the dedicated rocket-powered aircraft such as the Messerschmitt Me 163B. It was hoped that further development work would enable the unit to use standard jet fuel in due course. The fuel pumps on the 109-718 were the centrifugal type and ran at 17,000rpm, with the fuel pressure at 50 atmospheres. A special drive with universal joints was provided on the jet engine for these pumps, and ran at 3,000rpm. The fuel flow to the unit was controlled by spring-loaded valves operated by a servo motor, and a special automatic control was being developed for this purpose to prevent an inequality of thrust on twin-engine jet aircraft.

The 109-718 rocket units were tested on several prototypes including the Me 262 C-2b *Heimatschützer* ('home defender'), and the single-engined Heinkel He 162E in March 1945. (The *Heimatschützer* was the Me 262 C-1a with a single Walter 109-509 S1 fitted in the rear fuselage and exhausting under the tail.) Bruckmann informed Fedden that twenty of the 109-718 units had been constructed, and the production time for each one was around 100 hours.

Stand-alone RATO units were frequently used by the Germans for a number of reasons, either to gain additional lift at take-off for heavily-laden aircraft, to provide extra thrust, or to save jet fuel. The Walter HWK 109-500 *Starthilfe* ('take-off assistor') was a liquid-fuelled rocket pod which could provide 1,100lb (500kg) of thrust for thirty seconds – the thrust was doubled as they were always used in symmetrical pairs. Once the fuel was exhausted the pods were jettisoned by the pilot and returned to the ground by parachute to be serviced and used again. The HWK 109-500 entered service in 1942 and around 6,000 were manufactured by Heinkel. They were used extensively on a wide range of aircraft, including the under-powered Jumo 004-engined Arado Ar 234.

At BMW's rocket development department at Bruckmühl, Rosenheim, Bruno Bruckmann and W.J. Stern pose beside a BMW 109-558 liquid-fuelled rocket motor for the Henschel Hs 117.

SCHMETTERLING

The next rocket Fedden's team examined at Bruckmühl was the BMW 109/558 for the Henschel Hs 117 ground-to-air guided missile. The Hs 117 was codenamed *Schmetterling* ('butterfly'), although it looked more like a slender bottlenose dolphin with central sweptback wings and a cruciform tail. The nose was asymmetrical with the warhead extension on one side and a small generator propeller on the other. Designed by a Henschel team led by Professor Herbert Alois Wagner, the Hs 117 was a medium-altitude missile targeting enemy bombers flying between 6,000 and 33,000ft (1,800m to 10,000m).

The *Schmetterling* was launched from a modified 37mm gun-carriage with two Schmidding 109-553 solid diglycol-fuel boosters, one above and one below the main body, giving a total thrust of about 6,000lb (2,700kg) for a duration of sixty-five seconds before falling away. After take-off the BMW rocket motor provided the main power, giving the 992lb (450kg) missile a speed of between 558 to 620mph (900 to 1,000km/h) taking it up to an altitude between 20,000 and 30,000ft (9,150m). In order not to exceed the velocity at which the missile was stable, the engine's thrust was regulated by sliding valves in the nozzle actuated by a small electric servo activated by a Mach meter. The Hs 117 was radio controlled by two operators using a telescopic sight and joystick. Once near to a target, acoustic and photoelectric sensors homed in

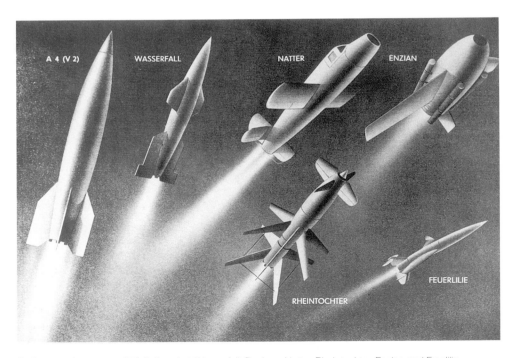

Surface-to-air weapons: V-2 (A4) rocket, Wasserfall, Bacham Natter, Rheintochter, Enzian and Feurlilie.

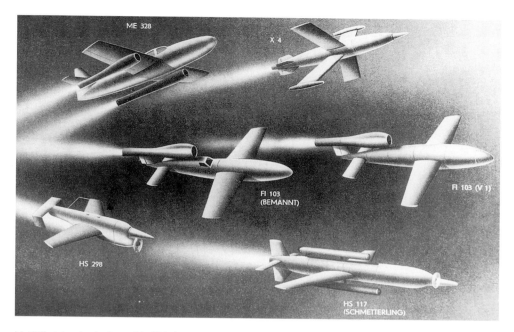

Hs 298 air-to-air missile, an Me 328 shown with Argus pulsejets, the Fi 103 R manned version of the V-1, an X-4, Hs 117 Schmetterling and the Fi 103 V-1.

automatically from a range of 33 to 66ft (10 to 20m), and proximity fuses detonated its lethal payload of 55lb (25kg) of explosives.

The BMW 109-558 rocket motor took the form of a long tube slender enough to fit within the missile's casing. It contained a compressed air tank, an SV–Stoff nitric acid tank, and a tank for the R–Stoff, a composite of hydrocarbon self-igniting propellant codenamed 'Tonka'. The combustion chamber was cooled by the nitric acid and was about 18in (46cm) long with a diameter of 5in (12.5cm). A photograph in the Fedden Mission report shows Bruckmann and Stern standing behind a complete rocket assembly which was 8ft (2.4m) long overall. According to Fedden:

> The whole equipment weighed 352lb (160kg), took forty to sixty hours to make, and the production price was 400 to 500 Marks. 120 had been made. It was stated that successful experiments had been carried out with this equipment, and the rocket motor which was a clean workmanlike job had started production in parallel with the Henschel flying missile.

A 'workmanlike job' is probably what passes for high praise in engineering circles. The Hs 117 underwent fifty-nine test firings, of which more than half failed. Even so, full-scale manufacture commenced in December 1944, with an eventual target output of 3,000 a month projected for the end of 1945, but production was cancelled by February 1945. Some Hs 117s were test launched from a Heinkel He 111, and there was also to be an air-to-air variant of the missile, the Hs 117H, which looked the same but did not have the booster rockets. This would have been air-launched from a Dornier Do 217, Junkers Ju 88 or Ju 388, but it never made it into operation.

WASSERFALL

Wasserfall ('waterfall') was a higher-altitude missile than *Schmetterling*, and it was also much more complex and expensive to build as it was, in essence, a scaled-down version of the A4 (V-2) liquid-fuelled rocket. As an anti-aircraft missile it required a far smaller payload and range/duration than the V-2, and consequently it was only 25ft 9in (7.85m) long and weighed 8,160lb (3,700kg); roughly half the size of an A4. In appearance *Wasserfall* resembled the V-2, with the same streamlined bullet shape for the body, but with four short wings or fins on the midsection to provide additional control. The fins on the tail also had control surfaces, and steering was supplemented by rudder flaps within the rocket exhaust.

Unlike the V-2, *Wasserfall* was designed to stand for several months at a time and be ready to be fired at short notice, something for which the V-2's highly volatile liquid-oxygen fuel was not suited. Instead the new rocket motor for the smaller missile, developed by Dr Walter Thiel, was based on Visol (vinyl isobutyl ether) and SV-Stoff fuel. This mixture was forced into the combustion chamber by pressure and spontaneously combusted on

The Fritz-X was a glider-bomb designed to pierce the armoured plating on Allied ships. *(JC)*

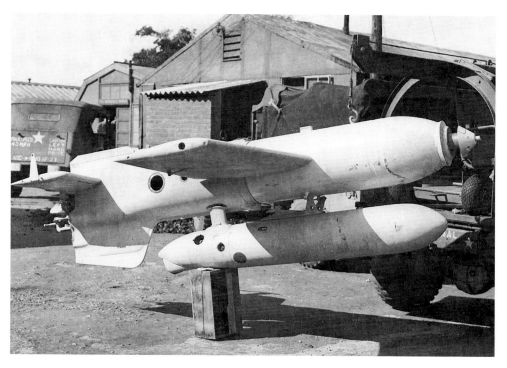

Another view of a captured Hs 293 anti-shipping bomb. *(USAF)*

contact. Guidance was by radio control, although for night-time operations a system known as Rheinland was developed, incorporating a radar for tracking and a transponder for location which would be read by radio direction finder on the ground. An alternative system using radar beams was also under development. Because of concerns about accuracy, *Wasserfall's* original 220lb (100kg) warhead was replaced by a far bigger 517lb (235kg) of explosives. Instead of hitting a single aircraft directly, the idea was that the warhead would detonate in the middle of a bomber formation and the blast effect would bring down several aircraft in one go. The missile itself was designed to break up to ensure that only small pieces fell on to friendly territory below.

Wasserfall was developed and tested at Peenemünde and in total thirty-five test launches had been completed by the time this facility was evacuated in February 1945. Subsequently the resources and manpower needed for the development of the defensive *Wasserfall* programme was diverted to the higher priority and offensive A4. It would appear that Hitler's quest for taking vengeance on his enemies, whether symbolic or real, overrode the need to defend the German homeland. Production of the *Wasserfall* had been scheduled to begin at a huge underground factory at Bleicherode in October 1945, by which time, of course, it was already too late.

The air-launched Hs 298 radio-controlled rocket-powered missile never entered full production and the project was abandoned in January 1945.

X-4 wire-guided air-to-air missile. Pods on two wing-tips contained spools for the control wires. *(USAF)*

THE *RHEINTOCHTER* AND *ENZIAN* HIGH-ALTITUDE MISSILES

In parallel to *Schmetterling* and *Wasserfall*, several other anti-aircraft missiles were also in development, in particular the *Rheintochter* and *Enzian* high-altitude missiles. *Rheintochter*, named after Richard Wagner's Rhine Maidens, was a multi-stage solid-fuel surface-to-air missile developed by Rheinmetall-Borsig for the German Army. Working from the top down it had four small paddle-like control surfaces near the nose for steering, plus six sweptback fins at the end of the first stage and a further four at the rear of the second, booster stage. It was 20ft 8in (6.3m) long overall including the booster stage, and the body had a diameter of 1ft 9.25in (54cm). Unusually the exhaust from the main sustainer motor was vented through six 'venturi' (small tubes) positioned one between each main fin. This was partly for additional stabilisation in flight, but also because the 300lb (136kg) warhead was situated behind the motor and would be attached before launch. The *Rheintochter* R-I was launched from a ramp or from a converted gun mounting. Guidance was via a joystick, radio control and line of sight observation.

After eighty-two test launches, further development of the *Rheintochter* R-I, and the proposed operational version R-II, was abandoned in December 1944 because it was only attaining the same altitude as the other missile systems. A third version of the *Rheintochter*, the R-III, was to have been a far sleeker affair with a liquid-propellant rocket motor for

Rheintochter III two-stage anti-aircraft missile. *(NARA)*

the main stage, and it did away with the second stage in favour of solid-fuelled boosters mounted to the side of the missile. Only six test firings were made.

TAIFUN

Taifun ('typhoon') was one of the smallest of the unguided anti-aircraft rockets. Its design was instigated by Sheufen, an officer at Peenemünde, who wanted to produce a back-up or alternative to the more complicated missiles. Further developed by the Elektromechanische Werke in Karlshagen, the *Taifun* was an unguided missile, 6ft 4in (1.93m) long and 4in (10cm) in diameter with four small stabilizing fins at its base. The simple rocket was fuelled by a hypergolic mixture of nitric acid and Optolin – a mix of aromatic amines, gasoline, Visol and catechol – pressure-fed into the combustion chamber. Burnout occurred after two and a half seconds, by which time the rocket was travelling at 2,237mph (3,600km/h) up to a maximum altitude of 39,370ft (12,000m). The rockets would have been fired in salvoes of up to thirty at a time from a rocket launcher mounted on an adapted gun mounting. Delays in the development of the rocket motor meant that *Taifun* was never deployed operationally. However, if this unsophisticated and unguided weapon had been ready earlier it could have caused devastation among the Allied bombers.

BMW 109-548

Schmetterling, Wasserfall, Rheintochter and *Taifun* were not the only surface-to-air or anti-aircraft missiles under development in Germany. Others included the Rheinmetall-Borsig Feuerlilie F-25/F-55 which Fedden had come across at Völkenrode, and also the Messerschmitt *Enzian* E-4 which, because of its antecedence in the Me 163 rocket aircraft, is covered in the following chapter. The third type of rocket motor shown to the Fedden Mission at the BMW works in Bruckmühl was the BMW 109-548 used on the Ruhrstahl X-4. Described by Fedden as an 'inter-aircraft rocket' – they were still finding the vocabulary for all this new weaponry in 1945 – the X-4 was a formidable wire-guided air-to-air missile suitable for use with the fast jets such as the Messerschmitt Me 262.

Developed by Dr Max Kramer at Ruhrstahl, the X-4 was designed to operate from a distance outside the range of an enemy bomber's guns. In flight the missile was stabilised by spinning slowly about its axis, at about 60rpm, thus ironing out any asymmetry in thrust. A joystick in the launch aircraft's cockpit sent control signals via two wires feeding out from spools or bobbins located within the pods at the end of two opposing wings, and small spoilers on the tail steered the X-4. The wire-guidance system was a means of circumventing the possibility of radio signals being jammed. The range for attack was 0.93 to 2.17 miles (1.5 to 3.5km) and the total payout of the wires was around 3.5 miles (5.5km). According to Fedden the compact 109-548 rocket propelled the X-4 at 620mph (1,000km/h) and had an endurance of up to twenty seconds. The X-4 was 6ft 7in (2m) long and had a wingspan of almost 2ft 3in (73cm) with four midsection fins swept at 45°.

Carrying a 45lb (20kg) fragmentation device in the warhead, the X-4 had a lethal range of about 25ft (8m) and positioning it accurately proved very difficult to judge for the controller. Accordingly a type of acoustically triggered proximity fuse known as a *Kranich* was also fitted, and this was sensitive to the Doppler shift in engine/propeller sound as it approach and began to pass the enemy bombers. Flight testing commenced in August 1944, initially wing-mounted on a Focke-Wulf Fw 190, but later on the Junkers Ju 88. The X-4 had been intended for single-seat fighters such as Messerschmitt's jet-engined Me 262, or possibly the Dornier Do 335, but the impracticality of the pilot managing to simultaneously fly the aircraft and control the missile were too great. Production of the airframe began in early 1945. This was designed to be assembled by unskilled labour, in other words forced labour, and incorporated low-cost materials such as plywood for the main fins. It is claimed that 1,000 were readied, but the Allied raids on BMW's production facility in Stargard held up delivery of the vital 109-548 rocket motors. Consequently the X-4 was never officially delivered to the Luftwaffe. A smaller version of the X-4, the X-7, was designed as an anti-tank missile, but there is no evidence of this ever being used.

'WINGED TORPEDOES'

The other main application of air-to-surface guided weaponry was against Allied shipping. A guided air-launched weapon greatly increased the potential range and accuracy of an attack in comparison with a direct attack using conventional bombs or torpedoes, especially on heavily guarded vessels such as warships. The Blohm & Voss company developed a series of 'winged torpedoes' or glider bombs, such as the Bv 143 which featured a pair of straight wings and a cruciform tail with guidance along a fixed course provided by an internal gyroscopic system. A feeler arm extending beneath the main body acted as a gauge, keeping the missile on a level glide just above the surface of the sea by activating a booster rocket within the fuselage. Four Bv 143s were constructed and tested in 1943, but the project was shelved until a more reliable automatic altimeter could be devised.

The Bv 246 *Hagelkorn* ('hailstone') was an un-powered glider bomber which did enter limited production in late 1943. Once released both of these glider bombs lacked external guidance input to ensure they hit their targets.

The most successful of the anti-shipping missiles were the fully guided Fritz X and the Henschel 293. The Fritz X was officially designated as the FX 1400, although confusingly it was also known as the *Ruhrstahl* SD 1400 X, the Kramer X-1 and the PC 1400X. Derived from the high-explosive thick-walled 3,080lb (1,400kg) SD 1400 *Splitterbombe Dickwandig* ('fragmentation bomb'), the Fritz X had a more aerodynamic nose, four midsection stub wings and a box tail at the rear housing the spoilers or control surfaces. Engineer Max Kramer had begun development work on the missile before the war, fitting radio-controlled spoilers to free-falling 550lb (250kg) bombs, and in 1940 the Ruhstahl company became involved because of their experience in the development and production of conventional unguided bombs.

Fritz X did not have a rocket motor and upon release it glided all the way to the target, guided visually from the launch aircraft via radio-control inputs from a joystick. The missile was designed specifically to be armour-piercing, up to 5.1in (130mm) thick, and the main targets were heavy cruisers or battleships. There was a micro delay in the fuse to ensure it detonated inside the target and not immediately upon impact. Minimum release height was 13,000ft (4,000m), although 18,000ft (5,500m) was preferred if conditions permitted, and it had to be released at least 3 miles (5km) from the target. The greater release height reduced the threat of anti-aircraft fire, which was especially important as the carrier aircraft had to maintain a steady course to keep the gliding bomb on target. It was essential that the device remained in sight of the controller and a flare was fitted in the tail to assist with this. In practice the carrier aircraft had to decelerate upon release, achieved by climbing slightly and then dipping back down, so that inertia would place the bomb ahead of the aircraft.

Fritz X had been launched from a Heinkel He 111 during testing, but in operation the Dornier Do 217 K-2 medium-range bomber became the main carrier. It was first deployed in July 1943 in an attack on Augusta harbour in Sicily, but its greatest success was with the sinking of the Italian battleship *Roma* on 9 September 1944. Bombers equipped with Fritz X also saw action at Salerno against American and British vessels. It is estimated that almost 1,400 Fritz X bombs were produced in total, including those used in flight testing.

Unlike the Fritz X the Henschel Hs 293 anti-shipping guided missile did have a liquid-fuelled rocket engine, slung beneath its belly, to allow operation at lower altitudes and from a far greater distance – estimated at up to 10 miles (16km). Designed by Professor Herbert Alois Wagner, the Hs 293 project was started in 1939 on the pure glide bomb principle, but Henschel und Sohn added the rocket unit which provided a short burst of speed. Over 1,000 Hs 293s were manufactured and a variety of rockets were used, usually the Walter HWK 109-507, producing a thrust of 1,300lb (590kg), or the slightly more powerful BMW 109-511 with 1,320lb (600kg) of thrust. The main element of the weapon was a high-explosive 650lb (295kg) charge within a thin-walled metal casing creating, in essence, a demolition bomb. Measuring 12ft 6in (3.82m) wide, it had a pair of straight wings with conventional ailerons for control, plus a tail with side fins and a lower fin. While the Fritz X was intended for use against armoured ships, the Hs 293 was specifically for un-armoured vessels, hence the thinner casing. The missile was radio controlled via a joystick control box in the carrier aircraft, and flares attached to the rear ensured the operator maintained visual contact.

The Hs 293 was the first operational guided missile to sink a ship. The British sloop HMS *Egret* was attacked and sunk in the Bay of Biscay on 27 August 1943, with the loss of 194 of her crew. Numerous other Allied vessels were also sunk in the Mediterranean.

The Allies' efforts to counter the German radio-controlled weapons by jamming the signals were given a boost when an intact Hs 293 was recovered from a Heinkel He 177

The Rheintochter RIII's liquid-fuel rocket engine on display at RAF Cosford. *(JC)*

which had crashed on Corsica, and improvements made to the radio jamming equipment had a major impact on the weapon's effectiveness. In response the Germans modified 100 Hs 293A-1s as Hs 293Bs with wire link, and as the television-guided Hs 293D, although neither of these were operational by the end of the war. The Hs 293H was an experimental air-to-air variant.

With the experience gained with the Hs 293, Henschel developed several other anti-shipping guided missiles along the same principle. The Hs 294 was designed specifically to penetrate the water and strike a ship below the waterline, and consequently it resembled the Hs 293 but with a sleeker conical nose and two Walter 109-507D rockets mounted tight up against the wing roots. On the Hs 293F the Henschel engineers experimented with a delta wing configuration without a tail unit. The Hs 295 featured an elongated fuselage with enlarged, slightly bulbous warhead and the wings from the Hs 294, while the Hs 296 combined the rear fuselage of the Hs 294 with the control system of the Hs 293 and the bigger warhead of the Hs 295.

BATTLEFIELD ROCKETS

Rockets were also developed to augment or supplant the army's conventional surface artillery. *Rheinbote* ('Rhine messenger') was developed by the Rheinmetall-Borsig company in 1943. Strictly speaking this slender four-stage rocket cannot be classified as a smart bomb as it was aimed solely by the positioning of the launcher and possessed no internal or external guidance systems. Apart from the V–2 (A4) this was the only other long-range ballistic missile to enter service during the Second World War.

The biggest drawback with conventional artillery is that the guns are often too heavy to be easily and swiftly transported to where they are needed, especially in a fast-moving battlefield. This had not been an issue in the opening stages of the war when the German Blitzkrieg spread with great rapidity thanks in no small measure to the Luftwaffe's overwhelming aerial superiority and the ability to provide airborne bombardment in support of the ground forces. But the big guns had other drawbacks. Their range was limited and while the biggest guns bombarding Paris in the First World War might have had a range of just over 62 miles (100km), their huge size made them virtually immobile.

A US Air Force officer examines an unidentified rocket-propelled guided bomb. Said to be just 8ft long (2.5m) it was most probably a test model. (CMcC)

Conventional artillery also required a constant supply chain to feed the guns. Rockets, on the other hand, had enormous range and were far more easily transported, although there might be an issue with accuracy. The *Rheinbote* project was initiated to put the battlefield rocket concept to the test.

In appearance *Rheinbote* was a slender spike 37ft (11.4m) long, with stabilising fins at the rear and three sets of smaller fins arranged at the end of each of the four stages. The rockets were fuelled by diglycol-dinitrate solid-fuel propellant and in tests achieved a blistering Mach 5.5, or 4,224mph (6,800km/h), the fastest speed of any missile at the time. *Rheinbote* was transported and launched from a modified V-2 (A4) rocket trailer which had an elevating launch gantry. The missile was aimed by orientating the trailer itself and elevating the gantry, although the accuracy of this method of aiming is highly questionable.

In tests the *Rheinbote* carried an 88lb (40kg) warhead, only 6.5 per cent of the missile's total mass, up to 48 miles (78km) into the atmosphere to a range of up to 135 miles (220km), but for shorter ranges some of the stages could be removed. Over 200 were produced and they were used in the bombardment of Antwerp from November 1944 into early 1945. After the war ended the Soviets helped themselves to the designs at Rheinmetall-Borsig's Berlin-Marienfelde headquarters, but in general the *Rheinbote* was considered to be lacking accuracy, thanks partly to the effect of the stage separations, and lacking punch as the payload was too small and the almost vertical high-speed delivery tended to bury it deep into the ground.

Time and time again the question is asked why these sophisticated and deadly weapons failed to turn the tide of war in Germany's favour. And just as with the aircraft the same answer invariably comes back: it was too little too late. Time and resources had been squandered in developing a multitude of missile projects instead of focussing on a few well-defined goals. Priorities were in a constant state of flux and by the time those projects which had any potential were put into production resources had either become stretched to the limit or they were being misdirected into other areas. As Albert Speer commented in his memoirs, *Inside the Third Reich*:

> I am convinced that substantial deployment of Wasserfall from the spring of 1944 onward, together with an uncompromising use of jet fighters as air defence interceptor, would have essentially stalled the Allied strategic bombing offensive against our industry. We would have been well able to do that – after all, we managed to manufacture 900 V-2 rockets per month at a later time when resources were already much more limited.

By the final stages of the war the measures to defend the Reich were becoming ever more ingenious, and more desperate.

nine

INGENUITY AND DESPERATION

OFFICIALLY IT WAS CALLED the Messerschmitt Me 163B, the *Komet*, but unofficially this stumpy aircraft was known among its pilots as the 'Powered Egg', although 'flying bomb' might have been a better description. Either way, it promised a lightning-fast ride to hell or glory.

Everything about the *Komet* was dangerous, particularly the fuel. The later production versions from June 1944 had the improved 'hot engine', the Walter HWK 109-509, which used two liquid propellants: 20 per cent C-Stoff, a mixture of hydrazine hydrate, methanol, water and a small amount of potassium-copper-cyanide, and 80 per cent of oxidiser, T-Stoff, which consisted of concentrated hydrogen peroxide. Brought together these form a hypergolic fuel; in other words they ignite upon contact. Refuelling required special care with the C-Stoff tank filled first, and then the whole system would be washed down with water before the T-Stoff fuel came anywhere near the aircraft. T-Stoff was an extremely unpleasant substance. It would spontaneously combust on contact with organic material and, gruesomely, it actually dissolved human flesh. Accordingly the Me 163 pilots were issued with special non-organic flying suits including headgear, gloves and boots.

The rocket pilots came from wildly differing backgrounds; war-hardened fighter veterans and rookie student pilots who were taking to the air after a few lessons under tow. The good news is that the Me 163B flew superbly well and they were far more likely to be killed in an accident during the take-off and landing than in combat. Before starting the engine the motor and jet pipe were flushed out with water. A small quantity of the catalyst was introduced into the T-Stoff which decomposed into high-pressure steam to drive the two fuels into the combustion chamber. The cockpit would fill with an ear-splitting screech and the little aircraft began rocking. The Me 163B took off on a detachable wheel dolly to save the weight of an undercarriage. Take-off was always into wind and on a hard runway surface as the wheels were close together and any bumps or ruts could cause the aircraft to veer to one side. At about 80mph (130km/h) the airflow was sufficient for the aerodynamic controls to kick in and at 180mph (290km/h) it took off. Jettison the wheel dolly too high off the ground and there was a danger it would bounce back up to strike the underside of the aircraft. Within moments the *Komet* was roaring towards the airfield boundary. (Should the engine fail at this stage, the chances of surviving an emergency landing in the fully fuelled aircraft were zero.) The trick was to fly straight and level at around 420mph (675km/h), taking care not to exceed the critical Mach number, and then pull back hard on the stick for an almost vertical climb.

The German test pilot Hannah Reitsch flew both the Me 163A and 163B and she described the sensation as being, 'Like thundering through the skies sitting on a cannonball, intoxicated with speed.' The only Allied test pilot to try the *Komet* under rocket power was Captain Eric Brown, commanding officer of the Captured Aircraft Flight:

> It was an aeroplane that made the adrenaline flow … I was normally used to a climb speed of 220mph (355km/h) and a climb rate of 3,000ft (915m) per minute, but when I flew this it had a climb speed of 450mph (725km/h) and a rate of climb of 16,000ft (490m). It was rather like being in charge of a runaway train.

Climbing at such incredible speeds the *Komets* could close in on the enemy bomber formations in a matter of minutes. The pilots didn't have time to spare as the rocket fuel would run out after six minutes and then the *Komet* would revert to a glider. With adrenaline pumping and a closing speed of around 400mph (645km/h) the German pilots had only seconds to fire off their formidable Rheinmetall-Borsig MK108 30mm cannon. (Some later *Komets* were armed with 50mm rockets which pointed upwards and were triggered by a photocell when the outline of a bomber passed overhead.) At that fleeting moment of contact the *Komet*'s great speed was suddenly its greatest drawback. A pilot had to think and act fast. New tactics were tried. Some would attack

The prototype Heinkel He 176 was the first aircraft to be powered by liquid-fuelled rocket motor when it flew on 20 June 1939.

from underneath the formation in a 45° climb, knowing that the turret gunners couldn't follow them. But the escort fighter pilots soon learned that they could pursue and attack an Me 163B on its fuel-less glide back to the airfield.

Landing was another high-risk moment for the Me 163. The retractable landing skid offered little protection, and it was essential that no fuel was left in system as a bad landing in the fast-moving but powerless egg could spell disaster. In an incident during one of the early un-powered flights, test pilot Hannah Reitsch had just taken off on tow behind an Me 110 when the Me 163's trolley failed to disengage and her aircraft began to shudder violently from the unexpected turbulence it created in the air-flow. After casting off from the tug at 10,000ft (3,050m) she desperately tried to shake the trolley off but it remained stuck. On the landing approach Reitsch made a crucial error, a side-slip which caused a stall, and the aircraft plunged into the ground before tumbling to a halt and leaving her with multiple fractures to her skull. Despite this incident she remained an enthusiastic fan of the *Komet*: 'The Me 163B had excellent flying qualities, better than I had found in any other aircraft.'

THE OPEL-HATRY RAK-1

The Me 163 was not the first rocket-powered aircraft to have taken to the skies. During the 1930s there was something of a fashion for strapping rockets on to all manner of vehicles including cars, rail riders and even snow sledges. One of the most notable proponents of rocket-power was Fritz von Opel of the Opel car company. In 1928

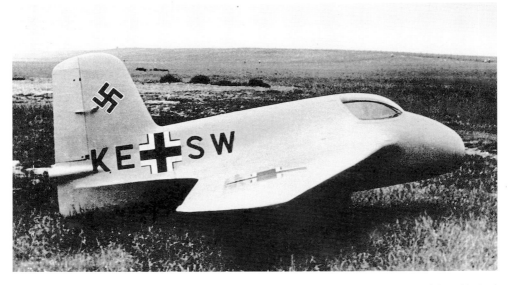

KE+SW, the Messerschmitt Me-163 V-1 prototype has a far more rounded nose than later models and lacked the single-piece bubble canopy.

Opel bought a Lippisch Ente glider from Alexander Lippisch, a young engineer with a fascination for aerodynamics. With two black powder rockets the Lippisch glider flew in 1928, although it was badly damaged on the second attempt when one of the rockets exploded. Undaunted, Opel bought a second purpose-built glider, this time from Julius Hatry. Christened as the Opel-Hatry RAK-1, it flew on 30 September 1929 at Frankfurt-am-Main with thrust provided by sixteen black powder rockets, but it was damaged beyond repair in a heavy landing.

Although Opel lost interest after that, in the late 1930s some of the mainstream aircraft companies were also looking into rockets, among them Heinkel.

THE HEINKEL He 176

When Wernher von Braun's rocketry team at Peenemünde needed aircraft for experiments with liquid-fuelled rockets Ernst Heinkel supplied them with an He 72 biplane and two He 112s; the latter a candidate for the Luftwaffe's 1933 competition for a new fighter aircraft. In 1936 the He 72 was used to test a Walter rocket motor using hydrogen peroxide and a paste catalyst, and in April 1937 one of the He 112s flew with a von Braun liquid-fuel rocket, but crashed on landing. Undeterred, Heinkel began work on a purpose-built rocket-powered aircraft which, it was hoped, might surpass the 621mph (1,000km/h) mark. The result was the Heinkel He 176, an extraordinarily modern-looking design with a rounded nose, a totally enclosed cockpit, and forward tricycle undercarriage. Unusually the entire nose section could be jettisoned in the event of an emergency at high speed. It was also very small, just over 17ft (5.2m) long with a wingspan of 16ft 5in (5.0m) – barely big enough to take the test pilot Erich Warsitz – and was built almost entirely of wood to keep weight to an absolute minimum. Within the streamlined fuselage there were tanks for the hydrogen peroxide and methanol propellants, plus the Walter R1 rocket which produce a regulated level of thrust between 1,102 to 1,323lb (500 to 600kg).

The first official flight under liquid-fuelled rocket power took place on 20 June 1939. The following day a flight demonstration was put on for Ernst Udet and Erhard Milch of the RLM and on 1 July it flew in front of the Führer. These displays were met by a resounding lack of interest from the officials and the project was cancelled by the autumn.

THE MESSERSCHMITT Me 163

Meanwhile Alexander Lippisch had been continuing to explore new aerodynamic forms under the aegis of the German institute for the study of glider flight, the *Deutsche Forschungsanstalt Segelflug* (DFS), and his tail-less *Storch* ('stork') was first flown in 1927. Further models on this theme led to the Delta I, which began flight testing in 1930 and saw a 30hp engine added in the following year. Development with the tail-less form continued with the DFS, on and off, but eventually culminated with the announcement of a rocket-powered version, the DFS 194, with an airframe built by Heinkel. This division of responsibilities proved untenable and in 1939 work on the DFS 194 was reorganised under one team under Lippisch's leadership and within the Messerschmitt company at Augsburg to create what became the Me 163.

In 1940 the first of the Me 163A prototypes was shipped to Peenemünde West where it was fitted with a Walter HWK RI-203 rocket motor, an improved version to the one on the He 176. In test flights the aircraft achieved speeds of up to 342mph (500km/h). The Me 163A V4 received the HWK RII-203 motor which used T-Stoff and Z-Stoff propellants on the cold principle, and in October 1941 it attained a new world speed record of 624mph (1,005km/h). This record was entirely unofficial as the project was so shrouded in secrecy that even the Me 163 designation had been taken from an earlier light aircraft. Five prototype Me 163 A-series were built, followed by eight pre-production aircraft designated as the Me 163 A-0. The flight testing wasn't without incident. There were problems with the detachable wheel trolley rebounding into the aircraft, and malfunctions of the hydraulic dampers in the landing skid resulted in pilot injuries. Nevertheless, the aircraft's performance couldn't fail to impress and, equipped with the newer HWK 109-509A 0-1 hot engine fuelled by a deadly cocktail of T-Stoff and C-Stoff propellants, the Me 163B *Komet* emerged in late 1941.

The *Komet* entered active service in May 1944, operating initially from the airfield at Brandis, near Leipzig, to defend the Leuna oil refineries to the south-west. The specifications for the Me 163B-1 were: length 18ft 8in (5.7m), wingspan 30ft 7in (9.33m). The Walter HWK 109-509A-2 motor gave a maximum speed of 596mph (1,060km/h), and the aircraft had a service ceiling of 39,700ft (12,100m). Improved endurance came with the HWK 109-509B and HWK 109-509C motors, although the latter was fitted to only a handful of aircraft. The final version, the Me 163C, featured a pressurised cockpit, enlarged wings and a lengthened fuselage with bubble canopy. There was also the Me 163S, an un-powered tandem conversion with the second seat for an instructor in the space normally occupied by the rocket motor. This was used for glider landing training.

Me 263 *SCHOLLE*

Due to the pressure already on Messerschmitt to supply Bf 109s and Me 262s, production of the *Komet* was dispersed among a number of locations and control of the work was handed firstly to Klemm and then to Junkers. The engineers at Dessau thought they could improve on Messerschmitt's work and their Ju 248 retained the pressurised cockpit of the 163C on a longer fuselage, to carry more fuel, which featured a retractable tricycle undercarriage. Only one prototype was built of the Ju 248 which reverted to a Messerschmitt designation as the Me 263 *Scholle* ('plaice'). Un-powered test flights were made in February 1945, but time ran out before it could be flown under rocket power. The Americans overran the Junkers plant in April 1945 and with the reallocation of territory within the Allied zones of occupation it fell into the hands of the Russians. The Me 263 is said to have been the inspiration for Russia's short-lived

Mikoyan-Gurevich I-270 rocket power interceptor, of which two prototypes were built immediately after the war.

The Japanese also constructed several versions of the Me 163 from plans supplied by the Germans. The Mitsubishi Ki-200 *Shusui* ('autumn water') was the equivalent of the Me 163B and was armed with two 30mm Ho 155-II cannon. A version produced for the Japanese Navy known as the J8M1 saw the Ho 155 cannon replaced with the navy's 30mm Type 5 cannon. Lacking the parts to complete their own motors, the Japanese aircraft could only be flown experimentally as gliders.

With only sixteen Allied aircraft credited to the Me 163B *Komet*, the operational record never lived up to expectations. In the end it was a glorious experiment in a type of propulsion that was not to enjoy a more widespread application. Just like its namesake, it had burst across the sky on a column of flame for only the most fleeting of moments. As Sir Roy Fedden stated:

> The Me 163, the only rocket-propelled fighter of the war, was a remarkable experiment capable of great development, and indicated the German plan of things to come for high-speed aircraft had the war continued.

Messerschmitt 163B, the 'Komet', the first and only operational rocket-powered interceptor.

THE *ENZIAN*

There is, however, an interesting adjunct to the Me 163 story. The *Enzian*, named after a type of mountain flower, was a guided surface-to-air missile designed to emulate the Me 163's mode of attacking the high-altitude Allied bomber formations, but without its inherent operational difficulties or risk to pilots, and at a much lower cost. The problem with the *Komet* was its short flight duration and even briefer opportunity to engage with the enemy. When it did encounter the B-17s and B-29s it lacked the means to aim and hit the targets at a closing speed of around 100mph (160km/h). Originally known as the *Flak Rakete* when proposed by Dr Wurster at Messerschmitt, the *Enzian* would be flown in front of the bombers and then the massive 500kg charge would be detonated creating a blast that could, in theory, bring down several aircraft in one go. In appearance the *Enzian* E-4 certainly looked like a scaled-down version of the *Komet*. The 7ft 10in (2.4m) fuselage had a low aspect ration and featured swept wings with trailing-edge elevons for manoeuvring, plus upper and lower fins at the rear. The airframes were designed for simple mass production and made as much use of wood as possible. Launched from an 88mm gun mounting, four Schmidding 109-553 solid-fuel boosters grouped around the fuselage gave a combined boost thrust of 15,400lb (7,000kg) and a far greater rate of climb than any human pilot could endure. The sustainer motor was to have been the Walter RI-10B which used SV-Stoff (mixed acids) and Br-Stoff (petrol) propellants, with

The shape of the unmanned Enzian surface-to-air missile bears more than a passing resemblance to the Me 163. *(JC)*

a small quantity of T-Stoff as the catalyst. In flight the thrust decreased from 4,410 to 2,205lb (2,000 to 1,000kg), enabling the controller to more readily fly it headlong into the bomber formations

Guiding such an approach remotely from the ground was the tricky part. It would be far more difficult than the straight line trajectory of competing missiles, such as Rheintochter, and initially the intention was to install a self-contained Elsass radar unit in the *Enzian*'s nose together with a proximity fuse. In tests the proximity fuse proved troublesome and an infrared system, known as Madrid, was proposed instead. This used several telescope mirrors to visually fix on the target. However, after thirty-eight test firings the *Enzian* programme was cancelled before Madrid could be made operational.

THE EMERGENCY FIGHTER PROGRAMME

Unknown to Sir Roy Fedden until after the end of the war, a copy of the secret report on his 1942-3 mission to examine American aircraft production had been leaked to the Germans shortly after its publication. In all likelihood this had been done quite deliberately to convince them that they could not possibly win the war in the face of such overwhelming industrial might. And that was Germany's greatest dilemma. Its war machine was being battered and starved of vital resources while the Allied bombers just kept on coming by the thousands.

In the summer of 1944 the Emergency Fighter Programme saw all aircraft production focussed on defensive fighters, in particular the Messerschmitt Me 262A fighter versions, and the only bombers allowed to continue in production were those powered by jets. But it was becoming clear that neither the Me 163B or the Me 262 could be expected to protect the Reich on their own. In August 1944 a design competition was launched by the RLM to create a jet-powered *Volksjäger* ('people's fighter') to deal with the Allied bombers. It must have only a single engine (the BMW 003 was specified), weigh no more than 4,410lb (2,000kg), should be readily manufactured by semi-skilled or even unskilled labour using only minimal resources, and had to be easy to fly by relatively inexperienced pilots. One suggestion was that members of the Hitler Youth could fly them after some preliminary training on gliders – a notion dismissed as 'unrealistic' by Ernst Heinkel after the war and symptomatic of the 'unbalanced fanaticism of those days'.

It was already very late in the day but Heinkel rose to the challenge and dusted down an existing design, designated P.1073, to create the He 162 *Spatz*, or 'sparrow'. The 162 designation was chosen from an earlier Heinkel project, and codenamed Salamander, to throw the Allies off the scent. Made primarily of wood with a sheet steel monocoque fuselage, the Heinkel He 162 wore its single BMW 003 jet engine on its back. Twin vertical tail fins were mounted on either side of a dihedral tailplane to provide clearance for the jet exhaust. It had high-mounted straight wings which were attached to the fuselage by four bolts, a tricycle retractable landing gear and an ejector seat for the pilot (vital to clear that big turbojet directly behind the cockpit bubble canopy).

Heinkel He 162, Volksjäger, captured at an airfield in France. *(USAF)*

Such was the urgency for the new fighter that Heinkel had a prototype in the sky on 6 December 1944, less than ninety days after the design had been selected. On the first test flight there was a problem with the wood glue on the nose cone and a number of other issues with pitch instability and side-slip due to the rudder configuration. On the second test flight the glue failed again, causing a fatal crash. There was no time for major design changes, so Heinkel made do with strengthening the wing structure and tweaking the tail design. On the third and fourth prototypes they introduced small aluminium wing tip droops in an attempt to improve stability.

The eventual production series, the He 162A-2, was armed with two 22mm MG 151 guns. Fuel duration was around thirty minutes and the aircraft could achieve a respectable 522mph (840km/h) at 19,700ft (6,000m); possibly a little more using short bursts of extra thrust although this ate into the BMW motor's already short service life. Assembly facilities were established at three main sites, at Marienehe, in a former chalk mine at Mödling, and at the Junkers plant in Bernberg, with components and sub-assemblies coming from all over Germany. Some of the wooden components, for example, were produced by furniture makers. An output of 1,000 aircraft a month was predicted by April 1945, and double that when production facilities at the Mittelwerk came on stream later on.

An active evaluation unit, *Erprobungskommando* 162, was formed in January 1945 at Rechlin. Then in February He 162s were delivered to the first operational unit, I./JG 1 at Parchim, to the south-west of the Heinkel factory. Officially the He 162 never entered active service as the paperwork wasn't ready in time but, unofficially, they were known to have engaged with Allied aircraft from late April 1945, only weeks before Germany's capitulation.

Another aircraft that bore a strong resemblance to the He 162, with a single turbojet mounted on the top of the fuselage and a dihedral tail, was the Henschel Hs 132. This design actually pre-dates the He 162 as its origins lie in a 1943 specification issued by the RLM for a single-seat dive bomber to attack shipping in the anticipated Allied invasion of Europe. The original RLM specification had called for a piston-engined aircraft, but Henschel believed that the performance requirement could only be met by jet power, in this case a BMW 003A. The 29ft 2.5in (8.9m) fuselage of the Hs 132 was a streamlined cigar shape having a rounded clear nose with the glazing extended almost as far as the wing roots. This was to provide a wider view for the pilot who was positioned slightly back from the nose behind a plate of armoured glass, lying on his stomach with his head right in the nose. The apparent advantages of this prone position were a reduced frontal area to minimise both drag and the risk of being hit by defensive guns, plus it was thought to improve the pilot's ability to withstand high pull-out forces. The thinner fuselage tube lacking any protuberances would also be easier to pressurise. The aircraft's wings were tapered slightly and, as with the He 162, the tail had a dihedral layout with end-plate twin fins to give clearance for the jet exhaust. The payload was to be a single 1,100lb (500kg) bomb, to be dropped in a shallow dive with the aircraft pulling out sharply just beyond the enemy ship's range of fire.

Other variations considered included the Hs 132B with a Jumo 004 engine and two 20mm MG 151/20 cannon. The Hs 132C was even beefier with the more powerful Heinkel HeS-011 and additional fire power.

Construction work on several prototypes, possibly four, was started in March 1945 with the first flight slated for June. Obviously events scuppered these plans and the Russians captured the Henschel's Schönefeld factory in May 1945. By that time the wings and fuselage had not been mated and the only surviving photograph of the Hs 132 V1 prototype, standing outside the works, might only be a mock-up according to some sources.

Designed as a dive bomber the Henschel Hs 132 looks very similar to the He 162.

THE LEONIDAS 'SUICIDE' SQUADRON

By early 1944 serious consideration was being given to the possibility of German airmen carrying out *Selbstopfer* or 'suicide missions' against important strategic targets. This proposal, which came originally from Otto Skorzeny and Hajo Hermann, had the enthusiastic support of the influential Hannah Reitsch, who had the ear of Adolf Hitler. At first he was dismissive of the idea, believing that it was not the right psychological moment for it to be acceptable to the German public, but he did agree to the formation of the Leonidas Squadron as the 5th Staffel of the Luftwaffe's *Kampfgeschwader* 200. The squadron derived its distinctive name from the King Leonidas of Sparta, who in 480 BC had resisted the invading Persian army with 300 warriors who fought to the last man.

The plan was to arm an aircraft with a 2,000lb (900kg) bomb in order to attack shipping in the Allied landings. The prime candidate for the role was a specially converted manned version of the Fieseler 103 V-1 flying bomb, but another design, the Me 328, was chosen instead. This diminutive aircraft was originally conceived by Messerschmitt in 1941 as the P.1073 as a cheap escort fighter, either towed by a heavy bomber or carried aloft, parasite fashion, on the back of an Me 264. Constructed almost entirely of wood, development of the Me 328 had been handled by the DFS and two versions were proposed originally, the Me 328A fighter and the Me 328B bomber. The fuselage was 27ft 7in (6.4m) long and it had a wingspan of 20ft 6in (6.4m). There were three options for propulsion; un-powered glide, Argus pulsejets or even jet power with a Jumo 004 engine. Test flights commenced with the glider version being released from a tow aircraft or sometimes carried piggy-back on a Dornier Do 217. Testing of seven prototypes fitted with two Argus As 014 pulsejets was started but soon abandoned, probably due to the excessive vibration the pulsejets caused. (An illustration of the pulsejet version is shown on page 127.) However, the Me 328 programme had already been suspended by this time and in order to save development time attention reverted to the manned version of the V-1, the Fieseler Fi 103R, known by its codename as the *Reichenberg*.

To accommodate the pilot a cramped cockpit was added immediately in front of the intake for the Argus As 014 pulsejet in the space where the compressed-air cylinders would have been on the unmanned V-1 missile. These cylinders were replaced by a single one positioned further back in place of the autopilot. The cockpit had only the most basic instruments. The wings were fitted with hardened edges to slice through the cables of any defensive balloon barrage. The idea was to carry either one or two *Reichenbergs* beneath the wings of a Heinkel He 111, releasing them near the intended target. In theory the pilots were to bail out shortly before impact, but the likelihood of doing that safely just inches away from the intake of the Argus ramjet were very remote.

Training commenced with ordinary gliders at first, and then progressed to specially altered gliders with shortened wings, and concluded with instruction on the dual-control Fi 103R-II trainer. There was no shortage of volunteers and seventy young recruits, Hannah Reitsch among them, signed a declaration stating; 'I hereby voluntarily apply to be enrolled in the suicide group as part of the human-glider bomb. I fully understand that employment in this capacity will entail my own death.'

Glider version of the Messerschmitt Me 328 considered as a candidate for suicide missions.

Test flights of the *Reichenberg* commenced in September 1944, with glider drops from a Heinkel He 111 at first, followed by fully powered tests. (It had become already standard procedure to drop the conventional V-1s from the bomber since the Allies had captured the missile's launch ramps in the Pas de Calais area.) But by this time the Allied advance upon Germany was in full swing and the original purpose of the suicide missions, to attack the invasion fleets, was no longer valid.

By October 1944 official interest in the *Reichenberg* had shifted in favour of the *Mistel* composite aircraft as a means of striking against Russian targets.

THE *MISTEL*

The concept of piggy-back aircraft, or pick-a-back as they were sometimes called, was nothing new. Shortly before the war Britain's Imperial Airways had begun experiments with the Short Mayo Composite which consisted of the S.20 Mercury twin-float seaplane riding atop the bigger S.21 Maia, a variant of the C-Class Empire flying boat. The plan was to use this combination to extend the range of the aircraft in order to establish a reliable long-range transatlantic service. In-flight separations, including one transatlantic flight, took place in 1938, but this line of development ended with the coming of war.

The German piggy-back, *Mistel*, was named after mistletoe for its obvious parasitic associations, although it was sometimes referred to as *Vati und Sohn*, ('father and son'), or more officially by the codename *Beethoven-Gerät* ('Beethoven device'). At first it was

This 'Bakka', a Japanese equivalent of the Fieseler Fi 103R manned flying-bomb, was discovered by US troops at Kadena Airfield, Okinawa. *(NARA)*

Mistel piggyback combination, with Fw 190 above an unmanned Ju 88, captured by the Allies at Bernberg, Germany. *(USAF)*

The Bachem Ba 349 'Natter' rocket-propelled interceptor shown on its vertical launch tower. *(NARA)*

explored as a means of increasing the range of the Luftwaffe's big paratroop-carrying gliders, with either a Focke-Wulf Fw 56 or Messerschmitt Bf 109E as the upper element. However, it was also apparent that the *Mistel* could be adapted to deliver a very heavy bomb load to a strategic target. The biggest bomb any existing aircraft could deliver was 5,500lb (2,500kg), but the *Mistel* composite aircraft could raise this to around 8,400lb (3,800kg) which was sufficient to seriously damage even the biggest and most heavily protected installation. Around 250 *Mistels* were built during the war, mostly a combination with various models of the Focke-Wulf Fw 190 or the Messerschmitt Bf 109 on top, and an unmanned Junkers Ju 88 to carry the bomb-load, although other variants were proposed including an all-jet Me 262 and Ju 287 combination. Contrary to expectations, the bombers were not well-used aircraft, but purpose-built for the task.

The method of operation called for the pilot in the parasite aircraft to fly towards the target and when at relatively close range to set the bomber on automatic pilot before firing the explosive bolts that held them together. In practice pilot losses were heavy and the slow-moving bombers were easy prey to the anti-aircraft defences. *Mistels* were used against the Mulberry harbours during the Allied landings at Normandy, although with little effect. In Operation Eisenhammer ('iron hammer') they were to have attacked the

On 4 May 1945 Allied troops caught up with the Bachem team as they attempted to escape to the Austrian Alps. *(NARA)*

more lightly defended power stations around Moscow and Gorky, but the Russians were already pushing into Germany before the plan could be implemented. In a final act of desperation in April 1945 *Mistels* were deployed as bridge-busters against the Russian bridgehead at Küstrin, but yet again they failed to cause any significant damage.

THE *OHKA*

American interest in the *Reichenbergs* in particular was concerned with the possibility of the Japanese deploying similar weapons in the continuing Pacific War. The Japanese culture was more familiar with the tradition of suicide missions and their equivalent of the Fieseler Fi 103R was the Yokosuka MXY7, known as the *Ohka* ('cherry blossom'), but nicknamed by American servicemen as *Baka*, the Japanese word for fool. At first sight *Ohka* looks much like the Fi 301R. In essence it was a 2,646lb (1,200kg) bomb with a 19ft 11in (6.06m) cylindrical fuselage, a pair of short wings, a double-tail and a cockpit, but it lacked the *Reichenberg's* rear pulsejet. Instead the *Ohka* was powered by three Type 4 Model 20 solid-fuel rockets fitted within the end of the fuselage. In operation the *Ohka* would be dropped from beneath a Mitsubishi G4M2e Model 24J bomber and then glide towards its target, usually an American ship. As it got closer the pilot would fire the three rockets, either one at a time or in unison, to increase the range and speed. On final approach the small aircraft was almost unstoppable as it closed in on the target at speeds over 400mph (650km/h), even more if in a dive.

Its range was 20 nautical miles (37km). Later models were designed to be launched from coastal airbases or even from catapults on board ships or submarines. Around 850 *Ohka* were built and they were used throughout the spring of 1945, mostly against American ships at Okinawa, where they sank or damaged seven vessels including the destroyer USS *Mannert L. Abele*. Other variations included the Model 22 fitted with a Campini-type thermojet, and also the Model 33 with Ishikawajima Ne-20 turbojet, but neither appears to have taken part in combat. The *Ohka* K-1 was a two-person trainer.

THE BACHEM Ba 349

The most radical design to emerge from Germany's Emergency Fighter Programme was the extraordinary Bachem Ba 349, otherwise known as the Bachem *Natter* ('viper'). Not a suicide weapon, it was the nearest thing the Germans had to an actual manned anti-aircraft missile. The Natter had evolved from Erich Bachem's earlier and unrealised designs for the Fieseler Fi 166, a twin-engined jet fighter launched upright piggy-back, almost Space Shuttle-style, on a liquid-fuel rocket. His submission in response to the 1944 call for fighter designs was equally radical. It didn't meet all of the Luftwaffe's requirements although, crucially, it caught the eye of the SS leader Heinrich Himmler. Consequently its development continued under the patronage of the SS.

The Bachem *Natter* was small, vertically launched and rocket-powered. IT could be flown by an untrained operator/pilot. 'Pilot' seems too grand a term as it would be taken into the flight path of the Allied bombers on autopilot; all the occupant was required to do was aim and fire the air-to-air rockets at the bombers. After an encounter the pilot would then point the nose downwards and descend to a lower altitude before levelling out. A latch released the canopy, which would flick backward in the slipstream on its hinges. The pilot would jettison the nose section, and both pilot and aircraft would float to earth under individual parachutes. It sounded so simple and yet so complicated. In its favour this system did away with airfield runways for both the launch and the landing, making it possible to locate the *Natter* wherever it was needed, reducing vulnerability to attack by Allied fighters.

The Ba 349 wasn't much to look at. A squat 20ft (6m) long, it had short straight wings with a wingspan of 12ft (9m), and a conventional-looking tail with control ailerons. The airframe was mostly constructed of wood, nailed or glued, and could be assembled by unskilled labour. The *Natter's* driving force came from the Walter HWK 109-509 A2 rocket motor, the same unit as on the Me 163, plus four Schmidding SG34 solid-fuel boosters strapped to the sides providing an additional 4,800kg of thrust for ten seconds before being jettisoned. It was armed with nineteen R4M air-to-air rockets, possibly increased to twenty-eight on later models, or 75mm Fohn assault rockets.

The first of the experimental prototypes was completed in October 1944, and test flights were undertaken towed behind a Heinkel 111 and also free-flying in glider mode. The first unmanned vertical launch took place on 22 December 1944 using only the solid-fuel boosters, and in late February 1945 a *Natter* was launched with the HWK 109-509 installed and it made a near-perfect flight. Near-perfect because the dummy pilot was returned safely enough but residual propellant ignited when the fuselage hit the ground, destroying the aircraft. Then on 1 March 1945 a young test pilot named Lothar Sieber bravely climbed into the cockpit for the first manned flight. In a cloud of steam the *Natter* rose out of the guiding rails on the launch tower with all rockets firing. Suddenly it pitched backwards and then continued to climb inverted at an angle about 30° to the vertical. At 1,650ft or so (500m) the cockpit canopy prematurely tore away and the *Natter* disappeared into low cloud. When the Walter motor stalled, at launch +15 seconds, the *Natter* nose-dived all the way to the ground. It is thought that Sieber had involuntarily pulled back on the stick because of the G-forces of acceleration, and he had probably broken his neck when the canopy holding the headrest flew off.

Development work continued, the rockets were upgraded, but claims that the *Natter* ever flew in anger are uncorroborated. It is thought that thirty-six *Natters* had been built by the time Allied troops had caught up with the Bachem team.

ten

OBERAMMERGAU

AFTER THE SCENES of devastation they had witnessed in the industrial regions in the north of Germany, particularly the horrors of Mittelwerk-Dora, it must have been with a sense of relief that members of the Fedden Mission travelled to Oberammergau in the picturesque Bavarian Alps on Friday 22 June 1945. The town is internationally famous for its passion plays which are presented in every year ending with a zero, although in 1940 the performance was cancelled because of the war. Otherwise this idyllic spot nestling in the hills seemed almost untouched by the war, which is exactly why Messerschmitt's research and experimental division moved here in order to continue its work in secrecy unhampered by Allied bombing raids. In 1943 Messerschmitt took over the Hötzendorf Jäger Kaserne, a large army barracks, having been evacuated from Augsburg. There

Aerial view of Hotzendorf Jäger Kaserne near Oberammergau, the extensive army barracks taken over by Messerschmitt in 1943.

were extensive tunnels, up to 22 miles (37km) of them burrowing into the side of the neighbouring Laber mountain, to augment the factory space, and the local winter sports hotel was commandeered as accommodation for the executive staff. In all, Messerschmitt had a workforce of around 1,800 people at Oberammergau, including 500 in the design department alone.

The facility had been discovered by an American infantry unit on 29 April 1945, and it was almost two months later by the time Fedden's group arrived by road on 22 June. Not surprisingly the Americans were in control and Fedden noted that a design team from the Bell Aircraft company had been working there for about five weeks on behalf of the USSTAF. But the Americans didn't have the place entirely to themselves. Fedden also encountered a party from the British de Havilland aircraft company, which included de Havilland's chief designer Mr Bishop. Immediately after the war de Havilland embarked on a series of experimental tail-less designs, commencing with the DH.108 which first flew in May 1946. These aircraft were used to investigate the behaviour of the swept wing in support of the DH.106 Comet and DH.100 Vampire programmes, though in the event the DH.100 featured straight tapered wings and distinctive twin-boom tail. After the war the Americans continued to occupy the Oberammergau site and, renamed as the Hawkins Barracks, it became the US Army School Europe until it was handed back to the Germans in 1974. It is now the primary training and educational centre for NATO.

Back in 1945 Oberammergau was an Aladdin's cave stuffed with some of Germany's most advanced aeronautical design and, unlike some of the cobbled-together short-term aircraft that had been thrown into the sky in the last-ditch defence of the Reich, here was a glimpse into the future. The Messerschmitt designers had been honing the shape of things to come.

Members of the Fedden Mission at Messerschmitt's experimental department, Oberammergau.

At Oberammergau Fedden was fortunate in being able to interview several members of the design staff, most notably Waldemar Voigt the chief designer, but also Hans Hornung and Joseph Helmschrott. At this time the company founder Willy Messerschmitt was being held in London for interrogation and pending possible charges relating to the company's use of slave labour. Fedden firmly believed that he was able to obtain a far better picture of developments at Messerschmitt by going to Germany and into the works in order to talk directly with the engineers. In particular he singled out Voigt, describing him as 'an extremely progressive engineer and most enthusiastic'. Fedden commented:

> He [Voigt] said that the recent work at Göttingen and Völkenrode had put an entirely new picture on interceptor fighters. He was strongly in favour of swept-back wings and of the opinion that the swept-back wing and the jet would accelerate the extensive use of tail-less type of aircraft in the near future.

Voigt took Fedden's team down to a workshop where they were shown the familiar shark-like Me 262. He talked at some length about the aircraft's flight characteristics and operational shortcomings, stating that because of inexperience among the pilots and stalling of the Jumo 004's compressors, there had been a number of accidents during flight development. There had also been instances of the engines catching fire, due to the incomplete combustion of the fuel in the combustion chamber. As far as he was aware there had been fifteen fatal accidents, but this was no higher than on other interceptor aircraft. This comment struck Fedden as rather contradictory unless, as he put it, 'the Germans accepted an appreciably higher accident rate than we do.' In Voigt's opinion automatic control of the jet engine was essential, but with a little more experience the Me 262 would have had an even greater potential as a fighter aircraft, capable of achieving speeds of up to 550mph (885km/h).

THE P.1101

The mission team saw a number of projects that were still in the developmental stage, in particular the P.1101, which Fedden refers to as the Me 1101. This was the prototype for a single-seater fighter produced in response to the 15 July 1944 Emergency Fighter Programme to create a second generation of jet fighters. Originally, the Messerschmitt people had produced a design featuring a wide fuselage, like an elongated egg, with a rounded air intake on either side at the wing roots and tapering off to a high slender tail clearing the jet exhaust and ending in a 'V' tail. The cockpit was right at the nose, flush to match the curved profile of the fuselage. The forward-mounted wings, shown in the original design drawings, had a compound sweep starting at 45° near the fuselage and changing to a shallower 26° towards the wing tips.

By August 1944 this design had changed, with a far sleeker extended nose, plus straight swept-back wings – borrowed from the Me 262's outer wings – mounted mid-fuselage. Other variations came in quick succession, including consideration of a pulsejet and

Messerschmitt's P.1101 prototype which the mission examined at Oberammergau.

rocket booster combination known as the P.1101L. Following wind tunnel testing a finalised design was submitted to the Construction Bureau of the RLM in early December 1944. On 28 February 1945 the RLM announced that it had chosen the competing Focke-Wulf Ta 183 as the winner of the Emergency Fighter order. The Ta 183, which was known as the *Huckebein* ('hunchback'), also featured a single turbojet within the short fuselage, cockpit above the engine and a high T-tail at the back. Work on the Ta 183s had commenced but none was completed by the time British troops overran the Focke-Wulf works on 8 April 1945. The Messerschmitt team, meanwhile, had continued with the development of the P.1101, but owing to the urgency of Germany's worsening situation they went straight to full-scale prototype while the detailed design for the production version was still being finalised.

The prototype P.1101 V1, which Voigt showed to Fedden at Oberammergau, featured a single turbojet within the main fuselage. There was an open-mouth intake at the front and the pressurised cockpit with bubble canopy was positioned above the engine near

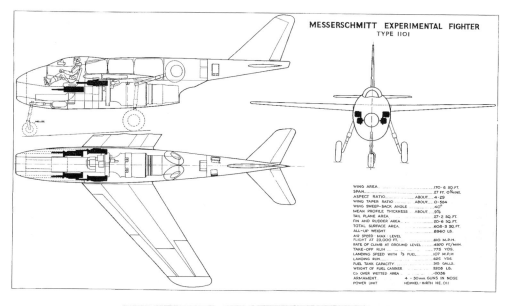

MESSERSCHMITT EXPERIMENTAL FIGHTER
TYPE 1101

WING AREA	170·6 SQ.FT.
SPAN	27 FT. 0¾ INS.
ASPECT RATIO	ABOUT 4·29
WING TAPER RATIO	ABOUT 0·524
WING SWEEP-BACK ANGLE	40°
MEAN PROFILE THICKNESS	ABOUT 9%
TAIL PLANE AREA	27·2 SQ.FT.
FIN AND RUDDER AREA	20·6 SQ.FT.
TOTAL SURFACE AREA	608·8 SQ.FT.
ALL-UP WEIGHT	8960 LB.
AIR SPEED · MAX · LEVEL FLIGHT AT 23,000 FT.	610 M.P.H.
RATE OF CLIMB AT GROUND LEVEL	4370 FT/MIN.
TAKE-OFF RUN	775 YDS.
LANDING SPEED WITH ⅓ FUEL	107 M.P.H
LANDING RUN	625 YDS.
FUEL TANK CAPACITY	315 GALLS.
WEIGHT OF FUEL CARRIER	2205 LB.
Cᴅ OVER WETTED AREA	·0036
ARMAMENT	4 - 30 mm GUNS IN NOSE
POWER UNIT	HEINKEL-HIRTH HE.011

Messerschmitt's drawing of the P.1101 published in the Fedden Mission report along with this photograph, left, showing the single turbojet.

An artist's impression of the P.1101 in flight.

Bell X-5, clearly inspired by Messerschmitt's P.1101 prototype. (Nasa)

the nose. The aircraft had swept-back wings and at the rear the fuselage tapered to a conventional tail but high enough to provide clearance for the exhaust. As part of the accelerated testing and parallel design programme the wings could be adjusted from between 35° to 45° before flight to assess the advantages of differing angles of sweep. This was a purely investigative measure and was never intended as an operational swing-wing feature. The fuel tanks were within the fuselage behind the cockpit, while the radio and oxygen equipment were in the rear section. There was a tricycle undercarriage with the main gear retracting towards the front. Armaments were to consist of either two or four MK108 30mm cannon, and/or under-wing mounted X-4 air-to-air missiles. This prototype had a Jumo 109-004B turbojet fitted for initial trials as the intended and more powerful Heinkel–Hirth HeS 011A was not ready in time, although the engine had been mounted in such a way that the two types were readily interchangeable.

Maximum speed was estimated as being around 612mph (980km/h), the equivalent of Mach 0.8 at 23,000ft (7,000m) altitude, and according to Voigt the prototype would have been flying by June of 1945. When the Americans discovered the Oberammergau facilities on 29 April 1945, the airframe – still without wings – had been hidden away in the nearby tunnels. At first there were suggestions that it could be completed but by this time some of the construction drawings had been removed by the French, and instead it was taken back to the USA – first to the Wright Patterson Air Force Base in Ohio and then, in 1948, to the works of the Bell Aircraft company in Buffalo, New York. It was fitted with an Allison J-35 engine but by then the aircraft had been damaged by rough handling in transit to such a degree that it could no longer be flown. Nonetheless, the unfinished German jet became the basis of the two Bell X-5 experimental aircraft which first flew in June 1951 and which bear more than a passing resemblance, in appearance at least, to their forebear, the Messerschmitt P.1101.

Some components of the German prototype were utilised for static testing, but the airframe was scrapped sometime in the 1950s. As we will see in the next chapter on captured and returned German aircraft, in the decades immediately after the war there was very little sentimentality or consideration given to preserving them for historical reasons and many unique aircraft were either dumped or scrapped.

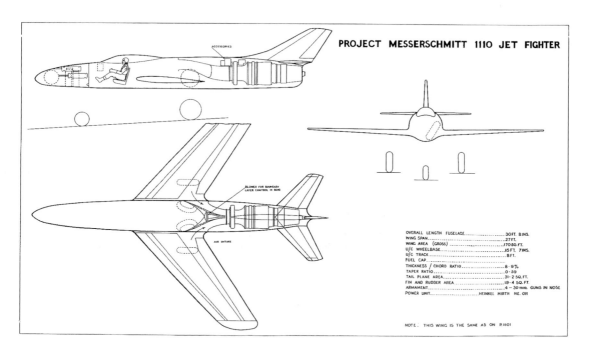

Messerschmitt's drawing for the P.1110 high-altitude fighter-interceptor published in the mission report.

Me P.1110

Fedden also saw design drawings for the next high-altitude fighter-interceptor, the Messerschmitt P.1110. These revealed an aircraft of incredibly modern design and shape (not unlike the British Hawker Hunter which first flew in 1951 and was derived from the earlier Hawker P.1052 of 1948). With the P.1110 it was as if aeronautical evolution had skipped a step and jumped a generation in one go. Instead of a single air intake into the fuselage, it was to have twin annular intakes ahead of each wing root. The result was a much more slender fuselage with the low-profile cockpit located between the intakes ahead of the Heinkel-Hirth HeS 109-011A engine. Voigt explained that although a central intake might give 4 per cent more air than the twin-intakes, this new layout saved 15 per cent on drag. Suction fans driven by the turbojet would draw the boundary layer air in through slotted ducts, and the exhaust was at the rear just below the swept tailplane – the next version was to have a butterfly V-tail. The wings were similar to the P.1101's with a 40° sweep. It was to be armed with three MK108 30mm cannon in the nose, with the possibility of another two cannon installed within the wings. Maximum speed was expected to be in the region of 630mph (1,015km/h).

To overcome the loss of ram air in the P.1110 design, together with the additional power consumption in sucking air from the boundary layer airflow, Voigt was investigating an alternative in which the two air intakes were located within the leading edge of the wing near the root. These intakes would join up behind the cockpit to feed air to the turbojet in the rear end of the fuselage. In January 1945 his design team had prepared designs for the P.1111 which had a sharply swept wing of 45° extending in a near delta-wing shape with just a vertical fin on the tail.

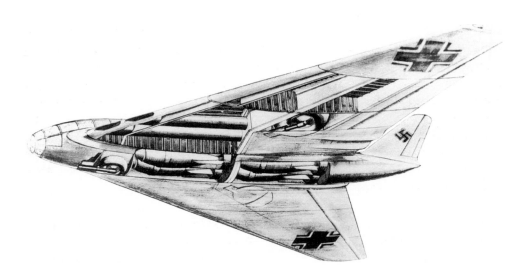

Messerschmitt's 1944 visualisation of the futuristic P.1108 Fernbomber project.

Me P.1112

One Messerschmitt design which had at least made it from the drawing board to initial mock-up stage was the P.1112. Started in February 1945, this was yet another swept-wing single-seat fighter/interceptor, but unlike the P.1111 it had the cockpit set well forward and streamlined into the fuselage with the pilot in a semi-inclined position. The indented air intakes for the Heinkel-Hirth HeS 109-011A turbojet were located roughly halfway along the sides of the fuselage, and at the rear there was a single vertical tail fin, although a V-tail had featured in earlier design drawings. Once again the aircraft had a very modern appearance, but although Voigt had predicted flight testing for the P.1112 by mid-1946, this design never got beyond a rudimentary wooden mock-up of the forward fuselage and cockpit area.

After the war, Voigt went to the USA where he contributed to the design of the Chance Vought F7U, a carrier-based fighter developed for the US Navy and known as the Cutlass, first flown in September 1948. While the profile of the Cutlass had the look of the P.1112, its most distinctive feature was the twin tail with a vertical fin located in the middle of each wing. The F7U proved to be a much-troubled aircraft. Under-powered, it was nicknamed the 'Gutless Cutlass' and suffered numerous technical and handling problems. Over a quarter of the 320 F7Us built were lost in accidents.

TAIL-LESS AIRCRAFT

The final design Fedden's group saw at Oberammergau was what the report mission refers to as the PL.08, although he may have been muddling the PL.08.01 with the similar designation numbers of the P.1108/II judging from his description, which includes four Heinkel-Hirth HeS 109-011 turbojets.

The PL.08.01, designed in 1941 by Dr Wurster who had worked closely with Alexander Lippisch, was a proposed long-range bomber which featured a compound swept wing and was to be powered by four Daimler-Benz DB 615 piston engines mounted within the trailing edge and driving pusher props at the rear, whereas the P.1108/II, another long-range bomber designed by the Lippisch team, was to have been jet-powered. (The P.1101/I design featured a conventional fuselage with swept wings and engines mounted in nacelles.) Although the P.1108/II project was still very much in the early design stage Fedden states that, 'the data available gives a good indication of the possibilities of large jet aircraft and the lines along which German design staffs were planning.' Clearly those lines were of the fast and tail-less sort:

> The aircraft was a four-jet long range bomber, with an all-up weight of about 30 tons and a bomb load of 4 tons. It was stated to have been designed to have a range of 7,000km [4,350 miles] at a cruising speed of 800 to 850km/h [495 to 530mph] at 9 to 12km [30,000 to 40,000ft] altitude. These figures are quoted as given to the Mission without any definite proof, and were described as only approximate, since all the data on this project has been removed

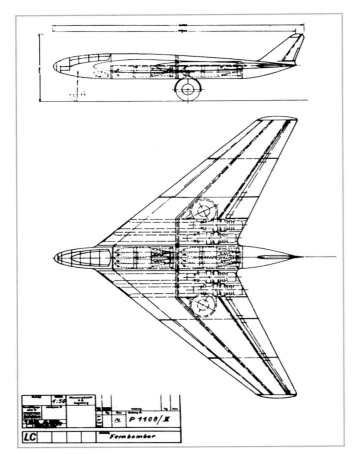

The P.1108 Fernbomber would probably have been fitted with four Heinkel turbojets.

by the French. The intended position of the four Heinkel 001 jet units on this aircraft were interesting. If the machine was made tail-less, the jet units would have been placed on the chord line at the trailing edge, near the wing root, with an influx pipe passing through the wing from the leading edge, or from a scoop on the upper surface of the wing. With a normal type of aircraft they would still have positioned the jet near the trailing edge, but with its axis somewhat below the chord line. The air intake would then be from the air flow beneath the wing, using a modified trailing edge in the region of the engines. The firm stated that these positions had been shown to be the best from the standpoint of minimum drag, and they did not contemplate any trouble from far aft position, as this would be compensated for by the heavily swept-back wings as far as the centre of gravity was concerned.

The design of the P.1108/II was well on the way to being what we would now term as a flying wing, although strictly speaking a full flying wing has no tail fin at all. If the P.1110 had represented a leap in design it is hard to be sure whether that of the P.1108/II was a leap into the future or the past. Much has been written about the advent of the truly tail-less aircraft, the flying wing, but it should be remembered that they had been a recurring theme in the aeronautical and popular science press of the 1930s which regularly featured designs for tail-less, or rather all-wing, aircraft. These were invariably depicted as futuristic airliners with lavish passenger accommodation contained within the deep leading edge of the wing. It is interesting to note that in his paper, 'The Future of Civil Aviation', which Fedden delivered at the Royal Aeronautical Society in the summer of 1944, and long before the wartime developments in Germany had come to light, he had given some prominence to the potential of the tail-less aircraft:

> The construction of larger machines might become feasible in ten years' time, using the tail-less design with improved materials and constructional techniques.

The paper was illustrated with drawings for three sizes of tail-less craft, ranging from an eighteen-seater with a compound sweep to its wing and four air-cooled piston engines buried within the wing to drive pusher propellers, to a thirty-two seater with a straight sweep, and even a small 'jet-propelled mail carrier'. The bigger versions were intended for long-distance travel, mainly transatlantic, and featured conventional rounded fuselages to accommodate the passengers. They bore a striking resemblance to the designs for the Messerschmitt P.08.01.

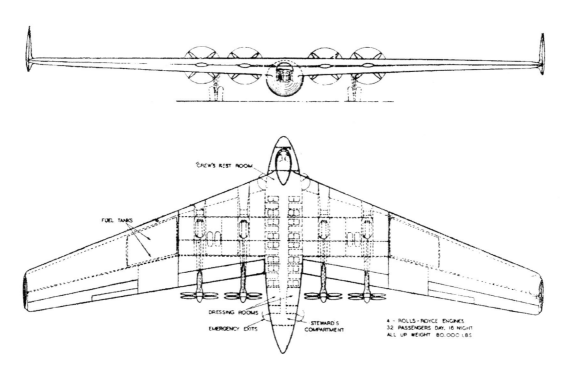

Design for a thirty-two seater tail-less airliner – in other words a flying wing – published in Fedden's 1944 paper *The Future of Civil Aviation*.

In fact, the concept of the flying wing was nothing new, even in the 1930s. It can be traced back to the dawn of heavier-than-air flight and a time when the pioneers were unfettered by any rulebooks of aeronautical convention. (In many ways this situation was replicated in the spirit of aeronautical experimentation found in Germany during the Second World War.) Several of the early European aviators took an all-wing approach to their designs, primarily with gliders, and some of these were moderately successful. However, complications arose when adding engine power to the inherent difficulties in controlling a craft without a tail. In September 1906 the Danish aviator Jacob Christian Ellehammer managed to get off the ground in a form of tail-less craft which resembled a biplane made up of two kites, the lower one fixed and the upper one flexible like a hang-glider, powered by an 18hp engine. This achievement is sometimes credited as the first powered heavier-than-air flight in Europe as it pre-dates Albert Santos-Dumont's flight some two months later, but Ellehammer's craft was tethered by wire to a pole and only managed a few circuits around a circular track without any directional stability or control.

The first free flight with a tail-less aircraft occurred in England. John William Dunne had also begun experiments with un-powered tail-less gliders and in conditions of great secrecy, because of the interest shown by the British Army's embryonic aviation department at South Farnborough, in the spring of 1907 he managed some brief hops with the distinctive V-shaped D.1-A glider. His experiments continued with a series of gliders which, in December 1910, resulted in the flight of the powered D.5 biplane. Further models followed, but ironically the great stability of Dunne's designs made them incompatible with the handling characteristics required in a more manoeuvrable military aircraft.

It was only after the First World War and the advent of thicker-winged monoplanes that designs for a true wingless aircraft, with engines, cockpit, passengers and so on housed within the wing itself were to emerge. In 1910 Hugo Junkers patented designs for a thick-wing aircraft and in the early 1920s the Junkers company produced conceptual designs for several large passenger aircraft. These were widely publicised, especially the J-1000 which was a colossal machine with a wingspan of 203ft (62m) intended for long-distance passenger services – possibly transatlantic – with twenty-six cabins accommodating up to 100 passengers, plus a crew of ten.

However, this all-wing design did feature an additional canard-style wing mounted on twin booms at the front, plus a pair of vertical fins on the trailing edge of the main wing. The J-1000 never made it off the drawing board, partly because of the limitations on permitted aircraft sizes imposed upon Germany in the terms of the Treaty of Versailles. Consequently the nearest a Junkers flying wing came to realisation was the 1931 G-38 Grossflugzeug; a four-engined airliner with three eleven-seater cabins, plus smoker cabins and wash rooms all contained within the thick leading edge and nose. The wing was very large, 6ft (1.8m) thick at the root and with a maximum chord – the measurement from the centre of the leading edge to the trailing edge – of 33ft (10m), but the G-38 still had a central fuselage and tail. Only two were built, the largest aircraft in the world at the time, and the prototype registered D-2000 first flew in November 1929.

The G–38s established several world records and the second aircraft, D–APIS, continued in service for Lufthansa until the outbreak of war. It was destroyed on the ground during an RAF bombing raid on Athens in May 1942. However, these aircraft did not lead on to further development of the wingless configuration. There was some interest in other countries, including from Jack Northrop and Charles Eshelman in the USA, as well as in the Soviet Union, while in Germany the main impetus remained in hands of three aeronautical designers; Alexander Lippisch and the Horten brothers, Walter and Reimar. (A third Horten brother, Wolfram, was killed flying a Luftwaffe bomber at Dunkirk.)

During the First World War Lippisch had flown as an aerial photographer and mapper, and when peace came he went to work for the Zeppelin company. It was during this time that he developed an interest in the aerodynamics of tail-less aircraft and during the 1920s and '30s this led to the design of a series of gliders. These included the *Ente* ('duck'), which in 1928 became the first aircraft to fly under rocket power and, as described in the previous chapter, Lippisch's designs led directly to the development of the Messerschmitt Me 163B rocket powered interceptor. While Lippisch was to steer more towards the delta-wing configuration, his innovative glider designs caught the imagination of the young Horten brothers. Enthusiastic sports flyers, they constructed their own glider which competed at the Ninth Glider Competitions in 1933. The H1 tail-less glider had a very simple wing form, tapered towards the tips but without sweep. Subsequent designs saw the refinement of the wing shape and by 1937 it had evolved into the Ho VII, a powered aircraft with twin 240hp Argus 10C engines on the trailing edge driving pusher propellers.

The great advantage of the slick wing configuration was a drastic reduction in drag which, in turn gave the potential for savings in fuel consumption and far greater range;

Horton 229 V3, a prototype jet-powered flying wing, handed over to Northrop after the war and now in storage with the Smithsonian.

characteristics that caught Hermann Göring's eye. In 1943 he issued a request for designs to produce a bomber that could meet his '3 x 1,000' requirements: Carrying a 1,000kg load over a distance of 1,000km at a speed of 1,000km/h. In other words he wanted an effective long-range bomber that was fast enough to be impervious to Britain's fighter defences. In response, the Hortens came up with an innovative design for a flying wing to be powered by two turbojets, the H.IX (later known as the Ho 229).

This design consisted of a central pod made up from welded steel tubing, with the wing spars built of wood. The wings, or rather wing, swept to an angle of 32° and with rounded tips, were covered with thin plywood panels glued together with a charcoal and sawdust mixture. There were control surfaces along the entire trailing edge. The cockpit was set well forward for maximum visibility past the wing, and the aircraft rode on a retractable tricycle undercarriage, with the front wheel on the first two prototypes sourced from a Heinkel He 177. Steering on the ground was via a small brake flap on each wing tip, and a drogue parachute slowed the aircraft upon landing. It was intended to install two BMW 109-003 jet engines, but as these were not available in time the ubiquitous Jumo 109-004 was used instead.

Given its official RLM designation as the Ho 229, the V1 prototype began testing as a glider in March 1944, and despite a mishap on landing it performed well. The second prototype achieved speeds up to 500mph (800km/h) but was wrecked after an engine failure. However, it had shown sufficient promise for the RLM to continue with the programme, although further design and development was handed over to the aircraft's builder, Gothaer Waggonfabrik, at Friedrichsrode, in Thuringia to the south-west of Nordhausen. Consequently the aircraft is sometimes referred to as the Go 229. The third prototype, V3, had a wingspan of 55ft (16.76m) and was fitted with the more powerful Jumo 109-004C turbojets, but had yet to fly when the US Army captured the works. The V4 and V5 prototypes intended for a night-fighter role were also under construction at the time. In addition, preliminary design work had commenced on a single-engine fighter version, fitted with the more powerful Heinkel-Hirth 109-011A and known as the Ho X. A test version of this aircraft fitted with a single piston engine was under construction at Hersfeld, near Kassel.

The legacy of the Hortens' flying wing has been much debated. After the war the Ho 229 V3 prototype was placed in the hands of the Northrop Corporation because of Jack Northrop's existing interest in the concept. Since 1941 Northrop had been working on the XB-35, a long-range flying wing capable of flying from US airfields to carry out bombing raids on Nazi-occupied Europe in the event that Britain had been overrun – a reverse take on Germany's *Amerikabomber* programme. It was to have a wingspan of 172ft (52.4m) – roughly three times bigger than the Ho 229 – and would be driven by four Pratt & Witney R-4360 radial engines, giving a maximum speed of only 393mph (632km/h) but a range estimated at over 8,000 miles (12,875km).

A one-third scale piston-engined prototype, dubbed the N-9M, first flew in December 1942. This test aircraft was used to gather flight data for the big XB-35 which was in the design stage. The war had already ended when the first of the YB-35s – the designation for the test model versions of the XB-35 – made its maiden flight in July 1946. By then

The YB-49, a jet-powered version of Northrop's flying wing, first flew on 21 October 1947. *(USAF)*

the emergence of the jet-powered aircraft from Germany at the end of the war convinced the USAF that a piston-powered XB-35 would be obsolete before it became operational. Prior to the YB-35's maiden flight the decision had already been made to replace the engines on two of the test aircraft with Allison J35 turbojets and these jet-powered flying wings became known as the YB-49 model. The first of these flew on 21 October 1947, but by 1951 the programme had been terminated following the loss of one aircraft and a succession of technical difficulties.

This was not the end of the flying wing, however. The Horten brothers had rightly surmised that its slim cross-section made a flying wing harder to detect by radar. They had even tried to enhance this characteristic by adding charcoal dust to the wood glue to absorb electromagnetic waves. What they didn't appreciate was that its flatter shape and the absence of radar reflecting vertical surfaces were the key factor in what we now term as stealth technology. In the 1980s engineers from the Northrop-Grumman Corporation made several visits to the Smithsonian Museum's facility at Silver Hill, Maryland, where the captured Ho 229 V3 prototype was still in storage. Their research led to the Northrop B-2 stealth bomber where the aerodynamic qualities of the flying wing are secondary to its low radar signature. The flying wing concept is also being reviewed and re-branded as the Blended Wing Body (BWB) with a flattened and more aerofoil-like shape to deliver lower drag and high-lift. The Boeing Phantom Works in association with Nasa's Langley Research Centre commenced flight testing with the remotely piloted X-48B in July 2007.

DELTA WINGS

The delta wing, named after the Greek character Delta which is represented by the Δ symbol, is so closely related to the flying wing that it can be regarded as a variation on the same theme. The main proponent of the delta wing in Germany was Alexander Lippisch of Messerschmitt Me 163 fame, although that aircraft wasn't a pure delta as the wings didn't extend to a full triangle. But such was the success of the Me 163 in terms of its aerodynamic qualities, bearing in mind that it always returned to the ground in glider mode, that Lippisch went on to experiment further with the design. This wartime work culminated in the Lippisch DM-1, or Darmstadt-München 1, a glider intended as a development model to test low-speed handling for a proposed super-fast ramjet-powered interceptor known as the Lippisch LP-13a. Eugene Sanger had already conducted flight tests with extremely powerful Lorin-type ramjets carried on the back of a Dornier Do 217E, and for the P.13a a ramjet that might be fuelled by coal dust had been proposed, possibly combined with rocket motors.

Development of the test glider was started by the *Flugtechnische Fachgruppe* (FFG) – an association of students and aircraft designers at the Darmstadt and München (Munich) universities – in August of 1944, but after the facilities were bombed they moved the work to Prien in Bavaria. The DM-1 featured a distinctive pure delta of 60° sweep, resulting in a triangular plan shape, mirrored by another triangle to form the high dorsal fin. In theory the compression shock at Mach 1 would occur on both the leading edge of the wings and fin at the same time. This single-seater, just 20ft 8in (6.32m) long, was constructed of steel tubing frame with a plywood skin, with the cockpit crammed into the space at the junction of the three triangular elements. In the final operational version

Lippisch DM-1 delta-wing with triangular dorsal fin. *(SDASM)*

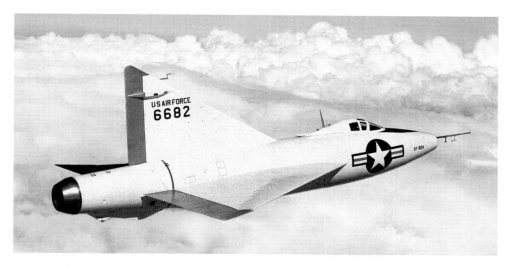

Convair's XF-92A delta-wing test aircraft first flew in 1948. *(USAF)*

the circular intake for the ramjet would have extended to the nose. The intention was to launch the DM-1 by piggy-back. Film footage exists of what appears to be a scale model of the DM-1 in flight, as the prototype aircraft was not ready by the time American troops arrived on the scene in May 1945. Work continued on the DM-1 under the guidance of the US military and in November 1945 Dr Lippisch and the completed glider were shipped to the USA. The model was scrutinised in the Langley Aeronautical Laboratory's wind tunnel and the data obtained from these studies led to the design of the Convair XP-92. Just as with the P.13a this aircraft was to have been powered by a combination of rocket and ramjet, but in the event a single test aircraft, the XF-92A, flew on 18 September 1948 fitted with an Allison J33-A-21 turbojet. The success of the XP-92 led Convair to feature the delta wing on a number of designs including the F-102 Delta Dagger, F-106 Delta Dart, B-58 Hustler, the F2Y Sea Dart produced for the US Navy, and the experimental FY Pogo VTOL aircraft.

Dornier Do 217E test-bed for the ramjet engine.

eleven

CAPTURED AIRCRAFT

THE BRITISH

EVEN AS SIR ROY FEDDEN and his team were examining the Nazis' aircraft design, research and development establishments, scores of the latest jets and other advanced aircraft were being spirited out of Germany. In the months leading up to and following Germany's surrender, technical intelligence teams from the three main Allied nations had been in a race to secure examples of some of the most advanced aircraft the world had ever seen. Each wanted their share of the aeronautical spoils of war and the line between cooperation and competition was frequently blurred.

For the British, at least, the process of gathering enemy aircraft had already begun in the early stages of the war, and their examination and evaluation played a vital role in formulating the tactics needed to deal with them in combat. These German aircraft had fallen into their hands through a variety of circumstances. The earliest examples were forced down because they had sustained damage or, in a surprisingly large number of cases, their crews had landed them at British airfields by mistake. This might be because of a navigational error or in some cases the pilots/navigators had become disorientated as the result of British electronic measures intended to mimic the German radio navigational beacons in order to deliberately lead the aircraft astray. (Imagine the sense of disbelief for any such German aircrew who thought they had got home safely only to be surrounded by British personnel.) It was usual for all captured aircraft to be taken first to the Royal Aircraft Establishment (RAE) at Farnborough. Flight testing of the aircraft was carried out by the Aerodynamics Flight of the Experimental Flying Department, although the Wireless and Electrical Flight (W&EF) also became involved when radar equipment was concerned. They would then be handed over to the Air Fighting Development Unit (AFDU), based at Northolt initially and later moved to Duxford and then Collyweston, for more thorough assessments of their performance characteristics. This would sometimes involve mock aerial combat sessions to provide realistic practical testing of the Allied fighter tactics. As the war progressed only new types would be fully evaluated or flight tested in this way, although the latest arrivals were always checked over for any recent improvements or modifications which the Germans might have introduced.

Wearing American colours, a Ju 88 captured in Italy in 1944. *(NARA)*

In 1941 a special unit was formed to perform flying demonstrations of the captured aircraft in order to familiarise Allied personnel, both RAF and the voluntary Observers Corps and so on, with the appearance, performance and even the sound of the German aircraft. Officially designated as No.1426 (Enemy Aircraft) Flight, and attached to 12 Group Fighter Command, the irreverently nicknamed 'Rafwaffe' was formed on 21 November 1941 and was based at Duxford in Cambridgeshire. Its first German prize was a Heinkel He 111H which had been shot down in Scotland in February the previous year. This was soon followed by a Junkers Ju 88A-5 that had force-landed at Chivenor, in Devon, and a Messerschmitt Bf 109E-3 which was already undergoing evaluation at the Fighting Development Unit (AFDU) at Duxford.

Flying an aircraft which might easily be mistaken for the enemy was potentially a risky business, and for most of the time the AEC 'circus' aircraft wore very clear British markings. For certain special assignments, such as filming work for the RAF Film Unit or for photographic sessions, they sometimes appeared in their original German colours. In March 1943 the unit moved to a new home at RAF Collyweston, near Wittering. The main part of its duties was presenting the aircraft at various RAF airfields, and from early 1944 the Enemy Aircraft Flight also toured USAAF bases in the UK. Tragedy struck in November 1943, however, when seven people on board the Heinkel He 111 were killed as the pilot tried to avoid a Ju 88 coming in to land on the same runway at Polebrook in Northamptonshire.

Following the D-Day landings in June 1944 the number of enemy aircraft coming into Allied hands grew rapidly, but conversely by the end of the year the familiarisation displays by the Enemy Aircraft Flight were no longer deemed necessary. The unit was

'711' was an Me 262A-1a surrendered at Frankfurt in March 1945 and taken to the USA for flight testing at Wright Field. *(USAF)*

disbanded on 31 January 1945 and the serviceable aircraft were transferred to the Central Flying Establishment at Tangmere in West Sussex.

As for the German jets, it was only after D-Day that the advancing Allied forces came across examples of the greatest prizes; the Messerschmitt Me 262, Arado Ar 234 and the little single-engined Heinkel He 162 *Volksjäger*. With the exception of some Ar 234B reconnaissance flights in late 1944 and early 1945, none of these types had ever ventured beyond the continental mainland to fly above English soil.

The first example of an Ar 234 was obtained in February 1945 when an American P-47 Thunderbolt encountered one limping along on a single engine following a flame-out, and forced it down to make a belly-landing, but still virtually intact. This was near Selgersdorf, to the west of Cologne and very close to the advancing Allied lines. The following day the 9th US Army captured the area and despite efforts by the German artillery to destroy the aircraft through heavy shelling it was successfully recovered and subsequently dismantled for transportation to RAE Farnborough. Although non-airworthy, this Ar 234 was the first complete German jet to be examined by the British.

With an end to the war in sight, in 1944 the Air Ministry's Branch AI2 (g), in consultation with the Ministry of Aircraft Production, drew up a Requirements List of the German aircraft that were of particular interest. This shopping list of aeronautical wonders was put in the hands of the Air Technical Intelligence teams working in Europe who were tasked with securing the aircraft during the Allied advance and in the immediate aftermath of the German surrender. Once an aircraft had been secured –

vandalism or accidental damage remained a possibility if they were left unprotected – the job of ferrying them back to England became the responsibility of a team of test pilots from the Aerodynamics Flight at the RAE, headed by the German-speaking Captain Eric 'Winkle' Brown. The airfield at Schleswig in northern Germany was selected as the main collecting point because it was well placed within the British zone and close to the area on the eastern side of the territory which had been allocated to the Russians but not immediately occupied by the Red Army. No. 409 Repair and Salvage Unit was set up at Schleswig, manned by RAF technicians and mechanics, and a ferry route to England was established with staging posts for refuelling at three airfields en route: Twente, Gilze-Rijen and Brussels-Melsbroek.

On 19 May 1945 an Me 262B (allocated the Air Ministry number AM 50) became the first of the German jets to fly into RAE Farnborough, having stopped on the way at Gilze-Rijen. The first of the airworthy Arado Ar 234s arrived at Farnborough on 9 July, having flown from Stavanger airfield in Norway, with a refuelling stop at Schleswig. The British pilots marvelled at its futuristic curves and the smooth finish, but flying these unfamiliar German jets back to England was fraught with risk, especially as they had invariably been found without any supporting maintenance records for either airframes or engines. The ferry pilots had no way of knowing if the turbojets were near to the end of their twenty-five hours of flight time, or past the ten-hourly inspection for that matter. Engine failure could be catastrophic in itself, and aborting mid-flight meant finding an airfield with a longer than usual runway. Two types of German aircraft not flown back were the He 162 and the rocket-powered Me 163B, which, because of obvious safety/serviceability concerns, were dismantled and transported by surface vessel and then road, or flown back on board one of the Avro Yorks of RAF Transport Command.

With RAF roundels painted over the German markings on 'Red 8', a two-seater 'Nachtjäger', or night-fighter, equipped with radar antennae. *(NARA)*

By the time the gathering of the aircraft was completed, in January 1946, around seventy-five German aircraft had been flown back to Farnborough, and another fifty or so were shipped or transported by air, including no fewer than twenty-three Me 163Bs and eleven He 162s. When they arrived at Farnborough the aircraft were placed in a pool and some were taken to the No.6 Maintenance Unit at Brize Norton, near Oxford, to be stored until selected either for testing or for exhibition.

There was a lot of interest in the captured aircraft, especially the jets, and from 16–22 September 1945 the British public were treated to their first close-up look when some examples were exhibited in a static display of enemy aircraft held on Hyde Park to coincide with London's Thanksgiving Week. Several aeroplanes from the Enemy Aircraft Flight's collection at Duxford were there including the He 162 and Me 163B, as well as other more conventional craft. *Flight* reported at the time:

> Seven aircraft are on view, among them the Heinkel 162A 'Volksjäger', and Londoners will be interested to see that this aircraft has a remarkable resemblance to the doodlebug flying bomb, this being due chiefly to the mounting of the power unit above the fuselage immediately aft of the cockpit.

This comparison was hardly accurate or relevant as the two flying machines actually had very little in common, especially as the unmanned V-1 was powered by a pulsejet while the He 162's engine was the BMW 109-003 turbojet. But it was the first time that the public, or the journalists for that matter, had had a chance to compare them at close hand. Among the more conventional exhibits on show were a Focke-Wulf 190A, a Fieseler 156 *Storch* light aircraft, a Messerschmitt Bf 108B *Taifun* which was a single-engine four-seater transport aircraft, plus the two largest aircraft, a Junkers Ju 88 and Messerschmitt Me 110G. For the purpose of the display those aircraft which had already been painted with RAF markings were restored to their Luftwaffe markings.

Arado Ar 234 in British markings.

Another Ar 234, this time with American markings. *(SDASM)*

The Hyde Park aircraft also formed part of a more extensive Enemy Aircraft Exhibition held at RAE Farnborough from 29 October through to 9 November 1945. The range of types on display was far broader than the limited number shown in London and this time the public were able to get right up close to the exhibits. The piston-powered aircraft included: Junkers Ju 88G, Ju 188 L, Ju 290A, Ju 52 transport aircraft, Ju 352; Focke-Wulf Fw 189A, Fw 190D (a shot-down example shown in derelict condition), Fw 190F, Fw 200C four-engined transport aircraft; a Mistel composite with the Fw 190A mounted on the back of the Ju 88A; a Dornier Do 217M; Siebel Si 204D; Messerschmitt Bf 108B, Bf 109G, Me 410B, Bf 110G; Dornier Do 335A; Tank Ta 152H; Fieseler Fi 156C; Heinkel 111H (a late comer to the show) and the Fieseler Fi 103/V-1 'Doodlebug'. Not forgetting the jet-set, there were two Arado Ar 234Bs and a Messerschmitt Me 262A, not including the flown aircraft mentioned later. If that wasn't enough exotic technology, an exhibition inside the shed included other aircraft in an assorted state of assembly including a Bf 109G, Fw 190A, Ju 88G-6, Focke Achgelis Fa 330 – a prototype for a lightweight helicopter/autogiro designed to be flown tethered from a U-boat – two He 162s (one partly sectioned), an Me 163B, the Horten Ho IV tail-less glider and a conventional Bv 155B glider.

During the exhibition several flying displays of the German aircraft were presented, flown by Captain Eric Brown's staff, and on the opening day two He 162s and an Me 262 roared above the airfield to dazzle the crowds. The main flying show was at the weekend, and on Sunday 4 November no fewer than ten German aircraft took to the sky including a Dornier Do 217, Focke-Wulf 190A, Büker Bu 181, Messerschmitt Bf 108, Junkers Ju 52 transport aircraft, Fieseler Fi 156C, Junkers Ju 88, the two He 162s and the Me 262. Not surprisingly the jets stole the show, described by the *Flight* reporter their performance was 'somewhat frightening':

Though lethal in appearance, the tiny 162, with a span of only 23.5ft, is, one gathers, quite a nice aircraft. It arrived at the far end of the very long runway with assistants at the wing tips and ran very nearly the whole length before becoming unsatisfactorily airborne.

Me 262A-1a, 'FE110'. The 'FE' markings were applied by the USAF on captured enemy aircraft after their arrival in the USA. *(USAF)*

Suggesting that the He 162 might benefit from some of RATO assistance, he was more appreciative of the Me 262 which he described as almost conventional in appearance:

> The pilot was seemingly very happy about it since his arrival after the demonstration was almost dashing for such a type. Evidently it has very good aileron control at even high speeds, and the demonstrated rate of roll was almost 'flick' in its violence.

But were the British pilots becoming over-confident with their captured jets? Tragedy struck on the final day of the show, Friday 9 November 1945. Flight Lieutenant Robert Marks, a former prisoner of war in Germany, was putting on a display of the He 162's aerobatic qualities when the rudder tore away and the aircraft tumbled from 800ft (244m) to plunge into the adjoining Aldershot Barracks where both Marks and a soldier were killed.

Public displays aside, the serious business of evaluating the aircraft began with a detailed engineering assessment followed by a limited flight test programme carried out by the Aerodynamics Flight. It concentrated mainly on the jets and only a handful of the piston-engined craft were ever flown for this purpose. Some of the more ordinary aircraft, such as the Ju 52 and the big Ju 352, were put to good practical use as transports, while some smaller ones such as the Fieseler *Storch* were utilised for personnel transportation. The test flying continued without major incident until 18 January 1946 when the double-engined Dornier Do 335A (Air Ministry AM 223) caught fire on take-off and crashed, killing the pilot. After that there were greater restrictions on flying the German aircraft, although some extended aerodynamic testing of the tail-less types – the Me 163b and Horten IV glider – continued until 1948 when an Me 163B was damaged beyond repair in a high-speed skid landing at RAF Wittering.

At one stage immediately after the end of the war the Ministry of Aircraft Production considered an extraordinary plan which involved constructing or completing eighteen experimental aircraft types for which only parts or drawings had been recovered in Germany. These included the Bachem *Natter*, the Horten Ho 229, the Ju 287 forward-swept bomber, the Ju 248 which was a development of the Me 163, the P.1101 seen by Fedden at Oberammergau, the Do 335 with a turbojet instead of the rear piston engine and known as the Dornier/Heinkel He 535, the Me 264, an Hs 132 jet dive-bomber, Junkers EF 126 pulse-jet fighter, Fi 103 with turbojet, and even a double-hulled version of the Do 335. In the event it was probably just as well that the idea was abandoned because of a lack of funds.

Once evaluation of the German aircraft had been completed there remained the question of what to do with them all. In the foreword to Phil Butler's *War Prizes*, Captain Eric 'Winkle' Brown recalls that there was very little sense of their historical importance at the time:

> Destruction rather than preservation was the order of the day, for everyone was fed up to the teeth with the war and all the attendant paraphernalia.

Many of the British-held aircraft were scrapped or simply left to rot, while other airframes were donated to various educational establishments as teaching aids. A good number did eventually end up in public collections and the aviation museums of the UK contain three Me 163Bs – at RAF Cosford, the National Museum of Flight in Scotland, and at the Science Museum in London – a couple of He 162s at the Imperial War Museum in London and the RAF Museum Hendon, and a solitary Me 262 currently resides at Hendon. (Incidentally, the RAF Museum at Cosford also has the most comprehensive collection of German guided missiles and rockets that you will find anywhere in the world.) The British were very generous in giving aircraft to the Empire/Commonwealth countries and examples of the Me 163B were sent to Canada and Me 262s went to Australia and South Africa. The South African National Museum of Military History, located in Johannesburg, has the only surviving example of the two-seater and radar-equipped Me 262 B-1a/U1

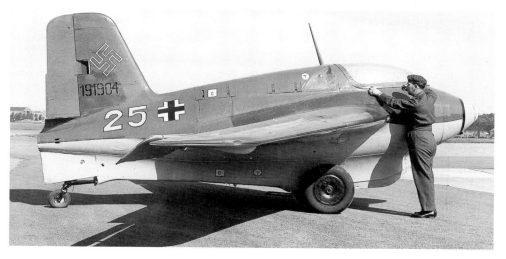

Me 163B Komet at an RAF airfield the UK.

night-fighter complete with Hirschgeweih stag's antler antennae. Unfortunately, however, the British didn't manage to hang on to a single example of the sleek Arado Ar 234 and you will have to travel to the Smithsonian National Air and Space Museum in Washington D.C. to see the only one left in the world.

THE AMERICANS

The Americans had a far more robust attitude to gathering the aeronautical gems scattered about Germany. In April 1945 the US Army Air Force Intelligence Service relaunched its wartime intelligence gathering for post-hostility activities under the codename Operation Lusty. There were several objectives to this operation: gathering technical or scientific reports and examining the research facilities in Germany, and the collection of aircraft and equipment. It is said that at the height of their activities the ATI teams were in competition with no fewer than thirty-two Allied technical intelligence teams in Germany and they would cross paths with the British Fedden Mission on several occasions. (The location and contentious 'recruitment' of German scientists and engineers was not a part of Lusty and came under the auspices of the Office of Strategic Services' Operation Paperclip, which is covered in Chapter 12.)

Leading the American Air Technical Intelligence effort was a Wright Field test pilot named Colonel Harold 'Hal' E. Watson. Equipped with a list of target aircraft, he divided his team into two. One searched for conventional aircraft while the other went after the

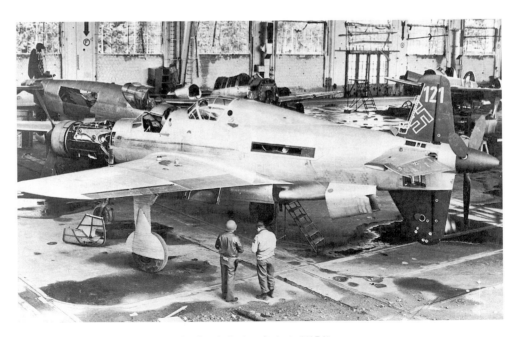

Do 335 examined by Allied personnel at Dornier's aircraft plant. *(NARA)*

jets. Intelligence reports indicated that these were to be found at Lager-Lechfeld to the south of Augsburg, Bavaria, and this was in fact the main airfield used by Messerschmitt. Watson immediately assigned Lieutenant Robert C. Strobell to head down to Lechfeld in order to get the jets into an airworthy condition, teach the US pilots how to fly them and the mechanics how to maintain the aircraft in preparation for their shipment back to the United States.

Arriving at Lechfeld at the end of May 1945, Strobell discovered that the airfield and most of its precious jets had been badly damaged; the former by aerial bombardment and the latter intentionally by the retreating Germans in a bid to keep their technology out of enemy hands. American soldiers from the 54th Disarmament Squadron had arrived a few weeks earlier and safeguarded as many aircraft as possible as well as gathering together members of the former Me 262 workforce to assist them. Pressed into service as civilian employees the Germans took great pride in their jets and proved to be willing and cooperative with the Americans. Strobell's team soon came up to full strength with six USAAF pilots, ten crew chiefs, plus the German nationals. He also succeeded in recruiting two former Messerschmitt test pilots, Ludwig Hofmann and Karl Bauer.

Of the airworthy Me 262s at Lechfeld, most were cobbled together from various engines and other components salvaged on the site, although at least two examples had been surrendered elsewhere and flown to the airfield intact. In addition there was a two-seater training aircraft still in good condition. In total, ten aircraft were readied for flight, but questions remained concerning who was to fly them as the Americans obviously had no previous experience with jets. In a ploy to deter any attempts at sabotage Strobell invited Bauer to make the first flight in an Me 262, which lasted around fifteen minutes, before he took his turn. Strobell found that the aircraft's slow rate of acceleration during the take-off run meant he almost ran out of runway before coaxing the jet off the ground. But once airborne the American pilot soon discovered for himself the sheer joy of jet propulsion:

> The next thing I noticed was the speed. Raw speed, exhilarating speed. Smooth speed. Unbelievable speed. It seemed effortless ...

With such an abundance of speed getting this bird back on to the runway required a little practice and on the first approach he shot right past the airfield. The second approach was little better and on the third he finally succeeded.

Once the USAAF pilots, including Watson, had been given orientation flights in the two-seater trainer the task of ferrying the aircraft began in earnest on 10 June 1945. The plan was to take them cross-country in two stages to Melun in France and then on to the port of Cherbourg where the Royal Navy escort carrier HMS *Reaper* – a former US Navy vessel on loan to the British – had been made available for their transportation to the USA. With the two German pilots making up the numbers all of the aircraft reached Melun without incident.

Among the American pilots there was a great sense of adventure in flying the jets and it didn't take long for America's first jet-fighter squadron to acquire its unofficial title of 'Watson's Whizzers'. The aircraft were christened with new nicknames daubed on their noses by mechanics of the 54th Air Disarmament Squadron and later amended and personalised by the individual pilots. These were either girl and family names, such as Wilma Jeanne and Vera, or more colourful tags including Screamin' Meemie, Jabo Bait, Happy Hunter II and Feudin' 54th. An impromptu squadron badge was produced depicting Donald Duck riding around the globe clinging to a jet engine. And, in recognition of their unusual status as jet-jockeys, it became customary for each newly rated pilot to have his metal USAAF badge removed and the propeller blades ceremoniously snapped off.

During their brief stay at the Melun airfield Watson's team put on a display for General Carl Spaatz. They also had time to investigate reports of additional Me 262s which had been recovered at other airfields. At the British-held Schleswig airfield they obtained an Me 262 two-seater trainer plus an Me 262B-1a/U1 night-fighter, and at Grove they located examples of the Arado Ar 234 twin-jet powered bomber, all of which were added to the hoard.

The next leg, to take the aircraft to Cherbourg, was conducted between 30 June and 6 July. One of the first to depart from Melun was V083, the prototype Me 262A-1a/U4 armed with a 50mm MK 214 tank-busting cannon, but when one of the Jumo 109-004 engine began spitting out turbine blades the aircraft was sent into a steep dive and the pilot, Ludwig Hofmann, was only thrown clear at low altitude. In another incident Lieutenant Robert J. Anspach descended through thick cloud in his Me 262 expecting to see Cherbourg but instead found himself over water. With fuel precariously low he barely managed to make an emergency landing on the island of Jersey. On a second ferry flight the unlucky Anspach experienced a dramatic landing at Cherbourg after the jet's nose-wheel failed to lower.

Forty German aircraft of all types were crowded onto the *Reaper*'s deck, each one wrapped in plastic film to protect it from the salty sea water. As was to be expected the list included several jets: there were ten Me 262s including an Me 262B-1a/U1 a night-fighter converted from a two-seater trainer, and four Arado Ar 234Bs. The array of piston-power included two Dornier Do 335 push-pull heavy fighters, three Messerschmitt Bf 109G fighters, nine Focke-Wulf 190D/F fighters and one Focke-Wulf Ta 152H-0 high-altitude fighter, three Heinkel He 219 night-fighters, a Junkers Ju 388 high-altitude reconnaissance bomber and a Ju 88G-6 night-fighter, plus several light aircraft including two Bücker Bü 181 single-engined trainers and a Messerschmitt Bf 108 *Taifun*. There were also three rotor-craft including the experimental Doblhoff WNF-342 with fin-tip mounted jets, plus two small Flettner 282 Kolibri helicopters. And, finally, there was one non-German interloper, a Mustang P-51 reconnaissance aircraft.

HMS *Reaper* set sail from Cherbourg on 20 July 1945 and arrived at Newark, New Jersey, eleven days later. Not content with his ship-bound hoard, Watson set off from Paris-Orly to fly across the Atlantic in a four-engined Junkers Ju 290 long-range heavy bomber/patrol/transport aircraft. With intermediate stops in the Azores, Bermuda and Patterson Field the aircraft finally reached Freeman Field the day after the *Reaper* docked in New Jersey. The Americans divided their German war prizes between the USAF and

Preserved He 162 at the Royal Air Force Museum, Hendon. *(JC)*

the US Navy. Those allocated to the air force were taken to Wright Field initially and many were then sent on to Freeman Field which acted as a subsidiary airfield to Wright and had been designated as the Foreign Aircraft Evaluation Center. Test flights of the German aircraft were conducted from both airfields. Apart from the technical value of the German aircraft, General Arnold, unlike his British counterparts, did recognise their historical significance and he ordered the preservation of at least one of every type of aircraft. It is only thanks to this measure that examples of the Ar 234, the He 219 and the Do 335 have survived at all.

In addition to the US military, some testing was done by other government organisations as well as by various aircraft companies. For example, the Me 262A-1a/U3 found by the Whizzers at Lager-Lechfeld and christened as 'Connie – My Sharp Article' and later changed to 'Pick II', was loaned to the Hughes Aircraft Division. Howard Hughes was a keen aviator and actually planned to enter the aircraft in air race competitions. During its time at Freeman Field it was given an extra smooth finish and in May 1946 its performance was put to the test in a direct comparison with a Lockheed P–80.

The Lippisch-designed DM–1, the delta-wing test glider for the ramjet-powered LP–13a super fast interceptor, was tested in the Langley wind tunnel by the National Advisory Council for Aeronautics (NACA – the predecessor to NASA) and influenced the development of the Convair XP–92. In a similar manner the Messerschmitt P.1101 found at Oberammergau was crated up and after evaluation at Wright Field in 1948 it was handed over to Bell Aircraft. By that time it had been fitted with an Allison J–35 engine, but sustained damage during ground handling which meant that it was never flown (see Chapter 10).

The only surviving AR 234 is at the National Air & Space Museum, USA, and is displayed with RATO units.

THE RUSSIANS

The Russians' stock of captured aircraft was far less extensive than that of the British or Americans even though the Soviet zone of occupation contained the lion's share of Germany's aviation plants, possibly more than half by all accounts, many of which were in the western side of the zone initially and had already been picked clean by the Allies before the Red Army arrived. Consequently only a handful of completed aircraft were taken back to Russia to be flown bearing the Soviet red star emblem. These included four Me 262s, three Me 163s including the two-seater trainer Me 163S, at least two He 162A-2s (possibly completed in Russia) and a single Ar 234. The Junkers Ju 287 jet bomber which featured the unusual forward-swept wing configuration was also completed and test flown in Russia (see Chapter 3). Several jets were test flown by the Russians and film footage from the period clearly shows an Me 262 taking off under jet power, and both the single-seat Me 163B and the two-seater Me 163S being flown on tow as gliders as there was no hydrogen-peroxide fuel available. One of these, the Me 163S flown by the test-pilot Mark L. Gallaj, was badly damaged on landing. In 1946 one of the Heinkel He 162s underwent flight testing at the Flight Research Institute by test-pilot G.M. Shiyanov, but apparently the Russians were dismissive of the jet's handling and the very long take-off runs.

However, the Russians did show more interest in the proposed Junkers EF 127 and the Messerschmitt Me 263 and these are said to have influenced the design of their own rocket fighter, the MiG I-270. Likewise, the Russian's Sukhoi twin-engined jet fighter closely resembled the Me 262. It first flew in November 1946 but was cancelled after only two prototypes as the aircraft's performance was disappointing in comparison with other designs.

twelve

SECRETS BY THE THOUSANDS

THE MAJORITY OF FEDDEN'S TEAM members flew back to Northolt on Sunday 1 July 1945, leaving just Stern and Flight Lieutenant Beeton still in Germany. Together with Mr Bruckmann they flew in the remaining Dakota to Salzburg in Austria, but with bad weather grounding the aircraft they were forced to continue their journey by road for the remaining 125 miles (200km) further south to Klagenfurt. On 4 July they were able to fly to Munich in order to make arrangements to conduct engine tests on BMW's high-altitude test bench and on Tuesday 17 July four members of the mission, including Fedden himself, returned to Germany for a further eight days. While in the country they also made return visits to various sites including Völkenrode, Göttingen, Stuttgart and Kochel, but it was the test bench in Munich that was of greatest interest. Codenamed Herbitus, construction had been completed in May 1944 but because of the Allied bombing raids it hadn't become operational until October that year. From then until the fall of Germany the Herbitus plant had mostly been employed on calibration tests for the BMW and Jumo jet engines, as well as some initial high-altitude trials on the BMW 801 piston engine. The man responsible for the design and direction of Herbitus was Christoph Soestmeyer who had been engaged on engine test plant design for a number of years. He informed the Fedden team that the RLM had also planned for four similar high-capacity test plants at Rechlin, Berlin, Stuttgart and Dessau.

At BMW's works in Munich the Herbitus plant was located in a separate building roughly 250ft (76m) square and 70ft (21m) high. At its heart was the altitude chamber, a steel cylinder about 12ft (3.6m) in diameter and 30ft (9m) long. Its rear end was detachable, allowing for engine units under test to be wheeled in and out on a trolley. A special cylindrical nose piece was positioned over the engine's air intake nozzle and a complicated system of pumps and cooling units created the air density and temperature conditions corresponding to those encountered in flight at any altitude up to 36,000ft (11,000m) and wind speeds up to 560mph (900km/h). Additional systems maintained engine temperature and ventilation, and dealt with the engine exhaust. Fedden reports that the plant was surprisingly quiet in operation and, thanks to the automatic control system developed by Siemens, easy to operate:

> The Herbitus plant is quite unique and has possibilities far in advance of any engine testing plant in England or America. It is the only test bench of sufficiently large capacity to test existing jet engines under altitude conditions.

During their initial visit to BMW Munich in June the Fedden Mission witnessed and participated in tests with the BMW 003/A1 which was the only German turbojet available for testing at the time. This engine had already undergone a series of fifty-four calibration runs, totalling about thirty hours, under the direction of the American authorities. A further set of nine calibration runs were carried out by the British team on 19 July, but the state of the BMW engine was such that it was not considered safe to run it for any length of time. With the Americans anxious to ship the jet engine back to the USA in running order, the subsequent tests carried out by the Mission were limited to thrusts of 200 to 500lb (90 to 227kg) and three of the runs were limited to below 100lb (45kg) thrust. As Fedden ruefully commented, they were in the nature of nothing more than token runs to demonstrate the working of the test bed. Undaunted, he managed to arrange with the Americans a loan of the Herbitus plant and the main purpose of the Mission's supplementary trip was to test two British jet engines, the Rolls-Royce Derwent V and a de Havilland Goblin, under high-altitude conditions.

Fedden lodged a strong recommendation with his bosses at the Ministry of Aircraft Production that arrangements should be made with the Americans for the transfer of the Herbitus plant to England at the end of the year, but without any success. Munich

Hermann Göring, the head of the Luftwaffe, is surrounded by reporters shortly after his capture on 6 May 1945. *(NARA)*

was within the American Control Zone and the plant was subsequently moved to the USA where, Fedden later observed, it was the model for the manufacture of larger high-altitude test equipment. In his opinion this 'undoubtedly played a major part in America's post-war gas-turbine development'.

Among the German equipment that the Fedden Mission brought back to England was an array of jet engines and rocket motors, various components including turbine blades plus a large quantity of drawings and documents. The main items were put on display at the offices of the Ministry of Aircraft Production and politicians as well as major figures within the aircraft industry were invited to inspect this storehouse of aeronautical riches. With the notable exceptions of Sir Stafford Cripps and Winston Churchill, most visitors to Stratton Street were determinedly unimpressed by what they saw. Fedden later wrote about their reactions:

> Many senior authorities came to look at this exhibition, but my colleagues and myself, who had had a stimulating and exciting time collecting all these exhibits together, were shocked by the lack of enthusiasm. 'What are you so excited about? We've won the war, haven't we?' was the general attitude.

With an end to the war the new era of peace brought many sudden and sometimes unexpected changes to the political landscape, not just in mainland Europe but also closer to home. Sir Stafford Cripps resigned from MAP at the end of May 1945 (just before the Fedden Mission left for Germany) to concentrate on the forthcoming general election and MAP itself wasn't to survive for much longer anyway. In August 1945 a minister was appointed with responsibility for both aircraft production as well as the Ministry of Supply, and by April the following year the MAP was fully merged into the new joint ministry.

To some extent the departure of Stafford Cripps might be seen as having robbed Fedden of the official support he had been receiving. Indeed, the justification of the entire mission to Germany may have been questioned in certain official circles. Having said that, Fedden still had the personal support of Stafford Cripps who took up a new post in Clement Attlee's government following the Labour party's surprise victory in the elections. Cripps was appointed as President of the Board of Trade. A staunch socialist and Marxist, he had previously been Churchill's Ambassador to the Soviet Union, from 1940 until he moved to the MAP in 1942. In this capacity he had played a key role in persuading Joseph Stalin to abandon his alliance with Nazi Germany and to enter the war on the British side. At one time there had even been suggestions that Stafford Cripps might succeed Churchill as prime minister once the war was over. Incidentally, in 1946 it was Cripps and the Labour government that agreed to hand over technical information on the Rolls-Royce Nene jet engine to the Soviets. Designed by Frank Whittle, in the hands of the Soviet engineers the engine was reproduced, albeit in a modified form, as the Klimov VK-1 engine used in the MiG-15 in the Korean conflict which started in 1950.

The political changes unfolding in Germany and Eastern Europe had even greater repercussions. Within days of the conclusion of the main part of the Fedden Mission to Germany, the Russians occupied the parts of their control zone previously held by the Americans and British. These included a number of key aircraft and jet engine facilities as well as the notorious Mittelwerk underground rocket factory at Nordhausen. While in the region Fedden had been acutely aware of the need for haste in advance of the approaching red tide:

> Our visits to various establishments at Dessau, Magdeburg, Stassfurt, Nordhausen and Eisenach had to be curtailed so that we should be away before the Russian troops arrived. Many other targets on our itinerary had to be abandoned as the Russians had taken over and no facilities were available for the British investigators.

The implementation of the changes to the Allied Control Zones was part of the process instigated at the Yalta Conference in February 1944, and ratified at the immediate post-war gathering of the 'Big Three' at the Potsdam Conference which began on 17 July 1945. This was at the epicentre of change on an unprecedented scale. Not only was the Europe that emerged from the Second World War deeply scarred by events, it was also divided

The Nazis on trial at Nuremberg. Sentenced to death, Göring evaded the hangman's noose by swallowing a concealed cyanide capsule. *(NARA)*

At the Potsdam Conference in July 1945 Clement Atlee replaced Churchill following a shock defeat at the hands of the British electorate, President Truman took Roosevelt's place following his sudden death, leaving only Joseph Stalin still in power. *(LoC)*

and forever transformed; not least by the influence of the weaponry and technology that came out of the ruins of Nazi Germany. In terms of industrial and military might the USA emerged as the most powerful nation in the history of the planet. The Russians, who had suffered hardship and loss of life on an almost industrial scale, regarded the west with renewed suspicion and insecurity. The result was a new arms race and fortunately for the Soviet Union it benefited more than any other nation from the influx of captured German hardware and expertise. Previously their aircraft had lagged behind those of the west; now they quickly caught up and the Soviet's jet fighters and nuclear arsenal would were soon on a par with those of its new enemies.

Aside from the redistribution of Germany's territories, the Allied leaders meeting at Potsdam also had to come to an agreement on how to proceed with the prosecution of Nazi war criminals. The leading figures in the Nazi party, or at least those who had not evaded capture, were put on trial at the Nüremburg trials which began in November 1945. Several of the accused had been important players in the story of Germany's aircraft and weapons programme. The first and most important of these was the former head of the Luftwaffe, Hermann Göring, who was subsequently found guilty of war crimes and sentenced to death. He managed to cheat the gallows by swallowing a concealed cyanide capsule in his prison cell on 15 October 1946. Albert Speer, Hitler's minister of armaments and war production from 1942 onwards, narrowly escaped the death penalty

Britain's twin-engined wartime jet, the Gloster Meteor, never saw combat against enemy aircraft. *(NARA)*

V-2 rocket being transported by the 1st Air Disarmament Wing in Wirsberg. *(NARA)*

and was instead sentenced to twenty years' imprisonment. After displaying his contrition at the tribunal Speer was often referred to as the Nazi who said sorry, and it was Speer who had countermanded the Führer's most excessive orders in the face of Germany's defeat. In mitigation the court's judgement stated that:

> … in the closing stages of the war [Speer] was one of the few men who had the courage to tell Hitler that the war was lost and to take steps to prevent the senseless destruction of production facilities, both in occupied territories and in Germany. He carried out his opposition to Hitler's scorched earth program … by deliberately sabotaging it at considerable personal risk.

Erhard Milch, the man who had overseen the development of the Luftwaffe and had been the founder director of Deutsche Luft Hansa, was convicted on two counts of crimes against humanity in connection with the ill-treatment and death of enforced labour and prisoners of war, and sentenced to life imprisonment; later commuted to fifteen years. Milch had shown Fedden around the various German aircraft establishments just before the outbreak of the war. Among the prominent aeronautical industrialists, Ernst Heinkel and Willy Messerschmitt were both charged with using slave labour in their factories. While Heinkel was acquitted, because of evidence outlining his anti-Hitler activities, Messerschmitt was found guilty by the tribunal and served two years in prison. Two notable absentees from the courtrooms were the rocketmen Wernher von Braun and Arthur Rudolph. Many believe that they should have faced justice because of their implicit involvement in the appalling treatment of the slave workers at the Mittelwerk underground weapons factory at Nordhausen.

THE NUCLEAR AGE

Following the terrible destruction unleashed during the war, with the coming of peace the world suddenly found itself on the brink of self-destruction. On 16 July 1945, the day before Fedden's return to Germany for the second leg of his mission, the first full-scale test of a nuclear device, codename Trinity, took place at Alamogordo Bombing and Gunnery Range near Los Alamos, New Mexico. At precisely 5.30 a.m. the world entered the nuclear age as the equivalent of around 20 kilotons of TNT sent a boiling mushroom

Jumo 004 scrutinised at the US Aircraft Research Laboratory of the National Advisory Committee for Aeronautics in 1946. *(Nasa)*

cloud towering 7.5 miles (12.1km) above the New Mexico desert. J. Robert Oppenheimer, scientific director of the USA's Manhattan Project to develop the atomic bomb, uttered these words from the Bhagavad Gita:

> If the radiance of a thousand suns were to burst at once into the sky, that would be like the splendour of the mighty one. Now I am become Death, destroyer of worlds.

Ten days later, on 26 July 1945, the Potsdam Declaration issued the terms for the unconditional surrender of Japan. (The declaration was not signed by Josef Stalin as the Soviet Union was not at war with Japan.) The ultimatum stated that if the Japanese did not surrender they would suffer 'prompt and utter destruction'. In response the Japanese rejection was couched in terms of '*Mokusatsu*', a policy meaning to ignore or treat with silent contempt. On 6 August the Little Boy atomic bomb was dropped on the Japanese city of Hiroshima, and three days later, on 9 August, Fat Man fell on Nagasaki. The extent and scale of the death and devastation was staggering, almost beyond comprehension, and on 15 August 1945 (Japanese time) Emperor Hirohito announced the acceptance of the terms of surrender. The official ceremony took place on 2 September and this date marks VJ-Day and the end of the Second World War. The war of science and technology.

PROFITS AND LOSSES

How do you draw up a balance sheet for an event as widespread as a world war? The cost in terms of the loss of life and the destruction of property was self-evident. But what of the other side of the balance sheet; who benefited most from Germany's defeat and the looting of its technology? The author of a news report published in the *Daily Express* on 9 October 1946 attempted to provide an answer:

Taken to the USA under Operation Paperclip, a group of 104 German rocket scientists, including von Braun and Arthur Rudolph, photographed at Fort Bliss, Texas

When all profits and losses of victory, and of the occupation of Germany, come to be weighed up there is one item which will deny an estimate. That is knowledge. The secrets of German industry and science. I put it at £100,000,000.

The amount of loot, in terms of war prizes, was immense. The US 9th Air Force Service Command's *Record of Accomplishment of Air Disarmament* confirmed that almost 2,000 tons of secret German air force equipment had been shipped to the USA, including the V-1 and V-2 missiles, the jet and rocket aircraft, as well as more exotic items such as the Horten flying wings. It stated:

> These and other similar items returned for study are contributing greatly to the advancement of Air Force research in new and improved aircraft for civilian and military uses as well as other weapons of war.

Fedden, on the other hand, was of no doubt that Britain had failed to get its fair share of the booty. While he was in Germany he had seen the Americans removing 'drawings, reports, test records, and experimental prototypes by the truckload'.

Quantifying the amount of material removed from Germany can be difficult depending on the category. This was not the case with the aircraft, however. Taking into account a degree of inaccuracy due to duplication of data, misidentification or examples spirited away covertly, it is possible to deduce the following approximate figures for the jet and rocket aircraft: at least twenty-four Messerschmitt Me 262s, fourteen Arado Ar 234s, thirteen Heinkel He 162s and almost thirty of the rocket-powered Messerschmitt Me 163Bs. Then there were the various experimental aircraft such as the Lippisch Darmstadt-München DM-1 delta wing, two Dornier Do 335s, the Horten Ho II, IV and 229V-3 (Go 229V-3) flying wings, the Junkers Ju 287 bomber with forward-swept wings and the Messerschmitt Me P.1101 from Oberammergau (Chapter 11 provides more detail).

There were the missiles and the rockets. Starting with the V-1 flying-bomb: France, the Soviet Union and the USA all continued with the development and testing of the V-1 and derivatives after the war. The French produced their own version for use as target drones. Known as the CT-10, this was a little smaller than the V-1, had twin tails and could be either ground-launched by means of a rocket booster, or air-launched from an aircraft.

The Russians captured a number of V-1s, mostly from the Blizna test range in Poland, but also a quantity of missiles found in various stages of completion at the Mittelwerk. From these they produced the Izdeliye 10 and testing began as early as March 1945 at a firing range in Tashkent. The Russians also continued development of the pulsejet-powered Junkers EF 126 Lilli manned aircraft, but abandoned the concept in 1946 after a test pilot was killed in a crash.

The Americans had reverse-engineered the V-1 from parts recovered in England since the summer of 1944. Thirteen prototypes of the Republic-Ford JB-2 Loons were completed; these closely resembled the V-2 although were slightly longer.

Walt and Wernher, an unlikely pairing. In 1959 von Braun took part in a Walt Disney film entitled *Man in Space*. *(Nasa)*

A naval version, known as the KGW-1, was also produced. The intention was to use the missiles in the anticipated Allied invasion of Japan, which obviously became unnecessary following the dropping of the atomic bombs. The KGW-1 was test launched from the American submarine USS *Cusak* in 1951 and both versions of the missile influenced the development of later surface-to-surface missile systems.

The big prize was Germany's Aggregate family of rocket designs, the V-2 (A4) in particular as these offered the potential to deliver an atomic payload to a far distant enemy. The first post-war tests were conducted within Germany. In October 1945, the British Operation Backfire saw the test launch of three, possibly four, V-2s from a site at Arensch near Cuxhaven in the north of the country. This was done with assistance of the German technicians.

The Russians also conducted test firings in Germany before transferring their rocket research programme to Kapstun Yar in the Soviet Union in 1946. This was part of their Operation Osoaviakhim which also saw the transference of personnel, as discussed later. The Soviets first missile, the R-1, was a clone of the V-2, but it also led to the development of the larger R-2 and R-5 rockets. There are suggestions that some test launches may have taken place at Peenemünde, giving rise to a number of sightings of 'ghost' rockets over Sweden and Finland at the time.

It was the Americans who grabbed the lion's share of the V-2s. Around 300 rail-car loads of complete missiles and parts were shipped to the USA. Between April 1946 and September 1952 sixty-seven V-2s were launched from the White Sands Proving Ground,

New Mexico, and two from the Joint Long Range Proving Grounds, better known as Cape Canaveral, in Florida. The US Navy attempted launches at sea from the aircraft carrier USS *Midway* in September 1947.

Then there was the value of the intellectual material. An article published in *Harper's Magazine* in October 1946 openly refers to the 'mountain' of documents involved. In *Secrets by the Thousands*, journalist C. Lester Walker explained that the 'captured' material was being handled at three main locations; Wright Field in Ohio, the Library of Congress and by the Department of Commerce:

> Wright Field is working on the mother lode of fifteen hundred tons. In Washington, the Office of Technical Services (which has absorbed the Office of the Publication Board, the government agency originally set up to handle the collection) reports that tens of thousands of tons of material are involved. It is estimated that over a million separate items must be handled, and that they, very likely, contain practically all the scientific, industrial and military secrets of Germany. One Washington official has called it the greatest single source of this type of material in the world, the first orderly exploitation of an entire country's brainpower.

Practically all the scientific, industrial and military secrets of Germany? The language of this mainstream article is staggering, almost beyond comprehension. At the time this back-door form of reparations was regarded as simply the spoils of war going to the victors; regardless of the effect on Germany's attempts to rebuild its own post-war industrial economy. In less civilised times a conquering army might pillage and loot a vanquished enemy for money or goods. Following the conclusion of the twentieth-century's most devastating conflict the greatest plunder was the enemy's secrets, not just the military ones, as you might expect, but just about every industrial or technological secret that might possibly offer commercial benefit or reward. This store-house of information covered textiles, chemicals, plastics, synthetic rubber, medicines, dyes, food, fuels, magnetic recording tape, infra-red sighting devices, miniaturised electrical vacuum tubes, you name it. Under the instruction of President Truman, the Office of Technical Services was tasked with processing the documents and, unless classified, making them available through a network of depository libraries throughout the USA. Customers queued up for the latest releases which cost just a few dollars each. Examples mentioned in the article included the Bendix company seeking the German patent on a record player changer, Pillsbury Mills wanting to study flour and bread production, Pacific Mills requesting I.G. Farbenindustrie's water-repellent crease-resistant finish for spun rayon, and the Polaroid company wishing to exploit the latest developments in German photography and optics.

Perhaps the most valuable war prize wasn't the hardware or the intellectual property; it was about the intellectuals themselves. The British, Americans and the Russians were all at it. Under a plethora of operational codenames they vied with one other to persuade the cream of Germany's scientists, engineers and technicians to come and work for them, either through persuasion or inducement. Fedden later wrote of his own frustrated efforts at recruitment:

Bell's rocket-powered X-1E being loaded under a B-50 Superfortress at Dryden Flight Research Center in 1951. *(Nasa)*

The Americans Hermes rocket programme saw continued testing of the V-2 (A4) and the A9/A4B Aggregat. *(Nasa)*

I collected a team of German jet engine specialists, who I felt would be invaluable to our country, but the delays after I had flown home to consult with the authorities about their disposition in Britain made them impatient. When I got back I found that some strings had been pulled in my absence. The German specialists had been whisked away somewhere else, and were lost to us. Only Britain of the wartime 'Big Three' victors could not be bothered to appreciate the implications of the new aeronautical technique which Germany had assimilated in such a remarkable way.

A full scale model of the Northrop MX-334 flying wing in the wind tunnel at Langley Research Center, 1943. *(Nasa)*

I think that it is safe to assume that when he says they were whisked away 'somewhere else' Fedden is referring to the USA and Soviets. Regardless of Fedden's attempts, under Operation Surgeon the British authorities had drawn up a list of 1,500 experts they proposed extracting from Germany 'whether they like it or not'. No small part of the motivation in this action was to deny their skills to the Soviet Union, but of those removed between 1946 and 1947 only around 100 chose to stay in the UK. In contrast, the Soviet policy had been more robust. In some cases entire workforces and their families had been evacuated from particular establishments and taken back to Russia. It is estimated that in October 1946 Operation Osoaviakhim saw the transportation of between 10,000 and 15,000 Germans along with their belongings. It is unlikely that they had much say in the matter, but in fairness the level of pay offered was generally not unattractive compared to the equivalent wages Soviet workers or those in Germany might earn.

The USA also had its eyes on the intellectual capital; if nothing else to deny it to the Soviets and the British. However, many Americans had qualms about dealing with individuals connected with the Nazi regime, let alone taking them back to the USA. In July 1945 the US Joint Chiefs of Staff had issued guidelines for the identification and seizing of key enemy nationals, in particular those who had worked on the V-2 rocket at the German army research centre at Peenemünde. Known as Overcast – the name was changed to Operation Paperclip in March 1946 – it was run by the Office of Strategic Services, the OSS. To circumvent President Truman's explicit instructions excluding anyone found to have been a member of the Nazi Party, or 'more than a nominal participant in its activities, or an active supporter of Nazi militarism', the Joint Intelligence Objectives Agency (JIOA) created false employment and political biographies of the scientists, and expunged the records of their Nazi party membership or affiliations. By this means hundreds of scientists arrived in the USA as 'War Department special employees'.

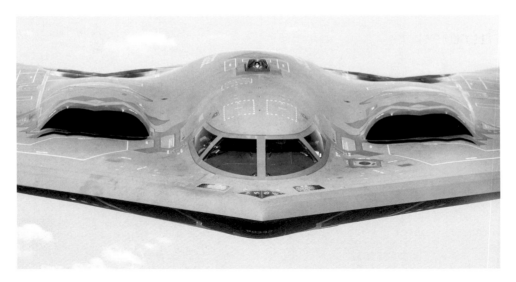

The flying wing concept lives on in the shape of the B-2 Spirit stealth bomber. *(USAF)*

Of the rocketmen among these were Wernher von Braun and Arthur Rudolph, who had been operations director in charge of V-2 production, while the aeronautical experts included several familiar names; Alexander Lippisch, Hans von Ohain, Kurt Tank and Adolf Busemann.

NASA came into existence in October 1958, and when the Marshall Space Flight Center in Huntsville opened in 1960 von Braun was appointed as the centre's first director. He went on to lead the team developing the Saturn 1B and the Saturn V rocket which sent man on the way to the moon. Whenever pressed about his wartime activities Wernher von Braun always denied any involvement in the atrocities at the Mittelwerk. He died at the age of sixty-five in June 1977. Arthur Rudolph was investigated for possible war crimes and in 1984 he agreed to leave the USA and renounce his citizenship.

Justification of the Allied plunder of Germany in the aftermath of the war was unashamed and came readily enough, as illustrated in this excerpt from the Control Commission for Germany in January 1947:

> The right of the Allies to use information collected by Allied investigating agencies is one of the consequences of Germany losing the war. The Allies are entitled to use this information as they see fit …

Regardless of the rights and wrongs of the war, there can be no doubt that the influence of the Nazis' research and technology permeates our modern world. The legacy of Hitler's X-planes – the jet, rockets and aerodynamic innovations – survives within the DNA of the aircraft and missiles of the twenty-first century.

thirteen

EPILOGUE

BY THE TIME THAT the Fedden Mission to Germany Final Report was issued in the late summer of 1945 Sir Roy Fedden had just turned sixty. The war years had seen an extraordinary upheaval in his fortunes with his abrupt departure from BAC, a knighthood for his services to aviation, and his appointment as the Special Advisor to the Air Minister. Now, with the coming of peace, he returned to the world of engineering; one which had been transformed by the technological advances and the upheavals of the Second World War. In anticipation of the war's end Roy Fedden Ltd had been formed in 1943 with his former Bristol colleague Ian Duncan taking the reigns as chief engineer, while Fedden remained occupied with his wartime work for Sir Stafford Cripps at the Ministry of Aircraft Production. Surprisingly perhaps the first project on the agenda was not an aero engine at all, but a car aimed at the post-war market, a sort of a 'British Volkswagen' in other words. And so it was by intention rather than serendipitous accident that Fedden made a little detour during his follow-up trip to Germany in the summer 1945 to observe test runs of jet engines at the BMW's Herbitus plant in Munich. On the way back to Völkenrode he took the opportunity to revisit the nearby Volkswagen works at Fallersleben − newly renamed by the occupation forces as Wolfsburg − in Niedersachsen, or Lower Saxony, in north-western Germany. Before the war General Milch had personally taken him to the plant in order to show off the new production line for the Volkswagen, the People's Car.

That Sir Roy Fedden had shown an interest in automotive design should not be all that surprising as this was the field in which he had cut his engineering teeth working for the Straker company in Bristol in the years before the First World War. And he certainly wasn't alone among a band of aero engineers who thought they could apply their talents equally successfully in this field. In Britain during the inter-war years Sir Charles Dennistoun Burney, best known for his involvement with the R100 airship, produced a design for a rear-engined streamliner. Thirteen of them were built by Streamline Cars Ltd in Maidenhead.

Likewise, over in the USA, William Bushnell Stout, designer of the famous Ford Tri-motor 'Tin Goose' and a number of Stout aircraft, came up with the Stout Scarab. This would probably be described as a minivan nowadays and just happened to be another rear-engined streamliner. In Germany Karl Schlör and the engineer Krauss Maffei had taken the rear-engine streamliner to the extreme with a slippery pod of a car known

Volkswagen's factory at Fallersleben was badly damaged by Allied air raids. *(NARA)*

as the Schlörwagen. Nicknamed the 'Egg' or 'Pillbug', it was built on the chassis of a Mercedes-Benz 170H and in pre-war wind tunnel tests conducted at the AVA Göttingen its efficient shape demonstrated an exceptionally low drag coefficient of 0.113. In 1939 the Schlörwagen was displayed at the Berlin Auto Show, as was the embryonic Volkswagen. (The fate of the Schlörwagen is unknown, although some sources suggest it may have been brought to Britain at the end of the war.)

The origins of the iconic Volkswagen Beetle, as it is now universally known, can be traced back to 1931 with Ferdinand Porsche's design for the Porsche Type 12 *Auto für Jedermann*, a 'car for everybody', which he produced for the Zündapp company. This featured the distinctive hump-backed streamlining and a rear-mounted water-cooled five-cylinder radial engine, although Porsche's own preference had been a flat-four engine. Three prototypes were produced, but all were lost in the bombing raids on Stuttgart during the war. (A replica can be seen at the Museum Industrielkultur in Nürnberg.) Porsche then began working on a similar prototype in 1933 for NSU Motorenwerke AG. Known as the Type 32, this had the flat-four engine, but when NSU decided to concentrate on its core motorcycle business the project was abandoned. Enter Adolf Hitler who, according to some sources, had produced his own sketch for a similar car while sitting in a restaurant in Munich in 1932. Hitler was a capable artist, certainly, and also a keen motoring enthusiast. However, it has been suggested that he may have stolen the general design from Josef Ganz's 'May Bug' car after seeing it at a show in 1933. Also featuring a rear-mounted engine layout the May Bug became the basis of the Standard Superior produced by Standard Fahrzeugfabrik in Ludwigsburg (not to

Der Kdf Wagen

The FDR Wagen was part of a lifestyle package the Nazis had promised to the German people, but in reality only a handful of the civilian version were produced by the outbreak of war.

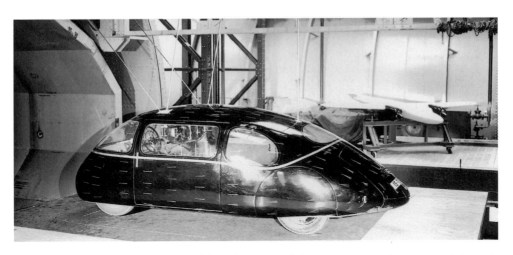

Karl Schlör's super slippery rear-engined Gebrauchswagen or Schlorwagen undergoing pre-war wind tunnel testing at AVA Göttingen. *(DLR)*

be confused with the British Standard car company) from 1933 until 1935. Another vehicle which bore more than a passing resemblance to the Hitler/Porsche design was the 1931 Tatra V570 prototype produced by the Austrian car designer Hans Ledwinka for the Czechoslovakian Tatra company. Hitler is known to have shown some interest in this car and even met with Ledwinka, and Porsche and Ledwinka regularly got together to discuss their respective designs.

The prototype Fedden 'F-car' was clunky in appearance and lacked the finesse of the VW.

Be that as it may, in 1933 it was Ferdinand Porsche who the Führer instructed to come up with a people's car capable of transporting two adults and three children at 100km/h (62mph), which should be cheap to produce and to purchase. It was to be part of the consumer lifestyle package he was promising the German people and the car would be made available for no more than the price of an average motorcycle. The latest design was designated the Porsche Type 60 and the first two prototypes were ready by late 1935. Following extensive testing with almost 100 pre-production models, the project was officially announced as the KdF-Wagen – standing for *Kraft Durch Freude* (strength through joy) – in 1938. Its main features were rear-wheel drive, a rear-mounted air-cooled four-cylinder 995cc engine, two-door bodywork with a flat windscreen and a small split oval window at the rear. Space for luggage was provided under the bonnet and also behind the rear seats. It was constructed on an almost flat chassis with a central structural tunnel, and the bodywork was attached by eighteen bolts. The engine, transmission and cylinder heads were of light alloy and an engine oil cooler ensured the optimal engine temperature. The independent suspension for each wheel was provided by means of transverse torsion bars.

To manufacture the car a new factory was constructed at Fallersleben, but this had only produced a handful of civilian versions by the outbreak of war. Apart from a small number produced for the Nazi elite, the main wartime output was for the military with the Type 82 *Kübelwagen* and its amphibious counterpart, the Type 166 *Schwimmwagen*. Car production at the Fallersleben plant was halted in early 1945 by the intensive Allied bombing and on 10 April 1945 American troops overran the town. When the Americans handed the area over to British control what remained of the plant was used by a detachment of the REME (Royal Corps of Electrical and Mechanical Engineers) to repair vehicles, both Allied and captured, and to overhaul engines.

When Fedden, together with his colleague Peter Ware, turned up in the summer of 1945 they saw for themselves the extent of the damage at the works. They met with Major Ivan Hirst of the REME and it was Hirst who allowed them to leave with a Type 60 rolling chassis. Hirst is credited as the man who saved the Volkswagen. Working against the official Allied policy for the de-industrialisation of Germany, which aimed to cap car production at only 10 per cent of the pre-war levels, Major Hirst recognised that it was vital to provide the Germans with a means of earning a living and he set about getting the plant back into running order. He had an example of the car painted in regulation khaki green and sent it up to the Rhine army headquarters for evaluation as a light transport vehicle – something which the army was chronically short of. The result was an order for 20,000 of the Type 60 under the former name Volkswagen Type 1. When Fedden got his Volkswagen back to England he found that, as with his exhibition of aero engines, he was unable to create any interest within British industry. No one was willing to take on the German car or the works in the difficult post-war market. (Henry Ford II is said to have rejected a suggestion to take on the Fallersleben plant because it was much too near to the Russian zone.) Fortunately under Hirst's leadership Volkswagen production did resume towards the end of 1945, and by the spring of the following year the output was up to 1,000 vehicles a month – a figure only limited by the availability of raw materials. The Beetle continued in production in Germany until 1980, when it made way for the VW Golf, and also in Mexico until 2003. By then over twenty-one million of the people's car had been built, making it the best-selling car in history. Having undergone several thousand minor tweaks and upgrades it was still recognisably the same little car that had emerged from the ruins of Fallersleben at the end of the Second World War.

Fedden's plans for a British version of the Volkswagen did not fare so well. It wasn't for any lack of expertise as he had gathered together a very capable band of engineers including Ian Duncan, Alec Moulton, Gordon Wilkins and Peter Ware. But despite the calibre of his team and Fedden's undisputed energy and ability to bulldoze his way through wartime restrictions on civilian vehicle development – largely thanks to his enormous standing in the engineering community and his high-profile connections – the 'F-car' as it became known was fatally flawed. The designers would later admit that that they had been led astray by Porsche's faith in the rear-engine layout.

The three-cylinder 1100 cc air-cooled radial engine at the rear of Fedden's post-war car with carburettor poking up into the void between the passenger compartment and the rear window.

At first glance the styling of the F-car, with its long bonnet and a curving rear end, had something of the shape of the Jowett Javelin which had also been designed during the war and went into production in 1947. However, that is where any resemblance ended. The F-car was rear-engined and drawing from his aviation experience Fedden opted for a three-cylinder 1100cc air-cooled radial engine, mounted horizontally, with sleeve valves operated by half-speed cranks off a vertical crankshaft. This was a less than ideal with the engine perched above a torque converter and the rear swing-axle assembly. Unusually the car was constructed in three separate sections. The self-contained passenger compartment or centre section had ample accommodation for up to six people on two bench seats. The front section carried the steering mechanism and suspension as well as providing space for the spare wheel, battery and any luggage. At the rear was the engine section, or 'power egg'. The body was a stressed-skin structure more familiar to the aircraft industry, but this type of construction had the distinct disadvantage of being far more expensive to repair and accordingly the three sections were each attached by four bolts. In theory this meant that the engine section could be completely removed in a matter of minutes, with the wiring connected by multi-pin plugs. But in practice the internal pressed steel struts that spread the loads gave the car a somewhat industrial feel.

Problems with the car were mostly caused by the positioning of the radial engine at the rear. Aesthetically it looked clumsy with the high-mounted carburettor poking up into a rear window void between the passenger compartment and the outer sloping window at the back of the car. The carburettor assembly was disguised beneath a metal cap, a 'top hat' as an *Autocar* journalist described it, but it was a far from elegant solution. Then there were further problems with vibration, excessive overheating and, worst of all, the road tests soon revealed that the engine – which had ended up at a hefty 70lb (32kg) above its design weight – tended to behave like an inverted pendulum. In a corner the car

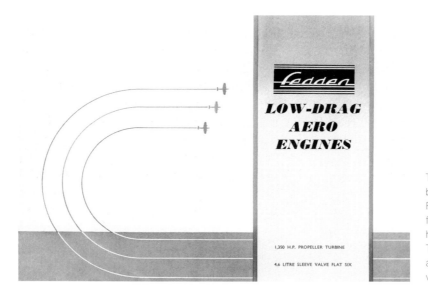

This post-war brochure for Roy Fedden Limited featured a 1,350 hp Propeller Turbine as well as a 4.6 litre sleeve valve Flat Six.

would become unstable causing a sudden and almost uncontrollable rear-end skid. Alec Caine, the main test driver, managed to cope with these handling quirks but inevitably the day came when he didn't catch it in time and the car executed a complete somersault, injuring Caine and his observer. The car was badly damaged and was still being rebuilt when work on the project was abandoned. Some preliminary designs were prepared on a range of successors, but in April 1947 Roy Fedden Ltd went into liquidation. The subsequent fate of the one and only F-Car prototype remains something of a mystery. There are some reports that it was seen stored in a shed at the Cranfield Aeronautical College until some point in the 1960s, but when the shed was demolished the trail went dry. Is it possible that this unique and extraordinary relic of automotive history is lying somewhere under a thick covering of dust in some long-forgotten storage facility?

Aside from the car, the main thrust of Roy Fedden Ltd had been the design and production of what the company brochure described as 'Low-Drag Aero Engines', initially a 4.6l horizontally opposed flat-six piston engine followed by a 1,350hp propeller turbine engine. The propeller turbine engine, or as it is more commonly termed nowadays a turbo-prop, was targeted at the builders of small to medium twin- and four-engine transport/passenger aircraft. According to the brochure:

> The complete power-plant is only 27in [68.5cm] in diameter and can be installed partly submerged in the leading edge of the wing where it provides the power needed for modern cruising speeds with minimum drag. Aircraft powered by turbines will carry more payload at higher speed than those using piston engines; they will cost less to run and maintain. The propeller turbine uses a little more fuel than an equivalent piston engine but the engine itself is so light that there is a saving in total weight on the engine and fuel under most conditions.

Clearly Fedden's discoveries in Germany and the discussions held with some of the German engineers had influenced this concept, especially those with Bruno Bruckmann on the topic of propeller-turbines. The brochure goes on to state that the Fedden turbine was especially suited for civil aircraft operating over short or medium ranges at altitudes up to 30,000ft (915m), at cruising speeds of 300 to 350mph (480 to 560km/h). For smaller aircraft or helicopters there was the Fedden flat-six, a six-cylinder 4.6-litre piston engine incorporating fuel injection and Fedden's sleeve valves. As with the turbo-prop this was designed to be mounted fully submerged within the aircraft's wings and was suitable for either tractor or pusher propeller configurations. (The installation drawings reproduced in the company brochure illustrated the pusher version.) Fedden believed that together these power units would open up a new field for the British engine industry and they offered 'stimulating' possibilities to the aircraft designers. According to Fedden's biographer, Bill Gunston, unlike the ill-fated F-car these engines were 'potentially great winners' and the piston engine was 'technically superior to the flat-four and flat-six produced in the United States'.

By the end of 1946 the first Fedden flat-six had been completed, in a remarkably short time, and had begun running on a testbed. Things were looking up and Fedden even managed to obtain a Ministry of Supply contract for the development of his 1,305hp turbo-prop. This became known within the company as the Cotswold, although it is not referred to as such in the company's promotional brochure. Weighing 760lb (345kg) it had an eleven-stage axial compressor and a two-stage turbine. With confidence growing, in February 1947 Roy Fedden Ltd moved to bigger premises at an unused government building at Stoke Orchard, to the north of Cheltenham, and at its height employed almost 200 people. It had grown very rapidly into a big engineering concern and in a memorandum, written by Fedden on 18 April 1947, he remained optimistic about its prospects. He even outlined an intention to extend the factory for the production of up to four turbine engines per week, and on the piston side the flat-six would be joined by a twelve-cylinder version with an output of twenty-five engines per week by 1952. However, such a big business relied on a steady flow of money, either from sales or other funding, and matters started to go downhill very quickly. By this time it was clear that the F-car, in its existing form, was going nowhere. A proliferation of aero-engine projects, in particular with a multitude of variants of the piston engine under consideration, meant that no single design was pushed to the fore and consequently the hard sales were not forthcoming. Then, to cap it all, in May 1947 the Ministry of Supply pulled the plug on its development funding for the turbo-prop. The company went into liquidation the following month.

Once again Sir Roy Fedden did not remain idle for very long. In 1950 he became an aircraft advisor on the planning staff of the newly formed North Atlantic Treaty Organisation (NATO), and afterwards worked as a consultant to the Dowty Group. He

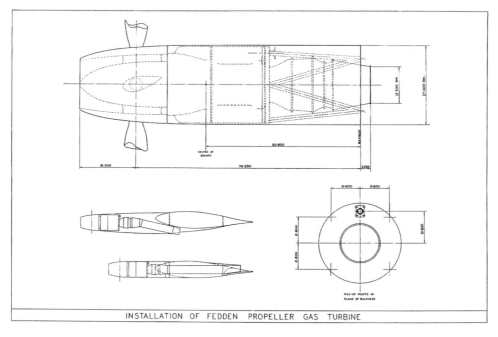

INSTALLATION OF FEDDEN PROPELLER GAS TURBINE

The 1,350 hp Propeller Turbine, or turboprop as this type of engine became known, illustrated in the Fedden brochure.

also found the time to write a book, *Britain's Air Survival*, which was published in 1957. Its message was straightforward enough: Britain needed to do more to assure it could adequately deal with the future threats it might face. More investment was required in training the engineers, and more resources should be invested in new advanced aircraft designs. But the well-intended polemic made heavy reading and to Fedden's critics it seemed that he was still harking back to the past. Out of the first eight chapters, two were devoted to the lost opportunities arising from the end of the Second World War:

> At the root of the disappointments of both our civil and military aviation programmes during the past decade is the neglect to put first things first. The lesson of the research facilities discovered in Germany at the end of the war and their indication of the pattern of future technical developments, far in advance of our own conception at the time, went largely unheeded by government and industry alike.

And once again the subject of piston engines came to the fore:

> We were on the threshold of the jet era, and in jet engines we held an undisputed lead. The jet age, therefore, it was to be; but confusing long-term planning and short-term needs, we prematurely abandoned the proven reliability of our piston engines.

Thankfully a considerable amount of Fedden's energy was being directed more usefully into establishing a British aeronautical college to train the next generation of engineers. It was Fedden who had first championed the idea after seeing the Institutes of Technology at Massachusetts and California during the Fedden Mission to America between December 1942 and March 1943. His vision was for a specialist college that would bridge the gap between the academic approach of the universities and the hard practical needs of industry. Upon his return to the UK his suggestions caught the ear of his boss at MAP, Sir Stafford Cripps, and in October 1943 Fedden was appointed as chairman of the committee which would submit detailed proposals for a School of Aeronautical Science to the minister. The ninety-eight page report was published in 1944 and, typical of Fedden, it went into the matter in great detail; the contents list alone ran to two pages. It covered the purpose, scope and character of the college, subjects of instruction, staff and their conditions of service, organisation and government of the college, location including buildings and equipment, finance, conclusions and finished off with multiple appendices. Included at the back were fold-out plans and drawings of what the college might look like. Inevitably the report became known as the 'Fedden Report' and, true to form, its contents managed to upset the existing educational establishments and aeronautical companies in equal measure. They hadn't been on the America mission and failed to see that there was any demand for such a college in Britain. Fortunately for Fedden, Sir Stafford Cripps remained firmly wedded to the idea and this explains why the establishment and equipping of the college was at the core of the mission to Germany in the summer of 1945. Fedden didn't get the purpose-built college he had pressed for, at least not at first, but the newly vacated RAF airfield at Cranfield, Bedfordshire, was

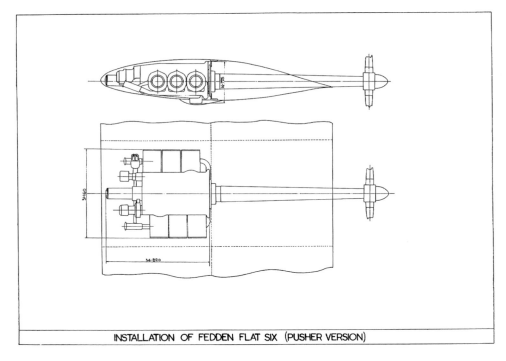

INSTALLATION OF FEDDEN FLAT SIX (PUSHER VERSION)

Fedden's 4.6 litre sleeve valve Flat Six mounted within an aircraft's wing with long drive shaft to the pusher propeller at the rear.

made available and the college received its first students in October 1946. Among the original equipment was a 3ft 6in (1m) double-flow wind tunnel and a range of precision measuring machines which had been liberated by the Fedden Mission in Germany. In 1993 the aeronautical college was renamed as Cranfield University.

Sir Roy Fedden died at the age of eighty-eight on 21 November 1973 at his home at Buckland Old Mill beside the river Usk in the county of Brecon. Coincidentally this date happened to be the 190th anniversary of mankind's first foray into the skies with the Montgolfier brothers' pioneering balloon ascent of 1783. Being born in 1885, Fedden had had the very good fortune to be an engineer at the time of the motor car's ascendency. His subsequent career had taken off with the flourishing of the aviation industry between the wars and his aero engines had made a lasting contribution to the progress of aeronautics. Nowadays his name is largely unknown outside of certain aviation and engineering circles, but the final word goes to the obituary notice published in *Flight International*. It described Sir Roy Fedden as a 'towering personality' and said that he was 'unquestionably the dominant figure in aircraft propulsion throughout the world between the wars'.

ITINERARY OF THE FEDDEN MISSION TO GERMANY, 1945

This is in the form as originally published in the Final Report.

Tuesday 12 June: The party assembled at 9 a.m. at MAP, Stratton Street, for transport by car to Northolt. On arrival, customs formalities were cleared and the Jeeps loaded into the aircraft, but unfavourable weather prevented a start being made until 2.15 p.m. Aircraft landed at Bückeburg in heavy rain at 4.30 p.m., but we were not allowed to leave aircraft there, and were asked to fly on to Würnsdorf, about 25 miles away. Delays with transport and heavy rain. Arrived at 2nd TAF Headquarters, Bad Eilsen, at 9.30 p.m. After dinner discussed programme of itinerary with RAF Liaison Officers. Drove on to 2nd Army Group Headquarters, Bad Oeynhausen for the night, where good arrangements were made.

Wednesday 13 June: Party went to Army Group Headquarters for instructions, and permits and decided to drive to LFA Völkenrode, Brunswick [Braunschweig] leaving the aircraft. Obtained additional Dodge lorry for luggage. This plan proved to be unsatisfactory, as party could have flown to Brunswick direct. Many delays owing to bridges broken down, and portions of the autobahn being damaged by bombing. Journey took almost the whole day and we arrived at RAF Headquarters, LFA, at 4.30 p.m. Billeted in Brunswick in American quarters for the night.

Thursday 14 June: All day at LFA Laboratories. General tour of premises and interrogation of scientists. Billeted for the night with RAF at the Laboratory Guest House.

Friday 15 June: Spent all day at LFA Laboratories, including tour of wind tunnels and Engine Laboratory. Took off from LFA aerodrome for Kassel at 7.15 p.m, a distance of 80 miles. Billeted at an American Intelligence Centre, Camp Dentine, 15 miles outside Kassel. Arrived 10.00 p.m.

Saturday 16 June: Party split; one aeroplane flew to Oschersleben, and then by Jeep to Magdeburg, where a tour was made of the Junkers Jet Engine Factory. The other machine went to

Göttingen, where the party visited the Laboratories, and made arrangements for Professor Prandtl and his colleagues to be available for interrogation next day. Returned to Camp Dentine for the night.

Sunday 17 June: The whole party went by road to Göttingen. A tour was made of the Laboratories, and several scientists were interrogated. A very satisfactory day. Returned to Camp Dentine for the night.

Monday 18 June: The party was split in two. One aeroplane flew to Köthen and its party went on to Dassau by road to interview technicians at the Junkers works, while the other party went by road to Eisenach to study the BMW Jet Engine Works. Returned to Camp Dentine for the night.

Tuesday 19 June: The party was split again, one aeroplane flying direct to Nordhausen, and then on to Munich, and the other flying to Öschersleben. Thence the party travelled by car to Stassfurt to examine an underground BMW Jet Plant, and afterwards on to Nordhausen to rejoin their aircraft, and returned to Kassel. Party at Camp Dentine for the night.

Wednesday 20 June: One aircraft took off from Kassel early and flew to Munich, and the whole party spent the afternoon at the BMW Engine Works. Billeted with American 3rd Army Intelligence Centre at Freising, 18 miles outside Munich.

Thursday 21 June: Party divided, some going by road to Rosenheim to inspect the BMW Rocket Development and then on to Kolbermoor to inspect the Heinkel-Hirth Jet Development. One aircraft flew to Frankfurt and Öschersleben and the other to Mengen, whence one party went by road to Lindau to get passes for the Stuttgart area. Returned to Freising for the night.

Friday 22 June: One aircraft returned from Öschersleben to Munich. The party was again split, one group going by road from Freising to Oberammergau with one of the BMW engineers, to visit Messerschmitt Experimental Department, and to investigate Jet Engine Installation, while some remained at Munich and others flew to Stuttgart to visit the Bosch works. All returned to Freising for the night.

Saturday 23 June: The party was again split, some remaining at BMW Munich, while others flew to Frankfurt, inspected certain factories, and went to SHAEF Headquarters. Aircraft returned to Munich. Another section flew to Stuttgart and proceeded by road to Esslingen and Reuthlingen before returning to Munich. Party divided for the night between Freising and Frankfurt.

Sunday 24 June: One party left Frankfurt at 9.30 a.m., flew to Munich and spent the morning at BMW. The other aircraft flew to Frankfurt and the party spent the night there. In the afternoon the Munich party flew to Salzburg, and returned to Freising for the night.

Monday 25 June: The party was again divided, some going by road to outlying factories near Munich, and also to Schloss Pullach, while others were in Frankfurt making investigations. One aircraft was away at Völkenrode and the other flew to Frankfurt for the night, arriving at 6.50 p.m. One section of the party went to Wiesbaden by road to get passes. All the Mission spent the night at SHAEF, Frankfurt, except one party which was at Völkenrode, on its way back to England.

Tuesday 26 June: The greater part of the Mission were in Frankfurt during the morning, while one machine was on its way to England from Völkenrode. The second machine returned to England via Brussels, on the evening of the 26th, arriving at Northolt at 6.45 p.m. Certain members of the Mission were left over in Germany for special duties, by arrangement with Sir Arthur Tedder, Acting Supreme Commander, until 2 July.

Wednesday 27 June: One machine returned from Odiham to Frankfurt. Visits made in the neighbourhood of Frankfurt, including Heddernheim and Kasselborn.

Thursday 28 June: The machine returned from Frankfurt to Northolt with those members of the mission who had been on visits in that area. This left Mr Stern and Fl/Lt Beeton in Germany on special duties.

Saturday 30 June: The machine which had arrived at Northolt on the evening of the 26th flew back from Odiham to Munich to pick up the two members of the mission still in Germany.

Sunday 1 July: Aircraft, with Mr Stern and Fl/Lt Beeton and Mr Bruckmann of BMW, flew to Salzburg.

Monday 2 – Wednesday 4 July: Party went by road from Salzburg to Spittal and Klagenfurt (crossing the Bavarian Alps), a distance of 125 miles, the aircraft having been unable to land there owing to bad weather.

Tuesday 3 July: Aircraft arrived at Klagenfurt, to link up with the party.

Wednesday 4 July: Aircraft flew from Klagenfurt to Munich and, after a further visit to BMW, returned to England, arriving Northolt at 6 p.m. and subsequently proceeded to Odiham.

Tuesday 17 – Wednesday 25 July: Four members of the Mission paid a further visit to Germany making Freising their headquarters, in order to witness certain tests on the High Altitude Test Bench at BMW, Munich, and also paid further visits to LFA Völkenrode. Göttingen, Stuttgart, Kochel, etc.

CAPTURED JET AND ROCKET AIRCRAFT REMOVED BY THE ALLIES

This list refers only to the jet and rocket-powered aircraft, which are listed by the country which first removed them and by type. Not all of these aircraft necessarily came from Germany itself as some were removed from other areas under German occupation. The aircraft listed here were taken as complete airframes and were mostly airworthy, although in many cases there is conflicting information regarding particular aircraft or a confusion of identities, and as a result there may be some duplication in this list. In a surprisingly large number of cases the fate of the aircraft is not known as many were discarded or scrapped after the war. In the UK Air Ministry (Air Min) numbers were allocated to most flyable aircraft, but not to every one for a variety of reasons. The Americans applied their own FE numbers for 'Foreign Aircraft'.

Surviving examples are highlighted in grey.

GREAT BRITAIN

	Werk Nr	Air Min. No.
Ar 234B Captured at Stavanger, Norway, on 10 May 1945.	140596	–
Ar 234B-2 Captured at Grove. Written off landing at RAE Farnborough at end of delivery flight.	140466	AM 24
Ar 234B Captured at Grove.	140608	AM 25
Ar 234B-1 Captured at Grove.	140476	AM 26
Ar 234B Captured at Schleswig.	140113	AM 54
Ar 234B Captured at Stavanger, Norway on 5 May 1945. Fate unknown.	140141	–

Ar 234B Captured at Stavanger, Norway. Fate unknown.	140493	–
Ar 234B Captured at Stavanger, 5 May 1945.	140581	–
Fieseler Fi 103/V1 – Reichenburg IV The manned version of the V-1 Doodlebug.	–	–
He 162A-2 Captured at Leck.	120221	AM 58
He 162A-2 – 'Yellow 4' Captured at Leck. Now on display at the Deutsches Technikmuseum, Berlin.	120076	AM 59
He 162A-2 – 'White 11' Captured at Leck. Crashed at the German Aircraft Exhibition at RAE Farnborough, 9 November 1945.	120074	AM 60
He 162A-2 Captured at Leck. On display at the Canadian Air & Space Museum (?)	120086	AM 62
He 162A-2 Captured at Leck. Fate since 1946 unknown.	120095	AM 63
He 162A-2 Captured at Leck. Reported in RAE Farnborough scrap area in 1946.	120097	AM 64
He 162A-2 Captured at Leck. RAF Museum, Hendon.	120227	AM 65
He 162A-2 Captured at Leck. Fate unknown.	120091	AM 66
He 162A-2 Captured at Leck. Reported in RAE Farnborough scrap area in 1946.	120098	AM 67
He 162A-2 Captured at Leck. On display at the Imperial War Museum, Lambeth, London.	Believed to be 120235	AM 68
Me 163B Captured at Husum. Believed scrapped in 1947.	191329	AM 200★
Me 163B Captured at Husum. Fate unknown.	191330	AM 201★
Me 163B Captured at Husum. Fate unknown.	191915	AM 202★
Me 163B – 'Yellow 13' Captured at Husum. Handed over to the French in 1946. Fate unknown.	310061	AM 203★
Me 163B – 'Yellow 11' Captured at Husum. Believed scrapped in Canada in the 1950s.	191454	AM 204★
Me 163B Captured at Husum. Believed scrapped in 1947.	191905	AM 205★
Me 163B Captured at Husum. Believed scrapped in 1947.	191902	AM 206★
Me 163B Captured at Husum. On display at RAF Museum Cosford.	191461	AM 207★
Me 163B Captured at Husum. Fate unknown.	191912	AM 208★

Me 163B Captured at Husum. Believed scrapped in 1947.	191315	AM 209★
Me 163B – 'Yellow 6' Captured at Husum. Identity has become confused: 191316 is displayed at the Science Museum, London. 120370 is at the Deutsches Museum, Munich.	191316 or more likely 120370	AM 210★
Me 163B Captured at Husum. Restored by the Canadian Aviation & Space Museum and now at the National Museum of the USAF, Dayton, Ohio.	191095	AM 211★
Me 163 Captured at Husum. Believed scrapped 1947.	191965	AM 212★
Me 163B Captured at Husum. Fate unknown.	191954	AM 213★
Me 163 Captured at Husum. In 2005 sold by the Imperial War Museum to Paul Allen's Flying Heritage Collection in the USA.	191660	AM 214★
Me 163B – 'Yellow 15' Captured at Husum. On display at the National Museum of Flight, East Fortune, Scotland.	191659	AM 215★
Me 163B Captured at Husum. Fate unknown.	191309	AM 216★
Me 163B Captured at Husum. Fate unknown.	191917	AM 217★
Me 163B Captured at Husum. Believed scrapped in 1947.	191654	AM 218★
Me 163B – 'Yellow 25' Captured at Husum. Returned to Germany in 1988 and now on display at the Luftwaffenmuseum in Berlin-Gatow.	191904	AM 219★
Me 163B Captured at Husum. On display at the Canadian Aviation & Space Museum, Rockcliffe, (?)	191914 unconfirmed	AM 220★
Me 163B Captured at Husum. Believed scrapped in 1947, may have gone to Canada.	191961 (or 191916)	AM 221★
Me 163B Captured at Husum. Now in the Australian War Memorial Mitchell Annexe in Canberra, Australia.	191907	AM 222★
Me 163B Already at Farnborough before the end of the war – source unknown – and allocated RAF serial number VF241 on 30 April 1945. Underwent gliding flight tests and was damaged beyond repair on 15 November 1947.	–	RAF serial No. VF241
Me 262B-1a/U1 – 'Red 12' Captured at Schleswig.	111980	–
Me 262A-1a – 'Yellow 5' Scrapped 1953.	500443	–
Me 262C – Heimatshutzer I prototype No known details.	130186	–

	Werk Nr	No.
Me 262 – Unidentified No known details.	–	–
Me 262 B-1a/U1 – 'Red 8' Rare two-seater night-fighter, captured at Schleswig. In 1947 shipped to South Africa and now on display at the National Museum of Military History, Johannesburg.	110305	AM 50
Me 262A-2a – 'Yellow 7' Captured at Fassberg. Now on display at the RAF Museum, Hendon, London.	112372	AM 51
Me 262A-2a – 'Yellow 17' Captured at Fassberg.	500210	AM 52
Me 262A No known details.	–	AM 79
Me 262A-1 – 'White 5' Captured at Fassberg. Destroyed in fire-fighting exercise, Canada 1949.	111690	AM 80
Me 262A-2a – 'Black X' Captured at Fassberg on 7 May 1945. Flown at RAE Farnborough, now on display at the Australian War Memorial, Canberra.	500200	AM 81

* Air Ministry numbers applied at RAE Farnborough

USA

	Werk Nr	No.
Ar 234B Captured at Grove. Shipped to USA.	140489	USA 5
Ar 234B-2 Surrendered to RAF at Stavanger on 5 May 1945. Shipped to USA.	140312	USA 50
Ar 234B – Jane I Shipped to USA. Scrapped at NAS Patuxent River.	–	202
Ar 234B – Snafu I Shipped to USA. Scrapped at NAS Patuxent River.	–	303
Ar 234B Surrendered to RAF at Stavanger, Norway. Shipped to USA and became FE-1011. Fate unknown.	140311	FE-1011/ T2-1011
Ar 234B Surrendered to RAF at Stavanger, Norway. Shipped to USA and became FE-1010. Now with the NASM.	140312	FE-1010/ T2-1010
He 162A-2 Captured at Leck. Shipped to the USA. Now on display in the Planes of Fame Museum, Chino, California.	120077	FE-489/ T2-489
He 162A-2 Fate unknown.	120017	FE-494/ T2-494
He 162A-2 Now with the NASM, Silver Hill, Maryland.	120230 (possibly 120222)	FE-504/ T2-504

Aircraft		
Me 163B-1a Believed to have been air-freighted to USA. Glide tests conducted in 1949. Now on display at the NASM Silver Hill Facility, near Washington DC.	191301	FE-500/ T2-500
Me 163B-1a Recorded as scrapped in 1946.	-	FE-501/ T2-501
Me 163B-1a Recorded as scrapped in 1946.	-	FE-502/ T2-502
Me 163B-1a Reputedly under restoration by Bell Aircraft in 1946. Fate unknown.	-	FE-503/ T2-503
Me 262A – 'Yellow 5' Captured at Fassberg. Shipped to England and later to South Africa.	500443	USA 1
Me 262B-1a/U1 Captured at Schleswig. Night-fighter converted to two-seater. Shipped to USA.	110306	USA 2
Me 262A-1a/U4 – Wilma Jeanne / Happy Hunter II Fitted with 50mm cannon. Crashed en route to Cherbourg.	170083	-
Me 262A-1a – 'Yellow 5', Beverley Anne / Screamin' Meemie Shipped to USA. Now on display at the National Museum of the USAF, Wright Patterson AFB, Ohio.	-	111
Me 262A-1a/U3 – Marge / Lady Jess IV Shipped to USA (?)	-	222
Me 262A-1a – Feudin 54th / Pauline / Deelovely Shipped to USA.	-	333
Me 262A-1a/U3 – Connie the Sharp Article / Pick II Captured at Lechfeld. Shipped to USA. Displayed at the Planes of Fame Museum, Chino, California, sold to Microsoft co-founder Paul Allen in 2000 and undergoing full restoration.	-	FE-4012/ T2-4012
Me 262B-1a – 'White 35', Vera / Willie Single-seater converted to two-seater trainer. Shipped to USA. Now on display at the Delaware Valley Historical Aircraft Association's Harold F. Pitcairn Wings of Aviation Museum, Willow Grove, Pennsylvania.	110639	555
Me 262A-1a/U3 – Joanne / Cookie VII Photo-reconnaissance version. Shipped to USA, crashed at Freeman Field in 1945.	500098	666
Me 262A-1a – Doris / Jabo Bait Shipped to USA and became FE-110.	-	777
Me 262A-1a – 'Yellow 7' / Dennis / Ginny H Captured at Lager-Lechfeld on 8 May 1945. Shipped to USA and became FE-111. Now on display at the NASM.	500491	888
Me 262B-1a/U1 – 'Red 6' / Ole Fruit Cake Two-seater night-fighter. Shipped to USA.	110306	FE-610/ T2-610
Me 262B-1a Two-seater trainer. Shipped to USA. Believed scrapped at NAS Anacostia in 1946.	110165	101
Me 262A-1a Captured at Frankfurt/Rhein-Main on 31 March 1945. Shipped to USA on the *Manawska Victory*.	111711	-

OTHER SURVIVORS

There are two more surviving aircraft, one surrendered to the Swiss and the other does not appear to match any records.

	Werk Nr	No.
Me 262A–1B – 'White 3' On 25 April 1945 Hans Guido Mutke landed his aircraft at Zurich's Dubendorf Military Airfield in neutral Switzerland. In 1957 it was handed back to the Germans and is now on display at the Deutsches Museum in Munich.	500071	–
He 162A–2 Said to be under restoration at the Musée de l'Air et de l'Espace, near Paris.	120015	–

OTHER EXPERIMENTAL AIRCRAFT

	Werk Nr	No.
Darmstadt–München DM–1 Lippisch delta-wing glider used for testing. Now in the collection of the NASM (?)	–	–
Dornier Do 335A–0 Captured 22 April 1945. Shipped to USA and now on display at the NASM, Washington DC.	240102	–
Dornier Do 335 A second Do 335 shipped to the USA on HMS *Reaper*. Tested at Freeman Field. Fate unknown.	–	FE-1012
Horten Ho II Taken to the USA. Dismantled and in storage at the NASM facility, Silver Hill.	6	–
Horten Ho IV Glider tested at Farnborough and then taken to the USA. Now at Maloney's Planes of Fame Museum.	25	–
Horten Ho 229V-3 (Gotha Go 229V-3) Shipped to the USA. In storage at NASM Facility, Silver Hill, Maryland.	–	FE-490/ T2-490
Junkers JU 287 Forward swept-wing jet-powered bomber. Taken to the USSR.	–	–
Messerschmitt P.1101 Found at Messerschmitt's design department in Oberammergau. Taken back to the USA. Plans to fly this prototype were abandoned, but it directly influenced the design of Bell's X-5.	–	–

GLOSSARY

AAF	see USAAF
ACC	Allied Control Council
ADC	Air Disarmament Command
ADS	Air Disarmament Squadron
AHC	Allied High Commission (created in 1948 to supersede the ACC)
AMG	American Military Government
ATI	Air Technical Intelligence
AVA	*Aerodynamische Versuchsanstalt* – Aerodynamic Trials Unit
Bf	Designation for Messerschmitt aircraft 1934–1938
BIOS	British Intelligence Objectives Sub-Committee
BMW	*Bayerische Motorenwerke* – Bavarian Motor Works
CIOS	Combined Intelligence Objectives Subcommittee
CIPC	Combined Intelligence Priorities Committee
EKdo	*Erprobungskommando* – Luftwaffe testing unit
FE	Foreign Equipment numbers applied by the Allies to captured enemy aircraft
FuG	Funker radar equipment
Fw	RLM designation for Focke-Wulf aircraft
Go	RLM designation for Gotha aircraft
Gruppe	Luftwaffe wing or group
He	RLM designation for Heinkel aircraft
Ho	RLM designation for Horten aircraft
Hs	RLM designation for Henschel aircraft
ICBM	Intercontinental Ballistic Missile
JABO	*Jägdbomber* – fighter-bomber
Jägernotprogramm	Emergency fighter programme
JATO	Jet Assisted Take-off
Ju	RLM designation for Junkers aircraft
Jumo	Junkers Motoren Junkers motor company
LFA	*Luftfahrtforschungsansalt* – aeronautical research institute
MAP	Ministry of Aircraft Production, UK
Me	RLM designation for Messerschmitt aircraft
MK	*Maschinenkanone* – machine cannon/gun
Nachtjäger	Night-fighter or hunter
NJG	*Nachtjagdgeschwader* – night-fighter group
Operation Alsos	US mission to capture the Nazis' nuclear technology

Operation Big	part of Alsos
Operation Lusty	USAF mission to capture and evaluate German aeronautical technology (LUftwaffe Secret TechnologY)
Operation Paperclip	US mission to recruit Nazi scientists
Operation Surgeon	British post-war programme to exploit Nazi aeronautical technology and forcibly recruit German expertise
RAE	Royal Aircraft Establishment (Farnborough)
RAF	Royal Air Force
RATO	Rocket-Assisted Take Off
RLM	*Reichsluftministerium* – German Air Ministry
RfRuK	*Reichsministerium für Rüstung und Kriegsproduktion* – Reich Ministry for Armament & War Production
Schnellbomber	Fast Bomber
SHAEF	Supreme Headquarters Allied Expeditionary Force
Shrage Musik	'Slanted Music' upward firing rocket array triggered by photoelectric cell
STAM	Special Technical Adviser to the Minister
Staffel	Squadron
Sturmvogel	Stormbird
USAAF	United States Army Air Force
USAF	United States Air Force (from 1947)
Vergeltungswaffe	Vengeance weapon
Versuchsmuster	Experimental/test
Volksjäger	People's Fighter, the He 162

BIBLIOGRAPHY

Bessel, Richard, *Germany 1945 From War to Peace*, Simon & Schuster, 2009.

Bower, Tom, *The Paperclip Conspiracy*, Paladin, 1988.

Brown, Eric, *Wings of the Luftwaffe*, TBS, 1977.

Butler, Phil, *War Prizes, Midland Counties*, 1994.

Charman, Terry, *The German Home Front 1939–1945*, Philosophical Library, 1989.

Christopher, John, *The Messerschmitt Me262 Story*, History Press, 2010.

Dancey, Peter and Vajda, Franz-Antal, *German Aircraft Industry and Production 1933-1945*, Airlife 1998.

Diedrich, Hans-Peter, *German Rocket Fighters of World War II*, Schiffer, 2005.

Ethell, Jeff, *Komet The Messerschmitt 163*, Littlehampton, 1978.

Fedden, Sir Roy, *Britain's Air Survival An Appraisement and Strategy for Success*, Cassell, 1957.

Ford, Brian, *German Secret Weapons Blueprint for Mars*, Pan/Ballantine, 1972.

Forsyth, Robert and Creek, Eddie J., *Messerschmitt Me 264 Amerikabomber The Luftwaffe's Lost Transatlantic Bomber*, Classic Publications, 2006.

Griehl, Manfred, *Luftwaffe Over America The Secret Plans to Bomb the United States in World War II*, Greenhill, 2004.

Griehl, Manfred, *Luftwaffe X-Planes German Experimental Aircraft of World War II*, Greenhill, 2004.

Gunston, Bill, *Fedden The Life of Sir Roy Fedden, Rolls-Royce Heritage Trust*, 1998. (Originally published as *By Jupiter! The Life of Roy Fedden*, The Royal Aeronautical Society 1978.)

Henshall, Philip, *Vengeance Hitler's Nuclear Weapon Fact or Fiction?*, Sutton Publishing, 1998.

Herbert Molloy, Mason, *The Rise of the Luftwaffe 1918–1940*, Cassell, 1975.

Hirschel, E.H., Prem, H., Madelung, G., *Aeronautical Research in Germany From Lilenthal until Today*, Springer, 2004.

Hooton, E.R., *Phoenix Triumphant The Rise and Rise of the Luftwaffe*, Weidenfeld Military, 1994.

Hyland, Gary and Gill, Anton, *Last Talons of the Eagle Secret Nazi Technology*, Headline, 1998.

Jones, R.V., *Most Secret War*, Wordsworth, 1978.

Judt, Matthias and Ciesla, Burghard, *Technology Transfer Out of Germany After 1945*, Harwood Academic Publishers, 1996.

Kay, Antony L., *German Jet Engine and Gas Turbine Development 1930–1945*, Crowood Press, 2002.

Kelly, *Andrew and Melanie, Take Flight Celebrating Aviation in the West of England Since 1910*, Bristol Cultural development Partnership, 2010.

King, J.B. and Batchelor, John, *German Secret Weapons*, Purnells, 1974.

Longden, Sean, *T-Force The Race for Nazi War Secrets 1945*, Constable, 2009

Lucus, James, *Last Days of the Reich The Collapse of Nazi Germany*, May 1945, Cassell, 2000.

Morgan, Hugh, *Me 262 Stormbird Rising*, Osprey Aerospace, 1996.

Nowarra, Heinz, *German Guided Missiles*, Schiffer, 1993.

Pavelec, Sterling Michael, *The Jet Race and the Second World War*, Praeger Security International, 2007.

Price, Alfred, *The Last Year of the Luftwaffe*, Arms & Armour, 1993.

Reitsch, Hanna, *The Sky My Kingdom*, Bodley Head, 1955.

Samuel, Wolgang W.E., *American Raiders The Race to Capture the Luftwaffe's Secrets*, University Press of Mississippi, 2004.

Smith, J.R. and Kay, *Antony, German Aircraft of the Second World War*, Putnam, 1985.

OFFICIAL DOCUMENTS:

The Fedden Mission to America Final Report, Ministry of Aircraft Production, June 1943.

The Fedden Mission to Germany - Final Report, Ministry of Aircraft Production, 1945.

Instructions for British Servicemen in Germany, Prepared by The Political Warfare Executive, Issued by the Foreign Office, 1944.

Technical Intelligence Supplement A Report Prepared for the AAF Scientific Advisory Group, Headquarters Air Materiel Command, May 1946.

Military Government Weekly Information Bulletin, Office of the Assistant Chief of Staff G-5 Division USFET, July 1945.

Underground Factories in Germany, Report published by the Combined Intelligence Objectives Subcommittee, G-2 Division SHAEF, 1945.

The United States Strategic Bombing Survey, Summary Report (European War), US Government Printing Office, September 1945.

ACKNOWLEDGEMENTS

Images have been obtained from a number of sources including the US National Archives & Records Administration (NARA), United States Air Force (USAF), Rolls-Royce Heritage Trust (RRHT), US Library of Congress (LoC), US Department of Defense (US DoD), Deutsches Zentrum für Luft- und Raumfahrt Archive (DLR), National Aeronautics & Space Administration (Nasa), the San Diego Air & Space Museum (SDASM), Campbell McCutcheon (CMcC), Nimbus227, MisterBee1966 and Rottweiller. New photography is by the author (JC). Thanks also to Shaun Barrington of The History Press for his patience, and to my wife Ute for her support, proof reading and assistance with translations.

INDEX